ADVANCE PRAISE FOR *IRVING LAYTON: OUR YEARS TOGETHER*

"I couldn't put down this vivid and sincerely rendered story of the tragic love between a beautiful, idealistic young woman and a brilliant aging poet. Relying on her old journals from the seventies, and letters and poems by Irving Layton, Harriet Bernstein has broken her silence of thirty-seven years to tell us what it was like loving a creative maelstrom who once dominated our literature. Readers and scholars alike will relish Bernstein's memoir."
—SUSAN SWAN, author of *The Wives of Bath* and *The Dead Celebrities Club*

"Bernstein writes compellingly this page-turner of a memoir, conjuring up her flower-power, ban-the-bomb, and burn-the-bra young womanhood in Toronto and Boston, but also those idyllic Greek islands where Leonard Cohen would drop by, all wry and ironic and sipping retsina. Not only is Bernstein a vital witness to that most vital poet, Layton, his gusto and genius, she is also the chronicler of that era—the 1970s—when women were becoming feminists and English-Canadians were beginning to believe that they could truly be Nobel-global poets and filmmakers of Oscar-award consequence. For me, she herself becomes a kind of reverse Elizabeth Smart, that Canuck woman writer who gave seemingly all of herself to the British poet George Barker. No, Harriet Bernstein always maintained a core independence from Layton, despite loving him indelibly, and this remains her own radiant, intellectual beauty, everywhere enlightening this sometimes tearful, and always wistful saga."
—GEORGE ELLIOTT CLARKE, 7th Parliamentary Poet Laureate (2016 and 2017)

"We are all destined to play a role in someone's life, be it big or small. But the role most likely to bring euphoric joy, ultimate glory, and incomparable pain is the role of lover and MUSE. Harriet Bernstein's candid, blunt and most compelling memoir will take you for a roller coaster ride into the passions of her body and soul. Bernstein holds

nothing back. A rare, intelligent, and creative free spirit who reveals the sensual and painful moments of her romantic affairs with some of the art world's most creative and dynamic men. But it is her irrefutable love and complicated relationship with Canada's most iconic bad boy of poetry, Irving Layton, that is a love story to sing to. If you thought you knew all there was to know about Irving Layton then you did not see him through Harriet's eyes. As lover, muse, wife, and mother to their daughter, Samantha, she offers a side of Layton rarely explored by academics. She exposes a man whose complicated, insatiable appetites and vulnerabilities were genius and whose generosity, and yet volatile behaviour, was giant. This is a love affair that refuses to end long after the flames are spent. A memoir to keep you turning pages long into the wee hours of the night."
—GIANNA PATRIARCA, *author of Italian Women and Other Tragedies* and *All My Fallen Angelas*

"Time does not heal all wounds. It can't. It shouldn't. Especially the wounds of true love. Time does, however, allow for reflection, for reckoning, for recounting and retelling. Harriet Bernstein's memoir *Irving Layton: Our Years Together* is a story about true love. It is unbelievable. It is maddening. It is passionate. It is sexual. It is sensual. It is torturous. It is extraordinary."
—VANESSA SHIELDS, author of *I Am That Woman* and *Look at Her*

IRVING LAYTON
OUR YEARS TOGETHER

Published in Canada by
Inanna Publications and Education Inc.
210 Founders College, York University
4700 Keele Street, Toronto, Ontario M3J 1P3
Telephone: (416) 736-5356 Fax (416) 736-5765
Email: inanna.publications@inanna.ca Website: www.inanna.ca

We gratefully acknowledge the support of the Canada Council for the Arts and the Ontario Arts Council for our publishing program. We also acknowledge the financial support of the Government of Canada.

Cover design: Val Fullard

Printed and Bound in Canada.

Library and Archives Canada Cataloguing in Publication

Title: Irving Layton : our years together : a memoir / Harriet Bernstein.
Names: Bernstein, Harriet, 1948- author.
Series: Inanna memoir series.
Description: Series statement: Inanna memoir series
Identifiers: Canadiana (print) 20190103124 | Canadiana (ebook) 20190103132 | ISBN 9781771336338 (softcover) | ISBN 9781771336345 (epub) | ISBN 9781771336352 (Kindle) | ISBN 9781771336369 (pdf)
Subjects: LCSH: Layton, Irving, 1912-2006. | LCSH: Bernstein, Harriet, 1948- | LCSH: Layton, Irving, 1912-2006—Marriage. | LCSH: Authors' spouses—Canada—Biography. | CSH: Poets, Canadian (English)—20th century—Biography. Classification: LCC PS8523.A95 Z56 2019 | DDC C811/.54—dc23

MIX
Paper from
responsible sources
FSC
www.fsc.org   FSC® C004071

IRVING LAYTON
OUR YEARS TOGETHER

A MEMOIR BY

HARRIET BERNSTEIN

INANNA
Memoir Series

For Samantha, whose presence is a bounty of joy for all who know you. With infinite love from your mama.

1.

IT IS 2014, AND I HAVE RECENTLY TURNED SIXTY-SIX. Sixty-six, the same age as Irving Layton was when we legally married each other. I was twenty-six when our love began; he was sixty-two. Now, reaching this age, I cannot help but think how incredible it was, he was, to have solemnized our relationship in a marriage. How scary it must have been to him, even more than it was to me. Right now, fireworks fill the night sky. I love and despise fireworks: love them because of their magic, their beauty; hate them because they remind me of the fireworks I saw in France, when I was there alone in 1976, on what I thought was the night of our final separation, and the end of our love affair. I don't know if I have ever felt so utterly alone as I did then, watching those fireworks. The life I thought we would have together was seemingly not to be. If I was not to be with him—where and what and how was I to be? These were the questions tormenting me. Because when Irving and I were together, everything else made sense, and if it didn't make sense, it didn't matter either. When we were together, the rest of the world fell away. Past partners, other children, families in crisis, concerns of every sort—all were small when held within the context, the embrace, the circle, and certainty of our love.

September 1974: the first day of classes at Toronto's York University. The room was packed, overflowing with students enrolled in the poetry workshop offered by Professor Irving Layton. We were required to bring a portfolio of our writing to Layton's classroom. I sat at a school desk for the first time in years, clutching the portfolio tightly to my chest. I had been working in the film industry and having left the film business due to an ethical crisis, I had taken some time out to travel. When I returned to Toronto, I was excited to learn that Layton was teaching at York. As a longtime devotee of his work, I was drawn to the idea of studying poetry under him. I decided to defer resuming my professional life to once again become a student with the goal of taking Layton's class, and also completing my undergraduate degree, which I had abandoned just short of matriculation.

That first day, he was late. I knew nobody there and, at twenty-six, I was a few years older than everyone else in the class. I sat waiting silently. How strange it felt to be back in a classroom and observe the others who seemed so much younger than me. Suddenly, Layton blew in. I say "blew in" and I mean exactly that. It was as though a blast of wind had pushed him through the door—he entered the room on a palpable gush of energy. I felt like I had been punched in the belly. I actually gasped. He literally took my breath away. His energy was huge, magnetizing. Immediately commanding the attention of everyone assembled, he launched into a diatribe about how there were too many people in the room for a poetry workshop, and he used various arguments to persuade us that we didn't really want to be there. A couple of students, discouraged, actually left, which surprised me. I thought that they couldn't have been too serious about wanting to study with Layton, if they were giving up so easily. The majority, however, remained.

Layton said he would make his decision on who could be in the class based on two things: our portfolios (which everyone knew was a prerequisite), and on a personal interview, which he would begin right then and there. He said he'd see each one of us privately for a few moments, so everyone had to exit the room, line up outside the door, and then be invited into the class one at a time. Dutifully, we filed out of the room. Everyone, that is, except me. I sat in that chair and made no move whatsoever. There was absolutely no way I was going to leave; I was determined to speak with this man, straightaway. After everyone else had left, he looked at me with those sharp, keen, light blue eyes and said in his strong voice, "Well, I guess

Harriet, ca. 1971.

you're first!" And that was precisely the beginning. Nine months later, we were in Italy for the first of several clandestine trips we took before our eventual marriage some four years later. Our relationship has been misidentified by media in some quarters as "whirlwind"; it certainly was not that.

Layton was a fabulous teacher; they just don't come any better. His greatest gifts as a teacher were his expansive knowledge and passion that inspired his students; his generosity both of spirit and with his time, which he gave unfailingly; and his dedication. Every time he "blew" into the classroom, each one of us felt our

3

Irving Layton with students in his poetry workshop at York University, ca.1974-75.

brains (and some nipples) commanded to stand at attention. His enthusiasm was unsurpassed, soaring, and not only for poetry: for literature, philosophy, knowledge, life in all its glory and horror. The breadth of his knowledge was incredibly extensive— he'd go from ancient Greek history to Blake to current politics without skipping a beat, and in the end it all led to poetry. His ability to impart some of that information and enthusiasm to his students was more potent than with any other teacher I have ever known. Bill Corbett, another poet who taught Romantic Poetry at Emerson College in Boston when I was a student there in 1966-68, also had that ability to supercharge. However, Corbett was a young man when I knew him, a man just beginning his professional life, whereas Layton was then in his sixties and going strong, stronger than almost anybody of any age. He taught us that a cathartic outpouring of emotion was not poetry, nor was journaling. In order to be called poetry, there must be a craft, an aesthetic present; there was form and language and precision. He was exciting; he challenged us, pulled things out of us that were better than we knew ourselves to be capable of. He brought humour, warmth, and passion to the very desolate landscape that was York University in 1974. He heated the frigid winter winds roaring across the barren landscape, transforming everything and everyone around him into something bigger and better.

There was not a student in any class he ever taught who would remain uninspired by him. Some of his students, including Moses Znaimer and our former Minister of Justice, Irwin Cotler, retain to this day not just fond, but loving memories of the best teacher they'd ever had. Irving and I by chance ran into Irwin Cotler one night in Montreal when we lived there (years before he became Minister of Justice), and Irving introduced Irwin to me as his "spiritual son." At Irving's funeral in Montreal in January 2006, Irwin held my hand gently and recalled that moment, and told me how much it had meant to him that Irving had referred to him in that way.

Blown away as I was by Irving right from that first encounter, and turned on as my mind was by what he brought to us, I was most of all just intensely happy that the man whose writing I had loved for so many years more than fulfilled whatever I had imagined he might be as a person. In my years as a publicist in the film industry, I had had many opportunities to meet and work with "the talent," big names in the business. While they were most often wonderful people who behaved entirely professionally, some turned out to be walking horror shows. Usually the top tier stars were great; it was the level just below that where challenging attitudes and issues arose. During that time, I learned that when we esteem someone highly, there is always a great risk of disappointment upon meeting that person in the flesh. I had read Layton's poems, watched him on television, had imagined what he might be like, and especially what it might be like to be the woman who inspired him to compose a particular love poem. Layton always more than delivered in the classroom, constantly challenging, encouraging and inspiring us. He brought worlds of knowledge to us, and breathed life into all the knowledge he shared, whether it was about ancient Greece or the current political climate. Eyebrows quivering, he would fix his penetrating blue eyes on one of us and challenge us to articulate what we felt about a topic, challenge us to really think about our opinions, to clarify and distill our thoughts, as we would learn to clarify and distill our creative process in the writing of a poem. Sometimes he

5

could also be intimidating; he knew so damned much, and he was such a giant presence. But intimidation was not his intention, not with his students anyway.

I wish that today there were more writers and teachers who would take the time to read unsolicited manuscripts, offer thoughtful feedback, and mentor. Irving always made time for that; it was one more thing that made him stand out from the crowd. His public persona attributed a kind of selfishness to him, but when it came to helping others who aspired to write, his generosity was as boundless as his energy. I did not fully appreciate at the time how unusual it was, this helping of others. I thought it was lovely, but I hadn't realized how rare it was. I have come to understand this better, as I progressed with my academic pursuits, and even more recently, as our daughter Samantha has journeyed through two Masters degrees, and has now completed her PhD in English Literature, at York University in fact. She has been fortunate to have had some wonderful, gracious, generous, and supportive professors, and academic advisors, who have taken time with her. Poets and writers ... not so much. She listens a bit wistfully when I tell her about how her father was, not only with his students, but with random people who would call him or send him their poems, how he always made the time to read their letters and their poems, respond to them with his best input, and always with encouragement.

It was several months before our relationship took its first shaky steps beyond that of student and teacher. It had never occurred to me that I could share anything with this man beyond my dizzying great fortune of being able to study with him. Our relationship was similar in some ways to the relationship between Suzanne Farrell and George Balanchine: Farrell could not imagine that Balanchine, this icon of choreography, would be looking at her with eyes of anything other than the master looking at his student. She came in time to understand differently, of course, and their relationship transformed as did ours. Irving had been in a marriage-like relationship for many years. Although never formalized with a marriage certificate (to the deep, enduring distress of his then companion), Irving was in some ways more bound to the relationship than if they had

6

Irving at a reading. Ca. early 1970s.

been legally married, or so he told me. That could easily have been an excuse, a way to sidestep his reasonable fear of a new love affair. There was, furthermore, the child that had come from this common-law marriage, his son David, who was an adolescent when Irving and I met.

As time went on, Irving and I were increasingly drawn to each other. We talked for hours on end in his office at York, and later in restaurants. I invited him to my home, introduced him to my parents. My mother, also an artist (a dramatic soprano: opera and concert soloist) got on with Irving like a house on fire. My businessman father was definitely less enchanted. He once said to me (with typical forthrightness and cruelty) that he wondered whether Irving's interest and support for my writing would be the same were I not so beautiful. I came to know that Irving had many of what he called his "coffee romances": women he would meet with and talk to in cafés, asking questions about their lives, drawing them out. He had a way of making a woman feel like she was the most interesting person in the world. When he talked to you, his blue eyes—that looked like the sea with the sun shining on it, or could be like ice—were fixed and you alone, you would feel flattered by his interest and you would open like

7

the proverbial bud to the sun. Many of these "coffee romances" were brief, some continued for years. In the case of Dorothy Rath, the relationship continued for years and she wrote a book about her time with him. Irving loved stories; unendingly curious, his gain was to have new blood so to speak, new grist for the ceaseless mill of his writing and his imagination. The women he met may have been represented in a poem, or he might alchemize them into another creature entirely. If he got a poem out of it, his time was well spent, he'd say. He could make poetry out of anything, from a new woman in his life, to roadkill that he may have chanced upon.

He told me he had never ever had a romantic involvement with a student, and I believed him. I had no illusions, however. I thought I was the "coffee romance" of the moment, which was fine with me. He was fascinating, and I readily told him any and all stories he seemed interested in hearing, and I wholeheartedly welcomed any stories that he cared to share with me. These became much more personal as time passed. We gradually began to get to know each other and each other's back stories, as woman and man, not just as student and teacher.

One day in a crowded elevator in one of the York buildings, as we were crushed against each other, Irving took hold of my hand and gently squeezed. It was molten fire between us, striking me in the pit of my belly. He felt it too, because he wrote a poem about it entitled "Because You Squeezed Back." It was a minor poem, but it captured that particular moment. It was a simple squeeze of the hand, yet we were like two exposed wires that barely touched but gave off big sparks. Our first kiss, standing outside in front of his college, followed shortly afterwards. Snow was gently falling as our lips met briefly. There were people around, but contrary to his public image, Irving was very private when it came to such intimacies. However brief it was, that kiss sent waves of passion through us, and I knew in that moment that I wanted to be with him.

I had no plan, no goal to try to "steal" him away and break up his turbulent long-term relationship. I just wanted to be with him, whenever and however. By my reasoning, I was a free woman and he was the one struggling in a relationship. I was a flower child at heart, and my free-spirited sensibility believed that our passion was a rare and precious thing, to be honoured and cherished. How I lived, what I then thought and felt, were inevitably products of the time in which I was living. It was "the sixties," when culture, politics, and thinking were exchanging the hard lines of grey flannel suits and ladies' gloves for flowing clothes as brightly coloured as the psychedelic posters adorning walls. The air was rich with the smell of marijuana, new music, and sex. As a teenager I deeply inhaled everything the sixties presented as part of my burgeoning womanhood.

Irving was a middle-aged man, living what I imagined was his version of that culture, with his open marriage and travels to India and Greece. Rumi's exquisite line: "There is a field beyond good and evil/ will you meet me there?" expresses how I felt about our situation. Irving was the one navigating the treacherous realms of his reality. I felt absolutely free to embrace whatever and whomever I chose. I took all my cues from Irving: if he pulled back, I understood and did the same, but if he moved forward, I was there for him, wanting him as much as he wanted me.

Again, contrary to his public persona, Irving did not enter lightly into an intimate relationship, at least not with me. He and his then partner had had many covert relationships during their long domestic life together, and perhaps the texture of those was different within the context of their open marriage. I did not know what the status of their relationship was when we first became involved. I knew that in the past they both had taken other lovers. Had I arrived at a time when they had made a pact to be monogamous? I did not know. Or, was the nature of our relationship distinct from previous casual affairs? In his own unique way, Irving was deeply devoted to his co-vivant and their son, David.

The feelings developing between us tortured him, even as they brought him what he declared to be previously unknown pleasures. What I understood from Irving was that our affair was different from the many dalliances he had had before. This one reached deep into the core of his being and allowed him to feel and be in a way no other relationship had vouchsafed. What precisely was it about the two of us that clicked? I am not sure this can be pinned down. Perhaps we can only accept the connection or understand it as a chemical, molecular, spiritual meeting; it certainly had everything going against it. And yet, there we were, undeniably drawn together. How irresistible and how absolutely romantic all of this was to a young woman already in love with the poetry and poet long before she met the man.

It must be remembered, however, that I was not a wide-eyed, naïve young woman who could be easily drawn by the glamour Irving represented. I had been for several years a self-supporting, independent businesswoman, well-travelled and sophisticated. I was not a woman defined by any preconceived or traditional notions of what womanhood meant. To me, my womanhood meant that I had the freedom to explore my femininity and sexuality in any way I desired, and with whom I desired. It was about being fully in the moment and enjoying it, rather than about future goals or aspirations. Any relationship I chose to engage in was my liberty. I was always very shaky when it came to planning the long-term future. "Be Here Now," a dictum of that time, was the credo by which I lived.

So there we were: a young woman, free-spirited, turning away from a supposedly bourgeois privileged upbringing to embrace a particular kind of freedom, and a very public poet and teacher, with a persona as egoist shit-disturber, involved in a long-term common-law relationship, living a life that was in fact bourgeois in many ways. The house that he and Aviva lived in at that time, on St. Clements and subsequently on Delavan (in the heart of lower Forest Hill Village), the trips, the mink coat he gave her, all smacked of a kind of bourgeoisie that seemed at odds with the rebel, pugilistic figure he projected. Perhaps we were both divided in that way. Perhaps the hyper-sexualized figure portrayed was an intention, rather than a reality.

2.

THE PATH THAT LED ME TO IRVING was a winding and unusual one. I left Toronto in the summer of 1966, refusing on principal to go to Grade 13 and thus making it impossible to attend university here. I fled to Emerson College, on Beacon Street in the heart of Boston. A cousin with whom I am close was registered there, and I was eager to leave Toronto, which had nothing to offer me except Yorkville, "the Village," centre of music, drugs, and bohemian life in the city. It had been great to run away from my parent's house and find a place that felt more like home to me in Toronto's Yorkville. I had been living in a room on Huron Street with my first great love, Danny Tripper, a musician, who had died too young several years earlier. However, there was still a restlessness in me, a desire to put geographic space between my parents and myself.

My parents were beyond delighted with supporting—financially and in every other way—my desire to attend college, anywhere! Anything to get me away from the Yorkville scene of hippies and druggies, they thought. I took the night bus from Bay Street in downtown Toronto. A girlfriend of mine from the Village came to see me off. She gave me a book of poetry as a going-away gift. My father, always suspicious, demanded to see the book. As he looked through it, a few joints fell to the ground. "Reefers!" he hollered, while I tried to shush him. He was horrified that a friend would bring me "dope," as he called it, when I had a border to cross and could easily wind up in jail. He was right, of course, although at the time I was annoyed to have lost the weed and thought it was a nice gesture on the part of my friend. As it turned out, I was stopped at the border. Apparently, I did not have the correct papers required to enter the U.S. as a student. I was let in provisionally, and given a deadline to provide the required documents to the authorities once I arrived at the college. At that point, in the border officer's booth, I thought it was a good thing the joints were lying on the ground of the bus terminal back on Bay Street.

Emerson was really an extension of the Yorkville scene, only couched in the guise of academe, with just as many drugs, and much more money.

In the autumn of 1966, it was pretty much the same on almost any university or college campus in North America or perhaps the Western world, in fact. On the heels of Timothy Leary's "Turn on, tune in, drop out" dictum, all over North America and Europe young people were united in a particular way that they have not been since. Racial integration, freedom of all flavours, women's lib, The Pill: everything was happening right then and there. In September 1966, I arrived in Boston, the epicentre, thanks in part to Leary. With my waist-long straight auburn hair, big brown eyes enhanced with dark makeup, and straight out of Yorkville, I was street savvy and not going to take shit from anyone. I was eighteen and fearless as only the young can be. I instantly loved the beauty of Boston, the Charles River, Cambridge, and Beacon Hill. Some of the buildings on the Emerson campus had once been grand old homes, and my classrooms had moulded ceilings and fancy balustrades leading up winding staircases, the sort of thing that inspired a sense of history and fancy. We lived at 100 Beacon Street. Our all-female dorm room overlooked the Charles River and the Feidler Bridge. We used to watch men hooking up at night through our crystal-prism glasses, while listening to The Doors and Jimi Hendrix, both of whom had just released their now iconic albums. I still have those vinyl gems!

Across Beacon Street was the Boston Gardens, with the swan boats and the flower clock in the summer. On the other side of the Gardens was Boston Common, venue for many a sit-in, as they were called, student demonstrations arranged in protest of whatever the cause of the moment was. The Commons were also the place where "smoke-ins" were held: gatherings of large

12

numbers of students advocating for legalization of marijuana. Everyone was getting high, and it was sweet because nobody could be arrested; if the cops arrived, you'd put your weed on the ground, and the police could not prove anything was yours. I think that witches were burned at the stake in the Commons, way back, and on misty wet nights in the fall, you could feel their ghosts still hovering. I particularly loved Cambridge and frequented the bookstores there, especially historic Groliers, where I picked up obscure books by Colette and Gertrude Stein, both of whom became lifelong passions of mine. On sunny spring days, the distinguished old streets would be teeming with fresh faces, young energy bursting out like the buds gracing the majestic trees that lined many of the streets. It was a beautiful time in a beautiful place. As cool as Boston was, the gypsy in me was still restless.

And so it was that in the summer of 1967, Andrea Gilbert, a friend from Emerson with whom I am still close, and I went to Europe. My father sponsored our trip to Europe; it was part of his well-intentioned goal of keeping me out of Yorkville. Yes, we were indulged. We spent some time in Rome, living in a *pensione* on Via Mario dei Fiori, just around the corner from the Spanish Steps. This spot became a fulcrum point later, when my affair with Irving was in its early stages, which is also why the story wants telling here. The intention, as masterfully arranged by my father, was for Andrea and me to experience working in Rome, and he had set this up with business contacts he had there.

At Cinecitta studio one day, I met a writer named Luciano Vincenzoni. He had written the screenplays for the now-iconic *The Good, The Bad, and the Ugly; A Fistful of Dollars; For A Few Dollars More*, as well as numerous other screenplays that were not spaghetti westerns. In collaboration with Sergio Leone, Luciano had become extremely successful. Back then, I could never have imagined that the phrase "the good, the bad, and the ugly" and the accompanying eight-note musical theme would become so embedded in our lexicon. Every time I hear the score, or read those words—and they are commonly used—I think of Luciano. He was that archetypical romantic: tall, dark and very classically handsome Italian, in his mid-thirties, always

Harriet, ca.1967.

impeccably dressed—and he smelled delicious. My olfactory sense is strong, and to this day, I confess that I find Dior's Eau Sauvage arousing.

Luciano had an elegant apartment on Via Veneto, decorated with fine paintings and costly *objets d'art*. He employed a housekeeper who kept the place immaculate, and prepared lovely meals for him and his guests. She was also well-trained enough to discreetly disappear at the right moment. The bedroom had blue gauzy drapes that billowed in the hot, sultry Roman afternoons. I would watch their gentle movement while lying on Luciano's bed, after he had taken me again. He was always solicitous afterwards, bringing me water to drink and a warm cloth to put on my pummeled, tender parts, as he murmured soft words of astonishment and gratitude at how aroused he was by me, how compatible he felt we were.

I was not particularly interested in Luciano when we first met, handsome and charming though he was. I was already involved with one of the members of The Living Theatre, an anarchic international theatre troupe founded and led by Judith Malina and Julian Beck. The Becks had their roots in New York, where they were part of the intellectual art scene emerging in the fifties and early sixties. Their circle included John Cage, Allen Ginsberg, and other cutting-edge artists and writers. Le Living, as the troupe was known in Europe, was theatre embodied, whether on or off the stage. When Andrea and I met them in Rome in 1967, they were rehearsing for a film with Bernardo Bertolucci, and were readying for performances in Paris at the famous Moulin Rouge in Montmartre. They were performing *Frankenstein, Antigone, Mysteries,* and *The Brig,* which had become their signature pieces. Funnily enough, Le Living happened to be staying in a *pensione* right around the corner from where Andrea and I were.

One night, when it was too hot to sleep, she and I had gone out for a walk, in search of cooler air and something cold to drink. We wound up in a restaurant where we found a couple of interesting men. One of them had long brown curls, and wore little round rose-coloured glasses; the other was a tall, built black man, who looked very cool. Before we had embarked on this trip, I had made Andrea a bet that, within a week of arriving in Rome, we would be able to find and plug into a "grooving" scene. It was 1967 after all, and I was still that hippie chick who had come from Yorkville. Our week was almost up. I went over to the dude with the rose-coloured glasses and asked if he was Italian. "No," he said, "I'm English." They were both members of the Living Theatre. We talked with them a while, then went back to their *pensione* for a smoke. I stayed the night, while Andrea, determined for the moment to hold onto some version of a routine and her chastity, stumbled around until she eventually found our *pensione*. In the light of the next day, we both thought it was hilarious that it had taken her so long to find our place, which was literally around the corner.

We began spending a good deal of time with the fascinating, colourful, international, wild Living Theatre folks. Andrea tried in vain to get us up early enough to go and visit the Vatican, which, by the way, we never did, even though we spent over a month in Rome. Thus, when Luciano came along, I was not particularly interested. He, however, was relentless in his pursuit, and wore me down, having his way, as he was clearly accustomed to doing. I was a free spirit, and as awful as it is to admit now, I could handle being with two men at the same time (in a pre-AIDS world). Although I did not adore being with Luciano—there was that ego in the way—he was interesting, intelligent, elegant, enticing, and very sophisticated. I learned many things from him. We became occasional lovers. He was generous and would have given me anything in the world. But I felt a commitment to return to college, so left Europe and all my lovers, returning to Boston when that summer was over.

I left Boston, however, before completing all the credits I needed to graduate. For two years, I took the courses I was interested in, and then—not giving a hoot about my degree—decided to leave.

Back in Toronto, I attended Seneca College, where I met Stephen Shuster, the only son of Frank Shuster, of the then well-known comedy duo Wayne and Shuster. Wayne and Shuster were big stars. They had appeared on the *Ed Sullivan Show*—at that time an arbiter of success—numerous times, and they'd had many CBC television appearances and specials. Stephen became, briefly, my first husband. It seemed like a good match. We came from similar backgrounds, we had a lot of fun together, and our families approved, which was a nice change for me. Our fathers had the entertainment business in common, and our mothers shared neuroticism. Stephen was very bright, very sweet, funny, kind, and adorable, but emotionally very young. We had been to Paris together for a holiday and it was fun. We thought we were compatible. I foolishly thought we could make a life together, but Stephen did not have a clear idea of what he wanted to do

Harriet and Stephen Shuster, wedding reception, November 1971.

with his life. I was convinced that all he needed was someone to believe in him, to stand by him, and he would be able to achieve whatever he wanted. How wrong I was.

We were married in November of 1971, in a Rabbi's study (high as kites on weed), and had our reception at what was then an elegant venue in downtown Toronto, The 54th. I wore a crushed velvet, multi-coloured, floor length dress with deep décolletage. Stephen wore a rented tux with a blue ruffled shirt that matched his eyes.

After a few months, it became clear that Stephen was not nearly mature enough for a marriage. I would arrive home after work to our little apartment on Avenue Road and find him stoned, playing music, the apartment a mess from his day and the friends he'd had over. It was as though he was having an endless party, which I was supposed to provide for and clean up from. We'd discuss plans, but he simply could not get motivated. He was a child and although a sweet one, this was not the marriage I had signed up for. He seemed unable to get his head around the

17

concept of being employed, or earning money in some way, of taking his share of responsibility for our marriage and what was needed to make it work. I saw no indication of his ability to step into the shoes of a man who actually was able and prepared to co-create a life together, and I was not prepared to be the only one working, cleaning, cooking, and being the "grown-up." I made the very difficult decision to cut my losses and walk away. It was shattering to both of us.

I moved, temporarily, back to my parent's home. It was a terribly difficult time. I was only twenty-three and, with a marriage that had ended after only a few months, I felt very wobbly about my future. Stephen did not want to divorce so that legal action took a long time.

Over the decades, we still spoke with some regularity. Stephen had a remarkable memory and would tell me things about our time together that I had no recollection of. He would remember songs that I liked and moments that we enjoyed together, and I was always amazed. Later in life, he did achieve some success as a stand-up comedian, working the Yuk Yuks' circuit and performing nationally. At his funeral, many professional comedians honoured Stephen, calling him "a comic's comic." But remembering Stephen, and our young and failed marriage, always makes me feel sad.

When that marriage ended, I had an opportunity for a new job that I jumped at, hoping to lose myself, and my pain, in work. I was hired to handle advertising, publicity, and promotion for International Film Distributors, or IFD, a Canadian independent distribution company. IFD was one of the fingers on the hand of Nat Taylor, a true giant and pioneer in the Canadian motion picture industry. Nat knew me because my father had worked for him at Twinex, a circuit of theatres representing Nat's exhibition finger. Nat was a lawyer, a gruff guy (his gentle and elegant first wife Yvonne used to refer to him as a diamond in the rough) with a big laugh, big nose, and big cigar in his mouth most of the time. He was a true visionary. In addition to his distribution company and his theatre circuit, he owned a ranch called the Circle M (the M was for Michael, his son with Yvonne) that he used for film productions. Nat also believed that Canada should have its own trade paper; he put his money where his mouth was and started one. Hy Bossin, a fine journalist who worked for one of the major Toronto dailies at the time, ran the *Canadian Film Weekly*, which evolved into the *Canadian Film Digest*, a monthly. It never made any money, as far as I know, but Nat did not give up and kept it alive for many years. Nat later went on to mentor Garth Drabinsky, with whom he started up Cineplex. Nat introduced me to the film business.

When I started the job, the woman I was replacing at IFD was supposed to be present, as was her assistant, to show me the ropes. Unfortunately, neither turned up, and I was on my own from day one. I had no idea what to do and there was no one giving me direction on advertising budgets or publicity directives, as is the common practice these days. This situation was "live or die," sink or swim. I was frantic. I checked binders on the shelves, looked up what advertising budgets had been for the pictures in the previous week, and searched for guidelines. It was harrowing but terrific experience.

Before long, I had figured out the rudiments of movie advertising, and I'd begun to put together what I thought were reasonable ad campaigns. I remember one day going into the office of the General Manager, Len Herberman, with my proposed advertising budget for a movie we were releasing. "Too much money," he said. I tried to argue that this expenditure was what it would take to properly advertise the picture. "How much film rental will we make?" he asked me.

"How the hell should I know how much film rental we'll make?" I retorted. That was a function of the sales department, not ad/pub.

None too patiently, he explained to me the ins and outs of advertising budgets and their correlation to film grosses and film rental. The film business by and large no longer demands this kind of knowledge from people here. All control now is mostly in Los Angeles and everyone dances to the tune of those L.A. executives and are grateful for the opportunity to do so. But in the 1970s, in independent Canadian film distribution, being in the film business meant knowing the business, and I set myself to learning it.

19

During this initiation, I also learned how to cut trailers and TV spots, which I used to do at the old Film House offices on Front Street. It was essential that I learn to do these things because many of the movies IFD distributed came from independent American or European companies, and they did not produce marketing materials for North America. Promotionally, I sometimes organized what was referred to (in the olden days) as "ballyhoo" or street exploitation. For example, with titles like *Tales from the Crypt* to market, I persuaded a funeral parlour to lend me a hearse and casket. (In those days, publicity and promotion meant you did not pay for things; instead, you persuaded people to give them to you for free.) I hired a driver to go up and down Yonge Street, while a mechanical hand rose out of the casket, with Bach's *Toccata and Fugue* blaring over loudspeakers. That got attention! For another picture, *Puppet on a Chain*, I contacted a company that made life-sized marionettes, and had one hung by a thick chain from the marquee of the now-demolished Uptown Theatre in Toronto. The film featured a speed boat race, so I co-promoted with a boat company to not only provide prizing for a contest we ran, but to install the speed boat in the lobby of the theatre. In those days, that sort of thing made a statement and got a lot of attention, and there was no L.A. Marketing Department person telling me what I could or could not do. Although my father was in the business, he was known to be very tough, and as tough as he was with everyone, he was tougher with me. Inevitably some people said that I got where I got because I was his daughter. Those were people who didn't really know either of us. I worked twice as hard as anyone so in my own heart I knew what I had achieved was because I had earned it. When *Puppet on a Chain* broke a house record (took in more money than any other movie ever had at that theatre), my father phoned me to tell me the news, and I knew he was proud, though of course he didn't actually utter those words.

When we released *The Richard Petty Story*, Richard Petty, the famous stock car driver, came to town to do some interviews. He flew in on his private plane with his manager, Bob Preddy, his pilot, and his son. Petty and Preddy were both big, tall "good ole' boys" from the South. I was driving a mid-size car then, a

Buick Skylark. I didn't know it at the time, but was subsequently told that the fact that Richard Petty had allowed himself to be driven by a woman was a very big deal. One evening, we were scheduled to do an interview live at the CTV studio during the sports segment of the late night news.

I had driven out to CTV many times, but for some reason this evening I missed a turn, and we were late. I was rushing so as not to miss this live-to-air interview. Richard Petty was in the back seat, his long legs scrunched up under his chin, hands covering his eyes. Bob Preddy rode shotgun. At one point, Bob drawled to me: "Um, darlin', I think we just passed a cop."

I asked, "Is he following us? Just let me know if he's still following us."

Bob replied, "Honey, we went bah so fayast, I don't think he even saw us!"

We arrived in the nick of time to a very nervous CTV staff, and the interview went live-to-air, nationally. Whew! After the P.A. (Public Appearance) tour was done, I received a lovely letter from Richard Petty Enterprises, thanking me for a wonderful job, and letting me know that if I ever grew tired of the movie business, they believed I had a great future as a race car driver and they'd be happy to work with me!

I do not believe there are many people today in the film business in Canada (only one or two come to mind) who enjoy the freedom I had in those days. Advertising is now farmed out to agencies that do media buying, not planning, because the studios do all the planning and give instructions for the Canadian people to execute. The Pub/Promo is so controlled by the studios that in most cases, if a picture is featured at the Toronto International Film Festival, the local Pub/Promo person often does not handle the talent with her press in her territory; a band of publicists— "handlers" from New York and L.A.—descend on Toronto to ensure that things are done "right." Good thing I am retired!

Back then, I had to do everything possible to ensure the picture "would open," since the life of any movie depends largely on how much money it grosses on opening weekend. One of the pictures I worked on was the re-release of *This Is Cinerama*. When it originally opened in 1952, it was a sensation, with new technology that made the audience feel like they were actually in the picture, and on the roller coaster that was featured in the film. I had worked hard on the re-release twenty years later and on opening weekend I went to the theatre to check out how the film was being received. I sat in the balcony, and as it happened, a family of two parents and three children sat in front of me. They didn't look like they had a lot of money, and my sense was that this movie was a very special night out for them all. During the film, it became apparent that they were not having a good time. I overheard them say they thought the movie was "a rip-off," and frankly, by then, so did I. This incident precipitated the ethical crisis in my professional life that I alluded to earlier. I simply did not feel good about my work anymore. I evaluated what I was doing in that job and concluded that being a rip-off artist was not the gig for me. Was this young and silly of me? Sure, but it was how I felt and I could not at that point in my life resign myself to selling people crap.

All this to say that I was not the typical starry-eyed, dewy freshman when Irving and I first met. I had been toughing it out in a tough business, and had made my way, learned to swim with the sharks so to speak. I had supported myself with my wits and my hard work, and I had learned to rely on those parts of myself. I was my own woman and did not need to account to anyone, beyond my professional responsibilities.

I had saved some money, so after quitting my job I decided to travel. I had become friends with Jocelyn Drainie, daughter of the renowned actor John Drainie. Jocelyn's mother, widowed by John's untimely death, had married Nat Taylor and it was through Nat that Jocelyn and I became friends. We met up in Lisbon with plans to travel for a few months in Portugal, France, and Gibraltar, but mostly in Spain. When we were in Madrid, we agreed that we were not enjoying the city so much and so we decided that before departing we should see some good flamenco, which we both loved. Our *Frommers* guidebook led us to a club called Torres Bermejas, not far from our *pensione* in the heart of Madrid. We went out on what was supposed to be our last night in Madrid. On the small stage, females were dancing. This was not tourist flamenco, with smiles and pretty flounces. The place and stage were small, the audience mostly Madrilenes. The music was heartrending, the faces tragic, the energy fiery, true gypsy. A male dancer came onstage, completely mesmerizing us with his precise balance of force and sensuality. I had always loved flamenco, the music brought my blood to a boil. Never had I seen anyone dance like this man. When he finished his act, he came off stage, and walked directly and without hesitation straight to our table. He looked at me and said "Shalom," and just stood there, looking into my eyes, waiting for my response. I was astounded. I thought, *Shalom? In a flamenco nightclub in Madrid?* His name was Antonio Vargas, and he was the man I loved beforeI stumbled onto the path that then led me to Layton.

That flamenco evening marked the beginning of a passionate affair that irrevocably affected my life. Antonio was a Jewish flamenco dancer and entrepreneur, born and raised in Morocco and in London. His grandfather had been the chief Rabbi in Casablanca. Antonio spoke Spanish, Arabic, Hebrew, and English with a British accent. He was intense, handsome, with almost black wavy hair and eyes that burned like bottomless pits of obsidian fire. When he danced, it was glorious; he is to this day one of the best, if not *the* best, male flamenco dancer I have ever seen. You can still see him, thanks to YouTube. He was a dramatic, romantic figure, commanding attention whether he walked on stage or into a café.

That first evening, we spent all night talking while walking the streets of Madrid. The first time we made love, he had me gasping in astonishment. I was hardly a sexual novice at that point in my life. Sex was always a big part of who I was, an essential component of my identity. I was open and relaxed about sexual matters. I enjoyed my body, I enjoyed men, and I enjoyed pleasuring them and myself. However, I had never felt anything like Antonio made me feel. He was fascinating and masterful, in and out of the bedroom. He was a passionate, questioning, and intense man, and he had an intellectual mind with a definite bent toward the dark side. And he was moody. He could swing from charm, laughter, and fun to despair and moroseness on the turn of a *peseta*. I learned from him about Madrid's café society, the nightlife, and the underbelly of the city. It was fascinating and exhausting. Jocelyn and I rented an apartment, having decided to stay in Madrid for a while. Antonio was addictive and I was addicted.

After a month or two of life in Madrid, Jocelyn and I decided we ought to continue our travels. After all, we were companions on a journey, and we had spent time sidetracked in Madrid, but where was all that going? I felt an obligation to try and pull away from Antonio, and to continue with the travel plans Jocelyn and I had made. The affair with Antonio was awkward. Jocelyn did not have a lover, and I was not getting any clear messages from Antonio that what we had was anything more than a passionate fling for him. So Joss and I left and headed for France. But it was no good, even in Paris. While I had always loved Paris and felt at home there, I was driven to return to Antonio. I needed to finish my business with him, get closure one way or the other—either make the commitment to stay together or end the affair once and for all. Also, our travel funds were getting scarily low, so Joss returned to Canada and I returned to Madrid. I went immediately to the club where Antonio worked. He looked like he had not slept in weeks. Our time apart had taken its toll on him as well.

Antonio and I lived together for a while. Being with him in this way was romantic and also dangerous. I was with him every night while he performed, which meant we had to sleep during the day. This made it hard for me to find work. Furthermore, I was not fluent in Spanish, so what could I do? I was afraid that unless I had something to do on my own, our relationship would suffer. I was, after all, used to working and being financially independent. The role of lover to the impresario and artist was not an entirely comfortable fit for me, as exciting as it was to feel his passion on and off the stage. Antonio was moody. He occasionally displayed a cruel streak: not physical violence, but a cutting tongue, and I thought I might begin to feel trapped in a situation for which there seemed no long-term workable solution. And yet I could not envision leaving him. Our lovemaking was addictive, exhausting, intense; we had become a couple. When he descended into his dark places, although he could be harsh he was also vulnerable, and I felt I could help him, hold him, be his woman. When he shone in all his glory, there wasn't another man I wanted to look at. Antonio commanded full attention. Being with him was a dilemma, but we were in love. So we stayed together and I tried to find a way to make it work and not be so utterly dependent on him. He never suggested I find work or make money. I think part of him enjoyed my dependency; it allowed him a sense of power, which he liked. However, as much as I loved being his woman, I knew I needed to carve my own path.

After a few months I got a telegram from my father, advising me that my grandmother was very ill and that I should return home; the ticket was being arranged. I left Antonio, temporarily we believed at the time. I cried on my way to the airport and cried all the way back to Canada. I had an image of Antonio in our bed, sleeping as I quietly left. We had made plans, though. We believed that we were going to be together long-term, that it was destined. He was going to come to Canada. I was going to help him set up a dance school here, use my publicity and promotional experience to arrange some performances. He was going to choreograph and teach. We were going to make a life together in Toronto. We exchanged letters and phone calls. Then he simply dropped off the face of the earth.

I was devastated. I had always been a full-figured, voluptuous woman, but I became thin, so thin I looked sick, as indeed I was: heartsick. I could not believe that we had lost each other and with no explanation whatsoever. I could not understand what had happened. I was ill for months, confused and lost. I did not see him again until many years later, in 1992, when I went to see a movie entitled *Strictly Ballroom*. The father of the female lead, a flamenco master, was teaching the young leading man a difficult dance step, the *paso doble*. The first scene of the father doing the steps was shot in shadows, but the moves immediately looked familiar to me. I thought to myself, "That is probably something like what Antonio would look like after all these years." In the next better-lit scene, I saw clearly that it was none other than Antonio himself! I nearly fell off my seat. I knew all those movements, every flash of the hand like a switchblade, each hip thrust, every step of those feet impeccably hammering out the dance, the exquisite, bold curve of that back.... I knew them all. It was indeed Antonio, my passionate lover who had disappeared eighteen years ago, whose disappearance ultimately led me to return to university—and to Irving Layton. Truly, truth is stranger than fiction.

In 2004, my curiosity overcame me, and I googled Antonio Vargas. Numerous pages popped up, with pictures, indicating that he was touring North America with a flamenco troupe, giving master classes as it were. After a bit of back and forth with people who manage the site, I was able to email a message directly to him. When he responded, the first words I'd had from him after twenty years, were: "Whatever happened to 'destiny'?" He had made a home in Australia, married, and had two sons. His wife told me she was surprised that Antonio had actually entered into a correspondence with me, as he was known for not writing. We spoke on the phone a few times, however, our moment had clearly long ago passed. He thought I had abandoned him, as I thought he had abandoned me, and he was as sad and mystified as I was.

We never solved the quandary of how we had lost each other. Was it karma? Did my parents intercept messages from him, which was certainly something they might well have done? Whatever happened to "destiny" indeed? Is there such a thing? I believe so, if only because I refuse to accept that random chaos is all there is. Maybe our destiny was not to be together, and that the breakup was what eventually led to my destiny with Irving.

And so, eventually, in the fall of 1974, after months of grieving the loss of Antonio, I had to return to the land of the living. I embarked on resuming my education to complete the degree I had abandoned midstream; to find my way in the world of the living again; and largely to pursue the opportunity of studying with the great Irving Layton.

There is one more piece of my backstory to be told here, as it may well detail another step along the path that led me to Layton. Another man proposed marriage to me. A man I had met earlier. And, again, had I accepted this proposal, I would have never met Layton. Although I might have instead instead lived *la dolce vita* ... sort of.

A few years later Luciano Vincenzoni was suddenly, and unexpectantly, back into my life. Destiny? One day the phone rang in my office, and there, out of the blue, was Luciano. He had tracked me down, I didn't know how. He was making a picture in Chicago with Peter Falk and Isaac Hayes, and he invited me to visit him for a weekend, and stay at the Ambassador East as his guest. I agreed thinking it would be a little adventure, and fun to see him again. There was also, of course, the flattery of his having sought me out and found me, after so much time. When I arrived at the hotel, the staff greeted me warmly, clearly having been informed by Luciano that I was coming and was to be treated with every respect, any wish fulfilled. In the beautiful suite, there was a lovely note and a lush basket of flowers from him, as well as a bottle of fine champagne. When he finished work that day and came to meet me in the suite, he said in his soft sultry tone: "When I knew you in Rome, you were a beautiful young girl. Now you have become a beautiful woman."

We spent an absolutely luxurious, romantic few days together, and I found him a much more sensitive and generous lover than he had been before. I had matured and he was as elegant as ever and much more gentle. We had fun together, we talked easily and comfortably and a lot. He was highly engaging and interesting. After all, he was a very successful screenplay writer who knew how to weave a tale. Towards the end of our visit, much to my astonishment, Luciano asked me to marry him! I considered it: the life he offered was enticing in all kinds of ways and I did have feelings for him.

Ultimately I declined, in large part because he had stated in no uncertain terms that he did not ever want children, whereas I did. I never considered that he might, over time, change his mind. I took him at his word and that was that. How young I was! Many years later I learned that he'd indeed had children. Nevertheless, I remain firmly convinced that having declined Luciano Vincenzoni's marriage proposal was also one more step along the path that ultimately led me to Irving Layton.

3.

THE FIRST TIME IRVING AND I SPENT an entire night together, we did not make love. In fact, there was no sex at all. We lay fully clothed on the floor of his office at York U., talking for most of the night, sleeping a little in each other's arms. There had been a huge snowstorm, the driving was almost impossible, and he had decided to just stay put. I was in his office when he called home and told Aviva he was going to stay the night at York. Irving and I had been spending more and more time together, and although we were not yet lovers, the rumours had begun to fly. People— even esteemed academics—love gossip and Aviva certainly knew of my existence by then. I assume she must have asked if I was there, because he vigorously said no, no, nobody was there; he was just staying at the university for the night because it was not safe to try to drive in the storm.

It was not the first time I had heard a man lie to a partner or wife, but I always took the position that that was between them. If a man wanted to cheat on his wife, that was their issue, not mine. If that man wanted me and I wanted him, we'd enjoy each other. How he handled his domestic life was his business. I didn't really care, hippie flower child that I was then, and still am in many ways. My daughter calls me "the last standing hippie." It was, after all, the culture of the time: live and let live, you do your trip and I'll do mine, no judgment, man. I wasn't amoral. I had my own sense of right and wrong. I just didn't believe in sitting in judgment on another.

Irving was actually quite faithful, in spite of his flirtations, and his many coffee romances. Contrary to his public persona, as

I've said, he was not a man who jumped easily or quickly into bed, no matter how enticing the woman may have been, or how available she made herself. And, oh, how available women made themselves to him! The persona he had created was alluring to women, and frankly I am surprised he didn't more often take advantage of the situation. Irving was a perceptive businessman as well as a great writer, and he knew that creating that persona of the lecherous, womanizing lover/poet would help boost sales of poetry in what he referred to as a "passionless WASP country." It was a marketing strategy, and as such, it was effective. He was a master at getting attention by being outrageous and provocative.

The morning after that first night together, we made our way through the snowdrifts in the brittle painfully bright frigid air, to the apartment of a colleague and his wife who lived on campus. I recall their raised eyebrows and suggestive looks as Layton and I came in to have showers (separately) and then coffee. I can fully understand how we must have looked, superficially at least. However, one might suppose that these keepers of the gates of higher learning could have peered with more discerning eyes at what was in front of them. Of course, they believed what they wanted to believe, as people generally do. What they wanted to believe fit with the public persona Irving had so steadily cultivated. For his part, Irving seemingly had no concern for what we must have looked like. If he had any thoughts about academic codes of conduct, he never mentioned it. He must have known how this adventure would enflame the gossip throughout the university community, that the story would inevitably reach the ears of his partner. He simply did not give a shit. And neither did I.

That day of course marked the dramatic rise of many more rumours about us and in due course there came to be truth to those rumours. Neither of us was in a hurry to get to that point. Irving was troubled about his long-term relationship because he was committed—to whatever extent—to another woman with whom he had a young son. He was also concerned that he was too old for me.

As for me, I had after all, only some months prior, emerged from the debris of my relationship with Antonio. I was still fragile and disinclined to so quickly lose my heart to another man. I didn't want to suffer loss again. I did not want to be that vulnerable. The only way to avoid it was to hold back. However, holding back with Layton? How long would that be possible?

Irving and Aviva went away for Christmas break. He told me he absolutely had to try to make things work. All the while they were away, he sent me daily postcards, expressing how bottled up he felt, how he missed me. I felt his conflict. I did consider the fact that while he said he "absolutely had to try to make things work," he was simultaneously sending me cards each and every day. Surely his attention and energy were divided? I put all this out of my mind. For the moment, it was enough for me to be with him as we were, to revel in our conversations, in how it felt to be together, as we slowly discovered each other, and allowed our burgeoning feelings to take shape.

It was exciting to be with him, sharing our secret time together, experiencing this new level of intimacy: his smell, the closeness, the vigour of his body. He was a powerful seducer with words and I was so cerebrally aroused that the physical could wait. We were aware that there was an electric current between us. It charged the air, palpable and obvious to everyone. However, I also understood that he was a highly complex man and I realized that to embrace the physical would raise the level of our relationship to a more profound and serious place. This was no frivolity, for either of us. Irving was bound to David and his son's mother in so many ways. So, while the relationship between us was confounding, marvellous, tempting, it was also terribly conflicting for him. Even though he was tortured, he refused to turn away from me. The torture, after all, was producing poems and that, for him, ultimately made everything worth it.

We began to visit with each other more during the days at school. I'd go to his office in Winters College at York, where we would talk and talk. This evolved into going out for coffee or for pizza. We spent more and more time together. Talking with Irving was in itself an education. His appetite was formidable: for reading, for knowledge, for learning about the person he was spending time with, for food, for everything. He grabbed each moment of each day and celebrated it, devoured it, tore into it like a famished beast.

Once we reached the point of physical intimacy, his appetite was as profound in that arena as it was in all others. We were immediately sexually compatible—astonishingly so. I hungered for him, desired him more than I believed possible, and he clearly was equally smitten. In those early days, the force flowing between us was so powerful, so surprising, that we were defenseless against the shock waves. Sometimes during a break in one of my classes, I'd go to his office for a quick visit, and return to class flushed, fresh from a brief embrace. We ravenously grabbed whatever time we could.

Many years later, I spoke with Clara Thomas, professor and author of *The Manawaka World of Margaret Laurence*, among other books. Clara had been one of my great professors at York, and she remembered the days when I would return to her class after a break breathless, and she knew I'd been to see Irving. She was one of the few, if not the only, profs at York at that time who did not stand in judgment on us, bless her heart. It was Clara who nominated Irving for his Honourary Doctorate. Clara warmly recalled those days, and confessed to me that she thought the affair was a wonderful thing!

Irving told me about his relationship with Betty Sutherland, how fresh and bohemian she was, and that her looks reminded him of Ingrid Bergman. Betty was related to the actor Donald Sutherland, and was sister to John Sutherland, with whom Irving had become associated in the days of his early poetry chapbooks. John and Betty had started the literary magazine *First Statement,* the two of them on the cusp of everything new and exciting about poetry in Canada. Irving told me that when he and Betty were married, he had walked into their kitchen one day and noticed that mould had been growing on their bread and was spreading across the kitchen counter. Irving liked his women sexy and bohemian, but he also liked his home kept in order. Although he chuckled as he told the story, it had offended his senses to see that mould. He also told me about a time when Betty had had a sexual indiscretion and told him about it, how it had actually enflamed his passion, how sometimes that kind of betrayal was a turn-on. I was puzzled, because I certainly had never felt turned on by betrayal. Whatever my relationships had been, they were honest.

It took me a long time to understand the darker, more perverse side of Irving, the one that could and would do hurtful things, so long as a poem could be dragged out of the experience. Anything was justified if a poem resulted—anything (short of murder).

Betty had gotten Bell's Palsy, and one part of her once-lovely face had dramatically drooped. Irving confessed to me that he sometimes thought that the affliction was retribution for wrongs done to him by Betty, and that it was the spirit of his mother looking out for him, getting even with anyone who hurt her son. The spirit of his mother was a force that stayed with him as long as I knew him. He was superstitious about her, and he told me many times that he believed she was watching out for him and rescuing him from dangerous situations. Her rough love was deeply embedded in his psyche and their relationship, in part, helps to explain his need and desire for women, and his simultaneous exaltation and rejection of them.

The marriage with Betty ended as his relationship with Aviva took hold. Irving, however, only divorced Betty many years later, when he and I were legally married in 1978.

While he longed for the solidity and security of a long-term committed and—certainly with me—monogamous relationship, a woman had to understand that she would be on her own much of the time, including as a parent. His first child, his first lover, would always be his writing. Irving felt, in retrospect, he had not been there for his children as much or as well as he would have wished. Free-spirited hippie that I was, I also loved to cook and I had a strong home-making desire; part of him longed for that too. It may have been "bourgeois" of me, but if it was, then it was "bourgeois" of him as well. Perhaps that contributed to his lashing out at me on occasions, that recognition that some of what I provided was actually some of what he wanted, whether or not he liked to admit it to himself. He was not going to get mouldy bread and dirty kitchens with me. He was going to get an orderliness that allowed room for his needs, a sort of domestic discipline that worked hand in glove with his writing discipline. He was going to get a clean home and good food, and dear reader do not for one moment think he did not like these things.

Anything that happened was grist for Irving's mill. Sometimes he would say something outrageous, just to try it on, like a devilish kid pushing the envelope to see how much he can get away with. Irving would say things because he liked to hear the sound of them, or he would do things simply to set something in action and see how it would unfold. He would watch it all happen, with neither concern nor regard as to whether anyone might get hurt along the way. It was like an experiment to him; he would use the experiment as fodder, devour it and then regurgitate it, as poetry. He repeatedly proclaimed, like a cock crowing: "I am a poet who turns shit into roses"; "I will immortalize you"; "I am a dreamer who makes dreams come true." I did not believe him. This last pronouncement he made so repeatedly that after several months I gradually began to think maybe he meant it. And his words did become truth. He *was* a dreamer who made dreams come true.

If he could be in difficult circumstances and create a good poem out of it, that seemed to confirm his ability to alchemize projections and abstract images into a reality that could be seen, felt, touched on the page. If he created a situation that felt horrible—for himself or others—and out of that situation would be birthed a good poem, that seemed to encourage belief in him, in his ability to make something—a poem, a love, a dream— come true. I suppose had I not had such a fervent love of his poetry, I would not have been able to love the man or his visions. But I want to articulate something here: I am not certain whether or not Irving actually had an inability to see other people as more than ends to poems. I tend to think that he sometimes looked at people and their situations as a scientific experiment; after all, he had obtained a Bachelor of Science degree, not a Bachelor of Arts. In the same way as he could be fascinated by a dead frog on the road and write a poem about it, he could be fascinated by the machinations of people finding themselves in whatever circumstances. He was endlessly fascinated; that is the truth, simple and complex as it may be.

We began to dream of going away together. He spoke more and more about us travelling together in the summer, when the academic year ended. We talked about where we could meet, where we would travel. I thought it was improbable, that his words were lovely but most likely just the ravings of a man inflamed by a new, passionate affair with a much younger beautiful woman. Poetic ranting, at best. I considered the trip itself highly unlikely to actually materialize. I supposed he was just feeding me romantic stories that he thought I'd like to hear, all a part of his seduction. While I enjoyed hearing the stories, I did not allow myself to believe them. They seemed fantasy, not autobiography. I continued to try to keep some small measure of emotional disengagement, to protect myself even as I yearned to capitulate. He continued talking about this dream trip, detailing every place he wanted to go with me, telling me that he felt like this was a new chance at life, that he felt more comfortable with me than he had ever felt with any other woman. Enlivened by our affair, he became inspired to write more poems. He nicknamed me Gypsy Jo—because I was still and always the gypsy, and because Jo was the name that had popped into my head one day, I'm not sure why. He said he really wanted us to be together. Over the course of that first winter we shared, our plans evolved. We were thinking of Italy, then his beloved Greece. My head was a tumult of ambiguities, doubts, hopes, refusals, desires, and belief.

The Spanish Steps, or Piazza di Spagna, had become one of my favourite spots in the world, dating back to the summer of '67, so Irving and I agreed on that as our point of rendezvous. That summer of 1975, David and his mother were going to Morocco. They planned to meet up with Scott Symonds, a Toronto writer from a wealthy Rosedale background, who was living in some kind of decadence in Morocco. Irving planned to meet me in Rome, and after a few days there we would begin our journey towards Greece, where he was accustomed to spending his summers. I had never been to Greece.

4.

H ARDLY BELIEVING THIS TRIP WITH IRVING was actually going to happen, I flew first to London to visit my friend Jocelyn, who was living with an art restorer in a groovy London loft. From there I flew to Rome, to rendezvous with Irving. Were we really going to be together?

Rome. A city I loved, a city that already held a piece of my heart and precious memories, a city that came to mean even so much more. Irving wrote about Rome in his poem for me, "Lady On The Piazza," where he says: "Love, so long as I draw breath/ this city is you/ and I shall always see you/ sitting on the steps of the Piazza/ surrounded by flowers and ruins." The day we were to meet was perfect: sunny and warm. I was wearing a long, white cotton skirt and white top, gauzy and flowing. I remember someone on the street stopping me on my way to meet Irving, saying I was *bellissima*, and that I looked like I was going to a wedding. In a way, I felt I was, as that day marked the beginning of our time together away from our respective homes, away from all the turmoil whirling around us over the past months. It would just be us and we would see how things went.

Irving had trepidations about being with a woman so much younger than himself, about his ability to satisfy me. However, in all honesty, most of his concerns were for David and Aviva, and Irving's ability to end their relationship. He repeatedly said that if we were good together for real, away from everything and everyone else, then he'd find the way to end his long-term relationship with Aviva, to finally break it off so that we could have a new life together. I believed him by this time. After all, he had made this dream of our travelling together come true, hadn't he? Why not believe the rest? Slowly, I was becoming a convert both to his dream—which was becoming my dream too—and to its becoming a reality. It was exciting to be part of his life, his creative process; to hear him say that I contributed to that creative process in a way that no other woman had, because the texture of our love allowed him a space, a freedom and peace to which he had been unaccustomed. He offered me an opportunity to be a part of that creativity; to see poems emerging out of our hours and days and nights; to participate in that inspiration, that stimulus, as his lover and muse. I could not see the future and I did not know whether I wanted to be married to him or not, it was too premature for all that. It was enough to be with each other, and to live the experience of being together.

I waited on the Spanish Steps for hours. Irving did not show up. Finally, I returned to the *pensione*, in a daze of anxiety and despair. Miserable to the core of my being, I crawled into bed, deeply troubled by all manner of worries, fears, and dark ominous thoughts. I'd never see him; he had changed his mind about us being together; something so terrible had happened that it prevented him from leaving to meet me. All I could think about were all the things that must have gone wrong to prevent him from coming. What was I to do? I had no way to reach him, even if I had known where he was. We did not have cell phones back then. Nor email. Exhausted, I finally drifted off into a restless and light sleep. After a while, persistent banging on the door dragged me out of my nightmares. When I opened the door there stood Irving, grinning from ear to ear.

To say I was amazed is an understatement. I could hardly believe my eyes. He was frazzled, tired, but tremendously excited, and so proud that he had found his way to me. He jubilantly proclaimed that he had always told me he was a dreamer who made dreams come true: we were together in Rome! It was a completely thrilling moment and we fell into each other's arms. At that instant, everything and anything *was* possible. Thus began our first travel rendezvous, the summer of 1975.

We stayed in Rome for a few glorious days and then headed by train to Florence. It was during that time that I began to keep a journal of our life together, a journal (1975-1981) that I kept though the years of our affair and our marriage, the birth of our daughter, and the end of our marriage. I am very happy I kept that journal because memory cannot be trusted to provide an accurate history. We are inclined to forget the rough parts, the hurts, and disappointments. Painful as it has been for me to read through my journals and use them to help me write this book, they do represent the truth, the truth precisely as I saw, felt, and lived it at the moment of writing each day. I recorded where we went, what we saw, the genesis of poems, Irving's observations about everything. Reading those pages, after more than thirty years, has been revelatory for me. I had put away so much, had forgotten details or chosen not to remember things that were too painful. I have rediscovered not only the personal story of Irving and myself and our years together, but also a recounting of the literary scene of the time: events we attended, gatherings of the glitterati of the CanLit scene, parties and readings, as well as all the torment of our on-, off-, and on-again tempestuous affair. I have kept the journals, and his letters, and they have helped me stay the path of honesty, no matter how uncomfortable it has been at times, uncomfortable for both myself and perhaps readers.

Some of my discomfort stems from the writing. I was a young woman besotted by this great passion, and I wrote straight from my heart, without edit or thought of how anything might sound. I only knew that I needed to record it all. Reading it now, I have to resist the urge to edit my words, for that would be untrue to the story, so I cannot permit myself to make any changes, other than omitting some lines here and there in order to not hurt others. If I quote from the journal, dear reader, you must know it is how it was written. It is not my intention to hurt anyone with this story. However, so much has been written and said by others, and most of it untrue, including terrible lies about me. So this is the truth, my truth, for the record, at last.

5.

JOURNAL, JUNE 4TH, 1975. "Irving and I are staying in a *pensione* in Florence. We explored the city for a few days. One afternoon it began to rain, so we took shelter in an open doorway of a house. Layton seated himself on the grimy old steps and began to write another poem. It never ceases to amaze me how he could just claim a spot, sit himself down, and begin scribbling, head moving with the rhythm of his writing, totally absorbed in his own internal dance of creativity. When the rain subsided, as we were leaving the building we noticed a plaque on the wall of the house, informing that Dostoyevsky had lived there. It frequently seemed as though benevolent spirits were guiding Irving. In Florence, a city of beautiful art and creative finery of all sorts, Irving claimed to feel claustrophobic. There were too many shops selling expensive leather, too many jewellery stands lining the Ponte Vecchio, where the Italian rumble is drowned out by the more piercing harsh tones of American tourists. We spent most of one day in the Uffizi. Irving said he would have loved to be a painter, the detail of a Bronzini or Lippi excited him so. But he also proclaimed there to be little originality in Renaissance art. A few masters, and the rest are only imitators, followers of a particular school, he said. I was fatigued by so much time in the galleries, while also fascinated that such a beautiful city could seem to be devoid of joy, aside from ours. It is a merchant's town. I am restless here, and so is Irving. After Rome, so rich in so many ways, Florence is not exciting us."

From these couple of days emerged the first poem in his book, *For My Brother Jesus,* "Florence," and it captures how we felt about the city. In my journal, I wrote: "Layton has written another great poem, about it all: the stink of money and fine leather, the absence of laughter and music." He also wrote "Adam" in Florence, the last lines of which are: "About the woman/ he has in mind for me/ we talk softly and for a long time/ and very, very carefully."

Irving was writing like mad, sometimes three poems in a day; the poems were matching stroke for stroke the pace of our lovemaking, as though one fuelled the other. His energy was astounding. In terms of his ability to satisfy me, it was easy to understand why his age was a non-issue. The only issues with regard to his age were the long string of unfortunate domestic histories (or hysterias) he dragged behind him like a jagged chain: the pain chain. He was struggling to unravel himself from that, even though, as Camus says, "We get used to anything." Irving had become accustomed to that particular flavour of pain. He made poems out of it, and as I've said, if anything provided the juice for a poem, it was worth it, whatever the "it" was. Perhaps in me, with me, he was finding himself capable of being a different version of himself, a happier creator, and perhaps he was uncertain of his ability to create out of a place of happiness instead of turmoil. Perhaps he was addicted to the pain and doubted his ability to break the addiction.

We left Florence early in the morning, after being devoured by bugs all night. Layton was singing joyously as we lugged our bags to the railway station. The train was crowded, but I wrote that "fortunately we managed to secure a window seat, which is important because there is a table which Layton uses to write on." We changed trains in Rome, "enjoying our usual lunch on the train, of food we brought: bread, cheese (gorgonzola or blue), salami, fruit, and tomatoes"; that was our favourite picnic. We met some interesting people on the train, one of them a dreamily lovely young American woman who told us about a place in Greece called Paxos, as yet undiscovered by tourists. Irving had never been there, in spite of all his years of going to Greece. As this would be a first for both of us, we decided to make that our next destination. We were travelling without a fixed itinerary and felt so free. We arrived at Brindisi on a Saturday night, and after the most incredible chaos I've ever been part of, finally made it onto the Adonis. The next morning, we arrived at Corfu. Irving had scribbled off "Adonis," a four-liner poem about our lovemaking on board the ship of that name. Our sexual craving for each other was absolutely insatiable and as we had neither a private room nor were able to find an available secluded corner, we resorted to the washroom to satisfy the clamorous demands of our bodies! Even as our passion surged and climaxed, we laughed, joyfully and totally appreciating the outrageousness of the moment. And, no, I am not embarrassed to remember it. It was a time filled with passion, joy, creativity, and an aliveness that few people ever experience. We had at it, full on. I thought and still think that "Adonis" is a giggle.

Irving was so happy to be back in Greece. It was his place, I think more than any other. His joyous nature soared there, as though the very air set his soul free. We stayed in Corfu for a couple of days, in a room that cost us about $1.50 a night. Irving's suitcase was broken into and several thousand drachmas amounting to over a hundred Canadian dollars were stolen. I wrote, "He says it's not actually the loss of money that so terribly distresses him, it's the heavy feeling of suspicion, the lack of trust, that the incident forces him to carry around." We made our way onto a small fishing-ferry boat, which took us to Paxos. "Layton has bought himself sandals, a new sailor cap, and sunglasses—which he claims will be his purchases for the summer—except for something he will buy me, I don't know what." He was not a big shopper, almost never a big spender, but what he did buy gave him enormous delight, and he was almost childlike in his exuberance. That exuberance was a core part of his being.

There was exactly one hotel in Paxos, which was then a tiny fishing village. "It is on a hill, and quite a climb up ... but the view once you get there is worth it. We passed goats and the occasional donkey on the way up. Layton has been writing like a madman. We spent yesterday morning looking for a house to rent, but didn't find one. There are a couple of new ones, with hot water (something of a luxury here), and all the facilities. But they are too large for us and cost too much. The owners rent out rooms, and thus make more money. Our hotel costs us $4.00

a night and the food is cheap. Last night we ate a big plate of fish, a salad of tomatoes, cucumber, olives, and feta, plus wine, and bread and it was about $5.00 for the two of us. We saw the boats come in earlier in the day with the catch, so the fish is really fresh." Subsequently, we looked at a couple of houses but did not find something that suited us, so we were able to negotiate a deal at the hotel: $7.00 a day each for the room and three meals! "One of our great delights is to breakfast on the terrace, enjoying a big pot of very hot strong tea, while overlooking the most glorious view of sea, trees, and flowers. On our way down the hill we often pass some goats or a donkey. This morning there was a big turkey tied up in the square. I suppose he'll be dinner for someone. We see the fishing boats come in with their catch of the day—and eat it for dinner. This afternoon we found a secluded beach where we sunbathed and swam naked. The sun and water were glorious. There is always a breeze so we don't scorch. This evening over dinner, Irving read to me from Petronius—'The Satyricon' and 'Fragments.' Irving said Petronius was one of the people he'd like to be with in the afterworld, and also Byron. Irving also said that although Keats and Shelley were greater poets, he wouldn't want to be with them, as they'd be too melancholy. He'd choose Byron, who was a real lover, who really lived before his too early death. We were also talking about the idea of starting a school here. We'd select about ten students who would live here say from April-September, or May-October. For those six months, we'd immerse ourselves in reading, talking, and Irving could be teaching. Two days for poetry, three days for reading great works: Petronius, Aristotle, Nietzsche, etc. He doesn't want to charge for the teaching as such—we'd just establish some sort of token fee to cover costs + a bit. Irving seems to enjoy this idea."

Those first few weeks of being away together, I began to really see Layton, the writer, in his element. Although I was twenty-seven and he was sixty-three, I wrote often in my journal of his incredible energy—he would climb hills and mountains like he had wings on his feet, singing heartily while I'd trudge up behind him, half-blinded by the sweat pouring into my eyes. He would write for hours on end, then enjoy a two-mile walk with me, swim, and then devour a meal with hearty appetite and strong stomach. After all that came our passionate love-making, many times every day, until our appetites were sated. He wrote poem after poem for me, inspired by me: "For My Incomparable Gypsy," "In Praise of Older Men," and "Daphnis and Chloe" in those early days and nights of our being away together. In "For My Incomparable Gypsy" he voiced not only the exuberance and ecstasy of newfound passion and its fulfillment, but also the warning notes of the poet recognizing the fragility of the muse in her exalted, airy perch and his resistance to her downward slide into a more mundane role: "Marriages are for common clay;/ for you I wish eternal day/ not pukes and the rounded belly./ Only in this embalming poem/ my unravished beauty be mine." He also playfully, humorously gave voice to his concern about our relationship, specifically our age difference. In his poem "In Praise Of Older Men," also composed during the first weeks of our trip that summer, he made fun of my supposed love of only old men (because I loved Picasso and concert pianist, Artur Rubenstein): "Despite my sixty-odd years/ my wrinkles are too few, my back's/ not bent enough/ my ways too rough and vigorous/ to ravish my darling." That summer also marked the beginning of the Jesus theme he would explore further in *For My Brother Jesus,* as well as *The Covenant* and *The Tightrope Dancer.*

In the spring of 2013, I was at an exhibition at the Tate Modern, in London, UK. The exhibit was entitled "Poetry and Dreams." Mostly a collection of surrealists, there were a few Picassos, and once again, as always in my life, I found myself resonating to his work. My daughter, also at the Tate, but at another exhibit, texted me just to check in, and I replied: "I'm fine, I'm with Picasso." The first line of Irving's poem "In Praise of Older Men" is: "It's a good thing Picasso's dead." That line, that poem, written at the beginning of our love affair, our first trip to Europe together, is so like Picasso's early paintings. I was, at the Tate, looking at an early Picasso portrait of Marie-Therese. It is all about her seductiveness, her sensual, compliant, submissive body that enchanted him for several years. She was so much younger than he was at the time he painted it in 1968. At the end of the exhibit there was also one of the last paintings Picasso did of his then wife, Jacqueline. Completed in one day, the brushstrokes are wild, rough. There are no neat lines; the work explodes off the canvas. The woman is an embodiment of sexuality, her legs spread; she is lying back, exposed, vulnerable in one way, tempting in another. The commentary by an art critic of the time questions whether her face is "ferociously defiant or heartwrenchingly vulnerable." Her face is beautiful and sad, as it must be when a young woman loves and is loved by a man so much older than she, a man with only a few years left to live. Compared with the earlier painting, which is, for all its sensuality, neatly composed, delineated, and contained (a man who thinks he is in control of his life), the lines clearly drawn, the portrait of Jacqueline holds and displays all the mess and messiness of life, and the realization that in spite of whatever passion he may still be feeling, it can no longer be directed in the same way. It is enough to be able to feel that passion. Try though he might, controlling that passion is utterly impossible. He ultimately knows there is no control, there is only passion, woman, and art. He needs woman for his art, though he may rage against that and against her. It is the ferocity of their relationship that keeps the life force pounding and pulsating. The desire is only to continue to feel it and to make art of it.

One journal entry reads: "Early evening ... Irving is having a pre-dinner sleep, after our afternoon in bed. This morning we took a vigorous two-hour walk to the top of Paxi, then had a swim. On our walk this morning, he was talking about some of his poems that have gone without the attention he feels they deserve; not with any bitterness whatsoever, just a smile and a shake of his magnificent head. On the winding steep road, we stopped at one spot; here there were the dried, brown branches of some bushes that had died. All around them were lush green, hardier ones that had survived. And thrusting upwards powerfully from the midst of it all was a tree, virtually growing out of rock. For Layton, this was what life is all about, he said, the whole thing summed up right there: death surrounded by life, not the other way around, and the will to live showing in that one tree. Looking across the mountain side at the water and sky, melting one into the other, he said he saw a fish wink at him.... Near the terrace of our hotel, the geranium bush is losing its fat red flowers, but next to it, a tree is blooming, a tree with long white flowers that grow upside down and hang from the leafy branch tips. There is an almond tree in the garden, so close I can pick the fruit from our window. All day the roosters crow to us and the sky, the birds sing, occasionally a donkey brays. It's a delightfully peaceful place and we're content here. Layton has even begun to talk about making inquiries regarding the cost of a plot of land, and building us a nice little house. Of course, he is still wrestling with A/David in his mind. He says he wants to spend the rest of his days with me. But he's so terribly attached to David, and he has a deep sense of responsibility. But the fact remains that he has never felt as relaxed, as spontaneous, as naturally happy with her as he claims he does with me. For my part, I would be happy to stay with him...."

A few days later, the journal entry reads: "I'm alone this morning; Irving has gone off poem hunting on the white gravelly roads up the mountain. It's virtually the first time we're not together, since we started.... With all his knowledge, wisdom, experiences, he retains an almost child-like wonder of the world. The sun, water, music—these things fill him with a profound ecstasy. It is very beautiful to be sharing it with him; he is a generous lover. He is also, of course, something of a liar. When I tell him so, he laughs, and says but of course he is—all poets are liars.... He was telling me yesterday that I'm too beautiful for him; that he's too old for me; that this is the supreme irony, the big joke that the gods are playing on him: to have finally given him everything he ever wanted, wished, and dreamed for in a woman—now, when he's too old. Or if not too old yet, will be soon. He says he lusts after me like a young man, he wants always to be holding, kissing, embracing me. Now his body is healthy, vigorous and strong— but he sees the time coming too soon when his desire will be greater than his capability. It's terribly sad and painful to hear him talk like that.... I know it's true too, but I don't want to look at it. Not now, when we're so happy and good together...."

Reading the entry now, it is of course obvious that he was not prepared to make the break with his domestic scene at that point. Truly, who could imagine he would have been, except a young woman swept away by the passion and poetry of the moment. He tried to put the "blame," as it were, on his age since that was the poignant thing to do, more so in the face of his amazing ego. He was also afraid to trust me; this too is easy to understand. Women had hardly been paragons of honesty with him. Given what he knew of my background, and my age in particular, how could he seriously trust that I would be able to live with him? I know that in his heart this tore at him for years. On the one hand, he desired me and wanted to believe he could have a life with me. On the other hand, he felt the fool for thinking that such a relationship could actually survive. Maybe he knew in his heart of hearts that he would inevitably hurt me, in spite of himself. Maybe hurting women had become a deeply embedded pattern in life by this point. He repeatedly warned me away, even as time after time he pulled me back to him. This was at the centre of our dilemma, aside from anything to do with his domestic issues, although those he tried to hold in another trunk full of demons that he could not keep the lid on. However, his creative juices were flowing, and as I was learning—and came to learn more deeply as our relationship endured—the poems justified and validated everything. This was undeniably true for him and for some time, also for me. This question, however, of whether those poems validate anything and everything for me became more pressing and perplexing as our affair continued.

A few days later, I wrote in my journal: "We have decided that I will return to Toronto in two weeks, and go to summer school and complete my degree. It has been a most difficult decision to make. So we will leave Paxi on Thursday, so I can see some more of Greece before I go: Athens, Delphi, Patmos, Hydra. All day yesterday Irving was hard at work on a long poem about Jesus. He's very excited about it. At this moment, he is in our hotel room, typing out the poem. I came to the square to buy some things, and have not had one moment's peace. Spiro [one of the men in town; he was loudly aggressive in his pursuit of me] is eternally on the make. He's married of course, and has two small boys. His only object in life all week has been to convince me to make love with him. He asks only five minutes, certain that this will be enough to convince me. I am getting very eager to see Irving's face. This morning he was telling me about his early adolescence, and about his first romances: Gertie and Suzanne, and Jenny. I have orders to steep myself in Nietzsche for the next few years. Layton says that he's been going back to him to re-read and re-read every summer for the past forty-five years or so, and that it is only recently he's begun to really know him. He says Plato and Nietzsche are the only two great poet-philosophers, the only two he repeatedly goes back to. Over breakfast, he compared for me the prophetic wisdom of Nietzsche as against 'silly Marx'.... Basically, that Nietzsche said exploitation was inevitable, whereas Marx said that it could be abolished by re-structuring society, doing away with classes. Russia today proves the folly of Marx's views. It was all kind of heavy for a beautiful morning, but, ever the teacher, that's the way he is, and I love to listen to him.... Yesterday he spoke to Aviva, who plans to go to Spain and then Morocco; there are friends to visit in both places. As I will be leaving in two weeks, Irving is now at a bit of a loss as to what to do with himself, where to go. I'm hoping that Leonard [Cohen, and friend to Irving] will be back in Hydra very soon....

"We plan to leave here on Thursday, heading for Corfu and then Patmos. Layton and I are not happy to be leaving—it's been so very beautiful here. We'll miss the great food the lady here cooks—and the long quiet walks—and the deserted beaches where we strip and lie naked in the sun, go naked into the bracing salt water. Layton is very taken with this island; he keeps saying he wants to come back and live here with me. He's a beautiful man to live with—a joy to wake up with in the morning. Imagine awakening to a smile, and words of joy and tenderness. I have never felt better in my life—although keeping up with him isn't easy. I ask him if he's sure I'm not too old for him.... He's still working on his Jesus poem, which has grown in length and gives him no rest. He gleefully anticipates the outraged reaction it will get."

Although my journal entry indicates that the decision for me to leave Greece was mutual, there is more to it. I actually got severe food poisoning in Athens, and was deathly ill for a couple of days. When I was finally able to get on the plane back to Canada, I remained sick for weeks afterward. A nasty parasite had invaded my system. Irving, instead, had a cast iron stomach. What nearly killed me gave him either no symptoms, or at worst, a mild case of diarrhea or gas. Did my illness make it easier for me to leave? Did my emotional turmoil contribute to my physical distress? Quite possibly this was so, although the food poisoning was a reality. Perhaps I also reacted to an emotional poisoning, a deep disappointment at Irving's vacillation. I think I must have sensed his ambivalence about our relationship, his lack of readiness to commit to me. Whatever the reasons, most of the poems in *For My Brother Jesus* were written during that summer, when we were together in Italy and Greece, and subsequently after I left him (the first of many times) to return to Toronto, while he went on to Spain and Morocco.

6.

I HAD DECIDED TO TAKE THE HIGH ROAD. From my position of love (and frustration), and in an attempt to make the situation easier for him, I returned to Toronto to complete my degree. It was an excuse, a way to graciously let him off the hook, so to speak. I wanted him to sort out his mess without the distractions, conflicts, and allures I provided. I knew I could not resolve anything for him; he needed to come to a decision on his own and I did not want to be in the way.

After I left, Irving stayed in Greece for a few weeks. During that time, he wrote some wonderful poems that could not have been written had I stayed. Nevertheless, as much as I adored the poems, I adored being with him more. By mail, he sent me "The Last Dryad" and "Of The Man Who Sits In The Garden," the latter of which has always been one of my favourites of all the many love poems he wrote for me. That was when I knew what it was like to be the woman who inspired his love poems. It was marvellous, tortuous, twisted, complex, and glorious, and I would not have missed a second of it.

I did indeed attend summer school at York, taking the two courses required to complete my undergraduate degree. One course was with Stan Fefferman, and the other with the lovely Irish writer John Montague. God only knows what they must have thought of me, distracted and half-crazed, receiving daily letters from Layton, letters that included drafts of poems (which I still have), as well as page after page of him pouring out his tortured soul. I remember going out of the classroom during a break one afternoon and sitting at the foot of a huge tree to read over again his most recent letter. It was not until my legs were covered with stinging bites that I jumped up and realized I had been sitting in a nest of red biting ants! I was a shell of myself, distant from everything around me, estranged from my own skin, to the point where I had not even felt the stinging bites. I was in a haze. How could it be otherwise? I thought. I felt as though the best of me was back in Greece with him. The entire situation confounded me.

On June 27, 1975, Layton sent me a postcard: "I'm in my hotel room, having just breakfasted, and preparing myself for the day's ravages of 'remorse.' Yesterday I felt as lonely as a leper.... In the evening I saw Denise Harvey (she's an Englishwoman who came to Greece eight years ago and decided to remain) whose Protestant conscience keeps her in continuous agitation, so she has neither time nor desire to attend to the vestiges of beauty that are still present in some of her features. She says the book can be out before Xmas, if Ted Sampson lets her have the translations in good time. I miss your lovely hands ... I miss your smile. I miss you. Period."

On June 28, 1975, Irving wrote: "I have just finished a poem which I shall type out for you below. [The poem was 'The Plaka'.] But why weren't you here when my imagination caught fire and I saw the Plaka as Id and the Acropolis towering above it as Superego. You can imagine my excitement when the image or notion first came to me, how I wanted you to be here as the first lines began to form in my mind. The beginning of the poem, of course, was Wednesday night when we supped and dined there and I saw feasters and tables unrolling before my eyes—that is, whenever I was able to take them away from your beautiful face. The 'garrulous old man' is Socrates who was famous for his irony. In fact, the phrase Socratic irony is to be met with in almost every essay or chapter written about him.... O why aren't you here so that I can have someone to talk to? A head of pressure builds up in me and you're not here to help me adjust the guage [sic]. I think I shall take off for Hydra tomorrow and spend several days there before going to some other island. Yesterday I wrote a letter to Desmond Pacey [author, literary critic, and historian, professor, and administrator at the University of New

Brunswick]—probably, alas, my last one to him. I also wrote one to Wynne Francis [professor at Sir George Williams College and later Concordia in Montreal. She was particularly interested in Layton's poetry and published her book, *Irving Layton and His Works*, in 1985]. What can you say to anyone who has lost her husband? I didn't try to comfort her but I told her a beautiful story about Lyman [Wynne's husband] and myself which she probably didn't know...."

My journal indicates that I was so miserable my family actually offered to pay for me to go back to Greece, back to Irving, when my courses were completed! Which was amazingly supportive of them, considering their own confusion about the situation. They asked me: "If he is sending you these letters and postcards every day, and saying he loves you, why is he not with you? Why is he going to Morocco?" I was hard-pressed to try and explain. I called Irving to speak with him about the idea of my returning. Not entirely surprisingly, he was less than encouraging. I could hear the surprise and confusion in his voice. On the one hand, he was sending me poems and letters daily, expressing his love and telling me how much he missed me. On the other hand, he had made arrangements to meet up with Aviva and David in Morocco, which I suspected but did not know for certain, and which he had not told me about—yet.

On July 3rd, Irving wrote from Hydra: "After our voices faded out, I went outside of the Phaedra [the hotel in the Plaka section of Athens where he liked to stay] to do some thinking. Your phone call surprised me as much as it disturbed me—and delighted me. It was great to hear your voice again and your laughter. I'd had you on my mind since you left and kept recalling things that we had done or shared. I never dreamt for a single moment that you'd call only two days after leaving [it was not two days] to say that you were contemplating a swift return. I think my voice must have betrayed my ambivalency. The propitious moment for deciding to stay was in Paxos when we were offered a house and could have lived the kind of life that we had talked about—or maybe it was only I who had. I was writing poem after poem and all the vibes were good. We were there, remember, because we were going to find out whether we could live happily together or not. I thought we were getting on splendidly when you brought up the business of getting your B.A, completely ignoring the fact that I'd counted on spending the whole summer with you. Of course I had my own ambivalencies, but I had them under control. It didn't seem to me that you had yours."

He most certainly did *not* have his "ambivalencies" under control: I knew how confused and torn he was when I had begun to think about leaving him in Greece and returning to school. Who would choose summer school over a committed lover?

His letter continues: "It also seemed to me—and here I might be doing you a great injustice—that I'd have a Forest Hill lady who wouldn't be able to hack it if ever the going got rough. I purposely told you the story of how Aviva and I put up with primitive arrangements: on THAT score I've never heard Aviva complain once. If the comparison seems invidious, it nevertheless has to be made. Human beings are complex and I don't profess to know what was going on in your mind. Do you know, when you became ill in Athens, I even thought it was some unresolved conflict concerning us that had brought on your illness. Stomach cramps—that's terribly suspicious! So after your phone call and after I'd done some cool thinking, I walked about six miles to find the telegram station to wire you not to come. I hope you got the telegram. I wanted some time to be alone so that I could think the whole matter through. I think you do know that I love you deeply and that I always feel intensely alive and happy in your presence. Never before have I ever been so physically alive and creative with a woman as I was with you. Even now I keep on shaking my head over the 'miracle.' But the fact has to be faced that I haven't cut my emotional ties to Aviva, and that leaving her and my son would be extremely painful. I've turned the matter over in my head a thousand times and each time the same red signal flashes through my mind: IT WOULD NOT BE FAIR [caps his]. For many reasons and for many guilts and for many memories, I couldn't justify a separation to my conscience—not yet anyway. My son needs me and Aviva loves me. David is growing into an adolescent and that's just when he'll need a father to give him some sound instruction and to provide him with an image or model. Where will he ever find a better model to imitate or rebel against? So I've decided to give it one more try. I shall leave for Tangiers the end of this month to spend August with Aviva and David. If I find the same old tensions returning—well, THEN I'll know it's hopeless and that I've done everything I humanly could to keep the family intact. This afternoon the person I'm negotiating to buy a house from will give me her decision. It's a beautiful house, one of the most lovely on the island. I've offered her $40,000. If she accepts I might move in by next Monday."

On July 6th, he wrote to me from Hydra. "Tomorrow will be one week that I've been here. Leonard hasn't come but Suzanne [Suzanne Verdal, Leonard Cohen's muse] is expecting him to arrive any day now. I'll stay on till Thursday or Friday and if he isn't here by then I'll make my vamoose to another island. I've a comfortable room downstairs and the use of L's study where I'm now typing this letter and listening to some Greek music on the radio which I bought at Corfu. Remember? The deal I wrote you about in my last letter has fallen through because the woman changed her mind. The house furnishings etc. had all been included for the sum I offered her—$40,000—but she turned around the following day and said she wanted another $1500. I took that as an omen and told her I was no longer interested.... Apart from that, staying on the island for a couple of days made me feel claustrophobic and running into the same people day after day only reinforced it.... In fact, if I'm ever sent to Hell, a distinct possibility, I shall immediately recognize the place as somewhere I've been before—Hydra! Or perhaps Limbo is a better ascription.... Along with this letter I'm sending one off to M.&S. telling them I've another volume of poems which they can have if they'll bring it out next February or March. I'm calling it *For My Neighbours in Hell*. Yup, it's all done, I've been fantastically creative this past week, writing as many as five or six poems each day. And what poems! I guess it must have been a spin-off from the impetus you gave my brain and gonads. I'm keeping the book down to sixty-five poems since I think it's a mistake to publish a book of poems that contains too many of them. It encourages a flipping of pages or at best a superficial reading of what's printed on them. If M.&S. accept this new one it will mean that I'll again have two books published in one year since *Sardonicus* is scheduled for publication in September 1976. Wow!"

Jack McClelland was not enthusiastic about publishing the poems in *Sardonicus* [the then working title of the collection] and not on Irving's proposed timetable either. So Irving gave that book to his former students Howard Astor and Seymour Mayne who published it under their Mosaic Press. Irving dedicated the book to "Jack and Mary," my parents.

The letter continues: "I miss you very, very much.... I can't get your dear face out of mind. Not that I want to, and that's what plagues me. Or your deep sexy voice out of my ear, promising all sorts of delights with each whisper. I'm in love with you and I cannot have you, not unless some good angel—or bad?—can show me some way to obliterate conscience, memory and practical common sense...."

Enclosed with this letter were drafts of three poems: "The Human Cry," "No Visitor from Outer Space," and "North American Poet"; all three appear in the same version, in *For My Brother Jesus*.

In his next letter, July 9th, he included a poem entitled "Island Circe," which is also included in *For My Brother Jesus*. He wrote: "It's two weeks since you left, so it's only right that I should write a poem to mark the bitter occasion. Ah-ha there I go, a hopeless prevaricating poet. But am I, really? Could I have composed the poem if somewhere in me there wasn't lodged the tiniest particle of truth—or a whole stone? ... [D.H.] Lawrence I think it was who gave us all this piece of advice: trust the tale, not the tale-maker...." He rants some more about his dissatisfaction with Hydra, and says, "I'd like to get off this island but there's a possibility Leonard might be arriving tomorrow, so I'm staying over. Furthermore, I loaned Suzanne three hundred dollars and I can't leave until she repays me since I'll need the money to keep me until August.... I've also written a fine poem for Leonard with the title 'Hydra.' It's a meditation on friendship, memory and art—a very complex poem but lyrical and moving.... Will you please phone Robert Weaver [writer, and for many years CBC broadcaster, also founder of the *Tamarack Review*] and ask him whether he received the seven poems I mailed him? 'For My

Incomparable Gypsy'—somewhat revised is among them...."

On July 12th, he writes: "My darling: Yesterday I went into Athens because I knew there'd be a batch of letters from you, and I wasn't disappointed. I was the green envy of all the furriners as they watched me walk away with my epistolary booty. Like a true sybarite, I put off the pleasure of reading them until I was on the boat taking me back to Ydra. Then I savoured it slow and sweet, every lovely syllable. The gulls accompanying the boat and flying directly above me would swoop low enough so that I could see their black-fringed wings and I would toss them some of the tidbits of gossip and news which they immediately snatched up and beaked on to the gulls farther down the line. All of them seemed as delighted as I was for they kept circling over my head and asking for more. I wrote the enclosed poem ["Gull"] after I'd finished reading and re-reading your letters and my heartbeat was back to normal again. My dear, shall I tell you again that I miss you and that I've turned quite glum and sullen since you left? No one to stoke up my fires, no one to cool my fevered brow when I'm in the throes of composition, no one to hold my hand or anything else.... Alas, there isn't a single soul here worth wasting a thought or a trope on (what's a trope, Ms. Bernstein? A trope is a figure of speech).... Among the letters at the Am. Express there was a telegram from Mary telling me Desmond [Pacey] had died last week. Though I've been expecting this black news I still can't believe I'll never see him again, never see him walk into my home with that broad lecherous grin on his face that he'd picked up somewhere in New Zealand. I've written a poem which I'm enclosing along with the 'Gull' one ['Desmond Pacey: In Memoriam']. I'd give a dozen poems to bring him back to life again. He was a beautiful man too, and the world is a lot poorer for his leaving it...

"Let me know how your courses (curses?) are all coming on? I believe Montague IS a poet, and I may have even met him, but I'm not sure.... Please tell Robert Weaver (this is important) that I mailed all seven poems to the CBC on Jarvis Street. You won't forget?"

Irving dedicated *For My Brother Jesus* "To the memory of Desmond Pacey."

On July 14th, from Hydra, Irving wrote: "My darling: I'm still here. Yesterday Leonard stuck his tanned face through the window just as I was muttering the words of my newest poem, the ant one which I'm enclosing, and we've been talking and exchanging compliments ever since. He's in great shape, looks better than he has in a long time and needs only my white hair to look as handsome as I do. We've spent the day reading our poems to each other and measuring everybody else's work by the light and radiance they shed. He's working on another book which he's calling *My Life and Art*. It will be a thick and very impressive book when it's completed, like nothing else he or anyone else has ever done. He writes a fantastic prose, combining delicacy and strength, and always surprising one. When he was finished reading one of the sections I said to him: 'Your spider web is made of steel.' If he can come up with writing like that, he must be doing something that's right. That mountain air he goes to breathe semi-annually must be pumping the right kind of ozone into his system. He gives to airy nothings shape and solidity; smoke blown from his lips assumes the most amazing contours. I guess that's because behind them all there is psychological truth, they're the embodiments of psychological states, very subtle and complex ones. His stuff makes almost everything else I read seem dull and lifeless as though his words and images had drained the colour out of them. Yup, it's going to be a great book; he's taking his time writing it because he's in no hurry and has no masters to serve....

"There's another extraordinary artist I've met on the island, Marcelle Marais, a French-Canadian living in Paris. She has a house on Ydra where she spends the summer months painting. She showed me a canvas she'd been working on for the last seven years. It's a painting of Ydra, a true masterpiece if I ever saw one. She expects to have it done by the end of August. She showed slides of other paintings she's done. If I had the money to buy some of her paintings I would but her prices are very steep, ranging from two thousand to five thousand and even beyond. The one she did of Leonard several years ago is the one which his French publishers used for the cover of his book of poems, a beautiful thing I'd love to own but she wants four thousand dollars for it.... Tomorrow I'll leave Ydra and go to Athens to pick up my mail. I hope there'll be a big batch of letters from you and one from Robert Weaver telling me that he's accepting all seven poems I sent him for publication in the fall issue of *Tamarack Review.* A couple of cheques from here, there and yonder would also give my aging heart a lift. I've been fighting off a depression which started when I got a telegram from Mary telling me of my friend's death. I can't talk to Leonard about it because he didn't know Desmond very well, having met him only briefly once or twice. In the last few years I've lost a number of friends and I'm beginning to have the feeling that I'm living with ghosts, some more vital than others. That's probably the saddest thing about growing old, the deaths of friends and relatives seem to become nails in one's own coffin. Or one thinks of them as a defence line that's being mowed down by some raging full-back intent on knocking you down, not on the ground but under it! Screw such reflections and images.

"I read Leonard the poems you inspired and he said they were terrific. He loved the 'Daphnis and Chloe' one, 'Of the Man Who Sits In The Garden,' 'For My Incomparable Darling' [which changed to "Gypsy" in final version], and 'The Hallowing.' He was astonished at their erotic vitality, and asked me what my secret was and I said "You" meaning YOU. He said that he could no longer be turned on by any one woman, that he was after something more metaphysical, something like the Feminine Principle, of which all women were imperfect embodiments, their cunts merely being means for standing (no pun intended) in its presence. We knocked that around for a while, your lovely face and form in my mind's eye all the time that we were talking. I hope I managed to keep the pitying sadness I felt for his not knowing you out of my voice as we compared the virtues of the ONE versus the MANY. I wonder what the pre-Socratic philosophers would have made of our metaphysical discussion if they had been able to overhear it. These dear souls had different notions in mind when they spoke of the One and the Many....

"How's York coming along? What are you teaching your instructors? Do you ever pass by my office and wonder if you and I are behind its door and if so what we might be doing.... I miss you terribly, my darling beautiful Sparkles."

I was involved in my two English courses at York, and having a very hard time being apart from Irving, especially as his letters kept kindling the fire, and they arrived almost daily.

On July 18th, he wrote from Poros: "I picked up another letter today at the Am Express, the one in which you speak of pills, sleeplessness and your memories of my morning good humour. The picture you limn, my dear one, saddens and depresses me. I'm not any happier either by our separation, as the enclosed poem ['For My Distant Woman'] and the one I sent you earlier, 'Of The Man Who Sits In The Garden,' should reveal to you quite plainly enough. I long for the sight of you, for the calming effect your beauty always has on me. There's not a day that has gone by that you haven't been in my thoughts, that I haven't gnawed away at images and memories of you. But contrasted with the full-blown experiences I had with you an eternity ago they're a starvation diet that is making my mind if not my body lighter than air. I long for you because I love you, Harriet. If I could erase my sense of justice I'd fly to your arms tomorrow. I read what you say of Montague leaving wife and children to take up with a young woman and I say, 'Bully for him!' I mean it. But I'm not Montague. I cannot bring myself to leave two persons for whom I have a deep attachment and who look to me to give them love and concern.... I've often told you that the tragedy of my married life didn't arise from the lack of deep affection and regard between Aviva and myself—that affection and regard have always been there—but from a mysterious tension that we seem to create whenever we're together. It may simply be that for all our mutual affection and regard we're incompatible and there's nothing we can do about it. But I do think it's worth one more try, a really good one this time, with myself doing all I can to make her happy. There have been times when I've been brutally inconsiderate of Aviva's needs and feelings or, not to exaggerate, insensitive to them. There are times when I think I've not been able to be my true self, which I like to think is a sweet and considerate one, because I lived with someone who didn't touch my centre as you always do. I suppose I didn't reach her centre either.... But,

but, but, don't stop loving me, be patient, and for all our sakes let me work this thing out without any pressures other than those of reason and compassion.... I had a letter from Max [Irving's first child, with Betty]. He's back at Sir George Williams and grateful for my assistance. He seems to be enjoying himself and as coincidence will have it he's also taking a course in Canadian prose and poetry and 'doing' me with an American lecturer who seems to think I'm pretty good. Life is sure funny: my son and my lover both studying my poems ... what playwright could ever have dreamed that one up?

"I'm going to stay in Poros for a couple of days and then return to Hydra to stay with Leonard's former woman, Marianne.....

"Have you phoned Robert Weaver? I rec'd a letter from him, acknowledging *three* poems, which is damned perplexing since I mailed him *seven*. Please get hold of him and tell him that I mailed all the poems to the CBC on Jarvis Street. He doesn't have his office there any longer, so it may be that he's unaware that there are some more envelopes containing my poems waiting for him to pick them up. If you do reach him tell him I want the title 'Saved' changed to 'Jacob and Jesus.'

"Poems sent to *Tamarack Review*:
Jeshua
The Hallowing
Florence
For My Incomparable Gypsy
The Plaka
Jacob and Jesus
How Many Days

"P.S. If Weaver is unhappy about any of the poems, you may tell him I have since written several fine things which I can send as substitutes: e.g., 'June Bug,' 'Of The Man Who Sits In The Garden,' 'The Arch.' All three are major poems."

I was still working through my two courses at York, trying desperately to think of something other than Irving, and our time together. I was miserable without him, however, I was valiantly attempting to convince myself that we had no future, as he had made it clear that he was returning to his life with Aviva and David for once and for all. But how could I separate myself from him emotionally, even though I had done so physically, when almost every single day brought at least one letter, or a letter and a postcard, in which over and over he was professing his love for me, telling me how much he missed me, how good he felt when with me, how creative he was with me, begging my patience while he sorted out his life, and begging me to stay in his life. We were both tortured now. At one point—when I felt I could no longer bear it all—I began to make plans to leave Toronto and flee to my family's condo in West Palm Beach to be by myself for a while, far away from Irving and all the mess of him, of us. I felt that perhaps the answer was to put a whole country between us, that maybe distance and throwing myself into a new environment, new work, was the only hope for me. Maybe I would continue my education in the States, I really didn't know. The situation was seemingly untenable.

Irving was somewhat frustrated with his critics and reviewers. He addressed this on more than one occasion in his letters. "When will my critics realize that modern Greece that I've written so much about is my *symbol* for the contemporary world, for I firmly believe the whole world is headed toward the condition of passionless, ever-consuming, useless, passive, bored and discontented 'Lotus Eaters.' And that in the same way, the Jew is both fact and symbol. Do you recall my *Galini* poem? Is there anyone (the man cried out peevishly) who can lift his eyes long enough either from my genitalia or from a reverent reading of 'Berry Picking' and 'Keine Lazarovitch' to take a good hard look at what I'm really doing? So far, alas, nobody."

Along with that diatribe, he included a draft of "The Last Dryad" with this commentary: "'The Last Dryad' was written on the boat taking me to Hydra. It began by my having fantasies of seeing you on the hills, beaches.... It's turned into a poem about the overthrow of Greek Paganism by Christianity, and now its return through the last Dryad—yourself. I'm just dying with impatience to lay all my treasures before you, and to kiss your smiling red lips and beautiful eyes ... I think of you always."

Such heady words for a young woman. Before the month of July had ended, he asked me one moment to meet him in Barcelona, and yet in another moment said, "I must give my marriage one more real, hard try. Being with you has shown me what a union ought to be—not just the absence of tension but aliveness, harmony and joy.... My love for you and my happiness in being with you—can you doubt them? Please believe me when I say once more that the month I spent with you was the *happiest* longest period I've ever spent with anyone in my life. It was pure joy from the first embrace to the last, and in-between: especially in-between. Hah, I couldn't resist that one.... No one has ever made me come (there I go again) so alive or made it so possible for all the inner chaos to come up roses. Let me not labour the point. But my feelings for Aviva and my son are still very strong and it would simply be unwise to make a move towards the embrace I long for if I can't take all of me into it. I know myself too well not to be able to anticipate the self-reproaches, etc. that would ensue, and I love you too deeply to want to inflict anything like that on you. If I thought my marriage was really dead, that I was trying to start a fire with ashes, I'd need no coaxing to get out of it. But whatever it is, it's not dead. There are deep feelings of mutual affection and regard; the great pity is that we don't seem to have been able to translate them into the kind of aliveness and peace that I experience so beautifully whenever I am with you. There are tears in my eyes as I write this, for I honestly wish it were different, that I could have with Aviva what I have with you. So tomorrow I'm off to Brindisi, the first lap of my journey to Morocco. The next month or so may tell the story."

By the time he left Greece, he was more than ready. He went to Spain where he fell in love with Barcelona, and where he expressed in a letter that he was thinking of changing the name of the book he had been working on to *For My Brother Jesus*. "The title alone ought to sell ten thousand copies of the book! No one is ever going to write a book like this one—not even I. I think with this book I'm ready to call it a day and leave the writing of poems to the spry fry who are treading on my heels—but not too close. The last poem in the book will be

'At the Barcelona Zoo,' since it enunciates about as neatly and beautifully as any poem of mine what my credo has been. Read up on Heraclitos and Anaximander to get the full richness of the poem."

As frequently happened, he also asked me to contact someone about the publication of another couple of poems. What was the man thinking? How did I become his designated person to contact people about the publication of his poems? Was he trying to make me feel like I was still an indispensable part of his life, or was he just using me? Surely there must have been others to whom he might have entrusted these tasks. It was bewildering, but I did his bidding. There was a part of it that was pleasing, of course. My parents, seeing the steady stream of mail from him— some of it postcards that they undoubtedly read—were at their wits end, both confused and angry. "Why," my father asked me again, "is this man writing you this way when he is en route to his wife and son?" Quite right, I thought, but all I could say was that he was trying to sort things out.

By August 15th, Irving had finally made his way to Essaouira, Morocco. He stayed with his friend Scott Symond, a Toronto writer, who gave him the first three chapters of his novel to read. "I've struggled through them with mounting irritation and distaste. He's got two things on his brain, COCK and CHRIST and they sort of meet and merge in his twisted Rosedale mind. Scott's religion can be summed up quite simply: Christ with an erection! For all his brave talk, I get the feeling he can't really accept himself as a homosexual and as a consequence of that failure is driven to divinize his 'perversion.' He'd like to be as natural and accepting and joyful about it as the Moroccans or Greeks, but his class and religious background make that forever impossible for him. I'm meeting him for some mint tea—to which I've become addicted—a couple of hours from now at one of the cafés near the beach and may the good Lord put the right words into my mouth if he asks me, as doubtless he will, my opinion of the three chapters of his novel...."

In the same letter, he writes to me: "How wonderful if I could reach out my hand at this moment and touch your cheek, your hair. Why does my heart fill up with gladness whenever I think of you and everything about me with light as if they had been touched by your radiance? It is now nearly seven weeks since you left me, and yet in a sense you never left me at all but have been in my blood or lying inside my head, taking up all kinds of shapes and attitudes. And always I see the beautiful curve of your chin and feel your tenderness. Hugs and many, many passionate kisses, beginning with your adorable lips." This from the man who was at that time in Morocco with Aviva and David, who was giving his life with them one more serious try.... What was I to think? He asked me to pick him up from the airport when he returned, so we could talk.

A few days later, he had found the way out of his dilemma with Scott. In a letter dated August 19th, Irving told me what he said to Scott: "[I told him] I thought his talents lay in the direction of poetry rather than novel-writing. Under the protection of what he took to be an enormous compliment, I was able to fire off one criticism after another at his Mss which I had manfully tried to struggle through. I wasn't being clever or devious—I really do believe he's tragically mistaken the nature of his gifts. If you can lay your hands on his book, *Heritage,* do so. It's a book about Canadian furniture and it's one of the most fascinating books I ever read."

While Irving was giving his relationship another good try in Morocco, I was desperately trying to pry myself loose of ours. That I loved him was unquestionable, to the point where I thought perhaps the greatest gift I could give him, out of my deep love, was to absent myself from his life so he could get on with his domestic business: David and David's mother, and with no Harriet in the picture to offer any hope, any distraction, any more dreams, any passion-inspired poems. I could not envision resuming our relationship as it had been and if we were not going to be together, I felt I had to be in another location, not the city where we had already begun to fill the streets with our stolen, passionate hours, the shadows of our embraces.

In my journal, I wrote: "He writes of his deep love for me, over and over. This he writes on his way to Morocco to meet with Aviva and his son. My emotional turmoil is exhausting. One moment I tell myself what a fool I am to expect any more of our love affair to continue: that this is the end now, in his going to meet her. And so I'm bitter and angry, momentarily, then unspeakably sad. And the hope comes back, the rush of positive feelings I always have had about us together. He writes always, beautiful poems, his letters are all sorts of positive reinforcement. But I don't know and there's nothing I can do but try to keep myself together—and wait. He writes he's coming back, flying from Rome, on August 29th so there's only three more weeks ... until what, I wonder?"

In subsequent letters he repeatedly asked me to meet him at the airport when he returned. I agreed. I deeply hoped for and needed resolution, one way or the other; the outcome hardly even mattered at that point, I just wanted the agony and uncertainty to end. I hoped that he would either tell me he was newly committed to his domestic relationship, and our affair had ended; or he had finally arrived at the point where he could put that old relationship behind him, and we could truly begin our life together.

He returned alone, and I met him at the airport.

7.

WE SPENT THE NIGHT HE RETURNED TOGETHER, in a hotel downtown. Part of the night we talked, and part of the night I was sick to my stomach, literally. It was immediately clear that Irving had not come to any decision whatsoever. He was still desperate to be with me, said he could not bear the notion of our not being together, but he was also still unable to make the break with his consort. He had just left her and could hardly wait to be in my arms. Yet she and David were returning shortly thereafter, and he intended to resume living with her. Further, he did not want to live with her and have me as "the other woman," on the side, his mistress as it were. That would still leave him torn. There was no solution. The circumstances were so intense, tortured, and agonizing that I was unable to physically handle the force of it. I spent a good part of the night hugging not him, but the bathroom bowl. In the morning I returned to my parents' home and crawled into bed, feeling like I was freezing in spite of it being a hot August day. As I recall, I lay in that bed unable to do much other than try to think about what on earth was I to do. I no more wanted to tear myself away from him than he seemed able to tear himself away from me. And yet I could not continue as things were, there was no question about that. I decided to throw everything into the hands of the gods and goddesses, fate, destiny—that word again. I let go, and let God.

I decided that I needed to make my academic life a priority, my own life, with or without him, and it seemed abundantly clear to me it was indeed going to be without him. I had after all left him in Greece because of his inability to move on in his own life.

I had completed the two summer courses and I would graduate and receive my B.A. degree in English Lit. It seemed specious for me to run away and not see things through, at least attend my graduation ceremony. I didn't particularly care about that ceremony or the graduation diploma, but it meant something to my parents. They had been good to me, financially supported my return to school, endured my going to Europe with Irving, then my return, followed by his endless stream of letters. I felt it was only fair to give them the pleasure of seeing me in cap and gown, finally graduating university, as neither of them had. But could I, should I, stay in Toronto beyond that point? Should I go on and aim for a Masters degree? Should I revisit the idea of holing up in Florida, going to college there? Incapable of clear thinking or resolution, I decided—half out of my wits at this point—that if I were going to continue to live in Toronto, I could no longer remain in my parents' home. I needed my own space once again. After all, I had lived on my own and supported myself for years before going back to school, and living in my parents' home was a sacrifice I had made in order to finish my degree. Having my own space at this point was essential; I needed quiet and to be alone. I needed a haven, a place where I could shut my door on all the chaos. Or, a place where I could at least be alone with my chaos. I needed a place where I would not have to answer any questions from anyone, at least until I could answer some of those questions for myself.

I had done nothing about looking for an apartment, of course. Classes were about to start again and it was time to make a decision. Although I don't remember the details, I must have applied to and been accepted into the Masters' program. I decided that if I were going to stay in Toronto and embark on my Masters' degree (which I discerned with some surprise I actually wanted to do), it was practical to live in the graduate residences on the York campus. That, at least, seemed eminently reasonable and clear. I would attend my graduation and then I'd immediately begin my Masters degree. Living on campus would be easier on me than daily commuting, and I intensely needed my own space. I was trying to find the way to look out for myself, re-assemble my life without Irving in it. But what was I to do? I had not filed application for an apartment in the on-campus graduate student residences.

The waiting list to get into the grad residences was long, with many more students than accommodation. And I had not even put my name on the list! This was where the fate, God, destiny—whatever—stepped in. I phoned one of my classmates from the previous year who had been in Irving's poetry workshop, a great guy named Jack Urowitz. I told him that I wanted to live in the grad residences but had not gotten my name on a list or anything, and asked him if he had any ideas. He said I should come right over and meet a friend of his, who in fact had placed his name on the list and was actually eligible for one of the precious apartments on Assinniboine Road. In the interim, this fellow had decided he didn't want it after all, but he had not yet officially given it up. It was like a miracle, a sign. I rushed over and met his friend, Will. Together we immediately went to the student office and I signed for the apartment, with Will as my "technical" roommate. The transaction was unbelievably smooth. My new address was going to be 8 Assiniboine Ave., Apt 501. I took it as a sign that I was meant to stay in Toronto, and further my studies at York. I had asked the universe for something completely unreasonable and that thing had miraculously materialized, smooth as silk and faster than you can say "fucking really?"

So, I remained in Toronto. I completely believed that my affair with Irving was over, in spite of his ongoing pleas for my patience. I could no longer handle being in the middle of his turmoil and I resolved absolutely to enjoy my newfound quiet space and dedicate myself to my studies. I enrolled in some graduate courses, and began my life as a grad student and single woman living on campus.

Irving was relentless. He called constantly, he wrote, he begged my patience and understanding, he said how wretched he was at the idea of our not being together. He was a powerful and seductive man. In spite of my resolve, I caved. Before long, he pulled me back to him. I was not strong enough to resist his continuous imploring, his endless stream of passionate notes, his seductive words, his formidable power. However, above and beyond all that—the bottom line—I was helpless to resist how it felt when we were together. I loved him and no matter how I tried to smother it, the fire kept blazing. I loved him then, and now, more than thirty years later, I love him still. Even though there was so much wrong with the situation, when we were together it felt like everything else simply evaporated.

He came to me there whenever he could—between classes or in the evening. I enjoyed shopping for groceries and cooking meals he devoured with great gusto, talking about his dreams over a bottle of wine. In December of 1975, I wrote: "Spent the day with Irving, who is fighting a cold. He just returned from Jamaica, and I returned from Florida. We praised each other's tans and luxuriated in being together again after what we termed 'two weeks going on eternity.' This apartment is our haven, our refuge. The afternoons and evenings we share are so precious— always free of any tensions, bitterness, bitchiness—it's so easy, simple for us to be joyous with each other. His unfailing energy level still amazes me, as do his sense of wonder, his limitless generosity, his humour; what it is to love such a beautiful man, and to be loved by him. We dream on of that village by the sea where we will together go some day. *For My Brother Jesus* should be out in February ... the book he calls mine, says would never have been written if not for me. When we hold each other, his huge silver head resting quietly on my breast, our bodies, minds, and souls exhausted and exhilarated, I have everything. We have everything. The tortuous wrestling with his 'domestic situation' continues. I take each day as it comes, am joyful in what we share and how we are when we are together. It's impossible for me to hypothesize or anticipate any more. We have our dreams. I believe in him, in his ability to make dreams come true. Sometimes we just reminisce about last summer. How it was in Paxi—the white beaches, the great meals on the terrace at our hotel, overlooking the view—the music—and Rome, where it began."

While he was in Jamaica with his family, he had again written me nearly every day, sending endless postcards, letters, and poems. "I wonder what your vacation is like, I hope a little less tense than mine." He said, "The only solution for me is to get myself an apt. close to York and begin the slow process of post-marital recovery.... I need Freedom, Solitude, Love: my holy

Harriet, graduation York University, 1975

trinity. Why are you in Miami and me here?" I was not in Miami, I was in West Palm Beach.

I graduated in the fall, a ceremony happily attended by my family. I was still twenty-seven years old. Irving was still sixty-three. With the B.A. finally under my belt, I settled down to work on the graduate courses I had registered for. It was odd living at York, which was a wilderness back then. I recall looking out my window one of many snowy nights, the wind howling uninterrupted by buildings or cars, just a vast winter wasteland of snow and ice; it appealed to me to be there. The landscape was such an abject dichotomy to what was going on inside my apartment, where our passion burned unabated and undiminished. What was supposed to be *my* haven and refuge became *our* haven.

Life took a new routine. I would go to the Italian supermarket that was then at the corner of Finch and Keele, and I'd buy groceries, tasty treats to share with Irving, like the salami and spicy olives he liked so much with red wine. Often I'd buy ingredients to make dinner for him. He'd come over to see me whenever he could, which was surprisingly often. I have no idea how he managed it, or what he told his partner: he didn't say and I didn't ask. Sometimes he'd arrive in the afternoons, between our classes; other times, in the evenings. I had once again given myself completely over to our affair, as my journal entries indicate. I did not have the strength to resist him and I had stopped trying. If anything, our passion grew as time went on and we gave ourselves over more completely to each other. We made love over and over and no matter how fulfilled we were, we craved more of each other. I was constantly amazed at his stamina. My sexual appetite was strong and he met me every inch along the way. We spent many hours together in that apartment, listening to some of our favourite classical records: Chopin, Schubert's "Wanderer," sharing all our thoughts, enjoying each other body and soul. It was as though the only peace we could find was with each other, there in that grad residence, in the wilderness of York campus.

As the New Year rolled in, I wrote in my journal: "He is so tortured, so loving, so incredibly beautiful. So great a poet, a man, a lover. Hadn't seen each other since Sat., and though we'd spoken on the phone every day, my god, it seemed like so long. We become more and more intimate, more joined, more sharing. Always we want more to be together more. We are alive and good with each other as with nobody else. I go to bed now, to dream of his dream—and mine—of our living together, sometimes here and other times in Italy or Greece, where he wants to go with me this summer, again.... Can it be, what I hope so much...."

And, a couple of weeks later, I wrote: "Irving is taking an apt, soon as he returns from Brussels, thank God, about time; he said his things were packed and in the car, he'd found an apt.—and she said that David had overheard them talking about separating and had been so upset.... Bam, right between the eyes. So he's decided that rather than make a complete formal split right now, he'll get a place, and spend some nights there, some here, and some at the house.... Wonder how that'll work out? He's planning seriously now on spending the whole summer with me in Greece and Turkey ... until maybe some time in August, when he'll go to her and David for a couple weeks. Next year: me here in the apt., he going along the same, more or less. After that, he'll have his sabbatical and pension, I'll have my Masters degree and we're supposed to leave. Go away, spend most of the year travelling—Russia, India, etc., etc. Says he's told her about it, he's going and that's that. She says she doesn't want to go, she wants her new house here. He says she brings my name up quite frequently now.... I wish she'd fall in love with some rich ordinary non-writing man and go away peacefully...."

A tiny beautiful stray kitten, a black one—my favourite kind— had somehow turned up at Winters College where Irving had his office at York, and he, a lover of kittens, had taken it into his office until it was time to bring it home. I was with him at his office and had snuggled the beautiful kitten. The next day, he told me the awful story of what had happened when he brought the kitten home. He had presented it to Aviva, who had initially expressed delight and cooed over it, snuggled it—and then abruptly tossed it down the stairs! Apparently, some of my scent had lingered on the poor wee thing, and when she smelled my perfume on it, she flew into a rage and literally threw the kitten away. I am not sure whether it lived or not, I do not recall now, but it is unlikely that it was kept. Irving was horrified, laughing in a very grim way as he related the story to me. I don't know, of course, that this was a true story, but it was what he told me, and why would he concoct such a tale?

Through the winter and spring of 1976, we were still seizing a "regular" one night a week, and speaking daily while he continued living with David and his mother. In retrospect, of course, it is easier to see things with the perspective of distance and time. I was a beautiful young woman, totally in love with him and he was a sixty-three year old who was unable (or unwilling) to extricate himself from a common-law relationship in which he said he was not happy. It's a time-old story, isn't it? However, even that unhappiness suited him in many ways: it provided him with a ready excuse for just about any infraction or whim he chose to exercise. It provided him with anguish, from which he distilled poems; it was the dark side to the joyous exuberance that was his light. Naturally he wanted to keep me: I was the perfect mistress and muse. I listened endlessly and patiently to his tortured ramblings and tales of his domestic absurdities. Then, having listened, I vowed to myself that I would not contribute to his torture, but would keep my own doubts, frustrations, and pains to myself in a noble attempt to take the high road at all times. I provided ecstatic, creative, immensely satisfying sex. I maintained my humour at all times. I was a good cook. And we stimulated each other mentally and creatively. He found in me a good editor and an outstanding muse. My publicity experience was a bonus, and he availed himself of my instincts and advice in that arena as well. Why wouldn't he do anything and everything to keep me? Of course, that's not even taking into consideration the possibility that he might have loved me as truly and deeply as I loved him—which ultimately was the truth, and was all that really mattered at the end of the day.

In March, I journaled that *For My Brother Jesus* was out, of course McClelland and Stewart had published it. My mind was flooded with memories as I read those poems. How he sat scribbling on the trains, on the beaches, struggling over some poems for days on end, presenting me with others after only a few hours, holding them out to me as most precious jewels. I remembered our rendezvous in Rome, the boat from Israel when it docked in Paxi, where we were swimming and sunning, how we approached the ship and spoke with the *kibbutzniks* and how it all became the poem "Galim".... I recalled the afternoon on the Adonis, when we were so aroused we had to keep searching for a private corner where we might satisfy our insatiable and irresistible desire for ourselves, enjoying simultaneously the hilarity of the situation and our passion in that moment, and the golden sun and sea air cooling off our sweat and sex-soaked bodies afterwards, the poem "Adonis" resulting: "My darling and I made love/ in the washroom of the Adonis/ and ship and I were as one/ as we rocked and ploughed the furrows."...Florence, too,

71

the long walks during the quiet nights and how all of that became this book. I remember him sitting in our *pensione* while I spread the food out on napkins, or washed some clothes, or sat on the bed just watching him, or scribbled away at my own poems, or my journal.

Sometimes he said that for us to be lovers was, after all, the best way; that if we were to live together, I would eventually and inevitably replace his partner. There was no way I could understand what he was saying; however, I knew for certain that never did I want to replace her, or play the role that she did, so if he said it, it was good enough for me. I did not dispute it. I somehow sensed, even in my besotted youthful passion, that what he said smacked of a hard and horrible honesty. I preferred to be his lover than his wife. Again, the telling of many love stories between artist and muse reflect that for the muse to become the wife is a slippery slope, one which few muses survive. Still, the temptation to buy into the fantasy is sometimes difficult to refuse.

From time to time, he'd have another huge domestic row, after which he would call me to say that he could not see me anymore. An entry from my journal in mid-March '76 reads: "Yesterday noon L. said 'I cannot see you anymore, period.' He'd had another super bad scene with her, and had decided that we must call it off, as he didn't feel he'd been fair to her. O.K. Then he called me twice later the same day to tell me how he loves me and wants to live with me and to beg my love and patience for the next few weeks while he works himself out. Fine. My love and patience he has, damn it, there's no way I can stop that. Today he calls, asking me to go to dinner with him tonight. I say—what is this, yesterday you said you can't see me anymore, period, and now what is this, what are you doing? And he says, yes, I said that, but I want to see you. So I said okay, though I don't know that I should have. I'm just making this entry because I can hardly believe all of this is happening. And there's nobody to talk to, and it's making me very nuts, all these changes in my head, and emotional traumas.... It's so outrageous, I'm hopelessly fascinated. Fool that I am."

A week later, I was busy clipping reviews and reaction to *For My Brother Jesus*, and Irving was busy with a flurry of TV and radio interviews. In the midst of all that activity, he had apparently told Aviva, while they were going to look at yet another house (to fulfill her "domomania" as he called it), and that, as I wrote in my journal, it would be "a house for her and David, not for him; he said that he wasn't coming back to live with her again after the summer. So, he says, that's it.... So, he says, he'll make reservations for him and me to Greece.... so he says.... I told him about Pablo Casals and his Martita—when they married, he was thirty years older than her father! Now L. talks sometimes about giving me children ... says he's making further inquiries about that house in Greece too...."

About a month after that entry, I wrote: "There have been some enormous changes in our relationship now. A few weeks back, L. left A. For a few days he stayed with me, in the meantime finding an apt for himself. He was concerned about her thinking he left 'for me.' Six days later, he was sitting here talking to me (I hadn't seen him for a day or so) and he blurted out something about wanting to come to say that he couldn't see me anymore, but I was too beautiful—and I went nuts and ran out [of the apartment]. Just left him, without a word, sitting there, talking to the walls. I ran and ran through the fields back of here, and went through hell for the next 24 hours. Received a note from him the next day, went to his office, couldn't help myself I cried and cried and we talked and talked. Now we are together again, and he's staying at the house with A. The big change is that now, although I love him, I no longer trust him, believe him as I used to. Which subtly/profoundly changes what my idea of what love should be—was. She'll never leave go of him. He's too good, too soft to just abandon her and—more—David. And he means too much to me for me to stop seeing him. So there it is, and so it seems it's gonna stay. The other day he was saying how I'm the best thing that's happened to him. That he thinks of me as his true wife, not her; he's a husband to her in name only, doesn't share nearly so much .... with her as with me. He's supposed to return from Saskatoon tonight and spend the night here with me. It was a most devastating few weeks, and I feel very aged from it. But I'm glad it all happened, because it's a fault I have to believe too completely in a man, to get so totally wrapped up in him that I lose sight of myself, get out of touch with myself. Now that the change has come, there is that separateness, that doubt, which probably is a good thing for me. Classes are over. How his students love him, Lord. He keeps saying how he's gonna keep the classes small next year (ruthlessly) gonna cut down readings, cut out reading manuscripts, etc. I wonder. He has such a hard time just saying no, it's quite amazing.... I've accepted work, as unit publicist for____ on a film shoot here. Work begins May 31, ends at the end of July. I'm to get paid $2,000 for that. After which I'll take it and supposedly meet L. in Greece. He promises we'll sail up the Bosporus—spend a month or six weeks in Greece and Turkey. I hope so."

A couple of days later, I wrote: "He came over ... and we listened to a radio broadcast on CBC-FM, Peter Gzowski's show, that he had recorded earlier. It was magnificent, like a great poem. It was in two parts—the first he talked generally about the plagues in society today, about the mindlessness, what is 'a Canadian (someone who goes around asking what is a Canadian!)', etc., ending with a reading of 'Adam.' The second part was about his new crusade, his reclaiming Jesus for the Jews, his view of Christianity being largely to blame for the Holocaust, etc., how the French turned the Jews over to the Nazis, etc. He said how they would have saved cats: 'the French, those great cat-lovers,' or the Germans would have risen to save persecuted dogs—but how they all took a hand in the slaughter of six million helpless men, women and children. How it was a Pope who initiated the yellow badge, etc.... And he ended with reading 'Displaced Person.' It was great.

"Then we had a good dinner and he talked and talked. He said he wanted to tell me something he had never told anybody—how reading Thomas Carlyle when he was fifteen or so influenced him, his whole life. That he read everything Carlyle wrote, over and over and how nobody (no critics, etc.) have ever mentioned noticing any of his influence. He spoke with Bill in Montreal for a while. He spoke—rather, prophesied—about his death. He said he sees himself being killed by a young Jew—say eighteen years old, a religious fanatic, who will stab or shoot him. In Israel. He also spoke a lot about how grateful he is that he's lived to this age of sixty-four. Because now he sees the pattern of his life, he sees with a clarity that he didn't have before, and feels a new confidence in himself. He likened it to being on top of a hill or mtn, and looking down on all the paths you've taken along the way—all the roads, the muddy and bad ones too—and as I said, seeing the pattern, the meaning of it all. He prophesied that within two years, Christians all over will want to be converting to Judaism. [This is interesting in light of the interest of so many public people—such as Madonna etc.—in the early turn of the century embracing the Kaballah].... That his opponents will be the rabbis and priests. But that he will get to them all with his poetry, because poetry is the most magnificent, the supreme articulation, the most clear, comprehensive way, the highest art, and cannot be refuted or confuted. He says, 'I'll get them with poetry and laughter. A life-affirming, atheistic religion. Because God is every man, God was the first imagist— he "created" man in his image.' How when Adam and Eve ate 'that Macintosh apple,' it wasn't the fall of man, but rather the beginning of man.' We said how if we have a daughter (which is what he hopes I'll give him), we should call her Eve. He said how I am his wife."

Irving was dancing at two weddings, as the saying goes. He actually said it himself in one of his letters: "Forgive me, bear with me, don't judge me. I've been trying to dance at two weddings and I haven't given a Fred Astaire performance at either of them." He clearly did not want to lose me, and he just as clearly was incapable of ending his life with his domestic partner. She stayed with him, I stayed with him, and he was unable to pull away from either of us. What a splendid mess. He was teaching, writing, publishing, and doing media right, left, and centre.

On May 13th, 1976, I wrote in my journal that he and I were booked on a flight departing June 20th to Athens. That weekend in May, he was off to Montreal again, from there to Ottawa for a day, Thursday back to Toronto and a reading at the St. Lawrence Centre, back to Montreal the next weekend, then a weekend in Collingwood with other poets, another honourary doctorate to come from Concordia in Montreal, and an Officer of Canada medal award from the government. It was a schedule that could do in a man half his age.

From my journal: "Over an ouzo in my York apartment, he had been talking about the people he gets himself involved with, how many people wanted a piece of him. He said that when he goes to Montreal now, it's a nightmare, there are so many people who want and expect to see him. He said that I was to be his saviour; he's got to get away from it all with me. I had told him about a super flat that might be coming available, and he said I should tell the people I'll take it. He said he'd pay rent etc. so I can live there and just write. It was very spacious, so he'd have his own work space, quiet and undisturbed. Meantime, we were looking for a house for A., who continued to guilt him with sobbing stories about how she was being taunted at York, how everybody was talking about us, and of course, the card she always played: David, how upset he was, how he knew something was going on."

On May 14th, Irving was visited by Desmond Pacey's son, Peter. He had read Irving's last letter to Pacey, as Pacey was dying the previous summer, and Peter told Irving how much his friendship had meant to Desmond.

More from my journal: "May 16th was my birthday, and Irving forgot. He was in Montreal, and busy with a gazillion things of course, but still I wished he had remembered. I went to hear Earl Birney read at the St. Lawrence Centre. I was keeping myself busy until we left for Greece. Irving had written to Ted Samson in Greece about a house on the Bay of Corinth, telling him he was interested, that we'd be arriving in Athens June 21st, and will want to see the house shortly thereafter. Irving suggested that after a couple days in Athens, we go to some of the islands— Crete, Patmos, Samos, Astipalia—then up the Bosporus for a peek at Turkey, maybe a stop in Israel, then maybe settle for the remainder of the summer in Greece, wherever we felt like."

Journal, May 20th, 1976: "Layton returned from Montreal and Ottawa on May 19th, and I met him at the airport. It was great to hear about all his successes: the reading in Montreal well attended and very moving; the interviews in Ottawa. The 20th was his reading at the St. Lawrence. As usual, I was enraptured. It had been his poetry that first drew me to him, and no matter what happened, it was always his poetry that kept me bound to him. When I had told him that, he had said that I was the only woman he has ever loved who had felt so about his poetry, who had ever understood so very well all of what it meant, his being a poet. It was because I was also a poet, he said. The turn-out at the St. Lawrence was disappointing, fewer people than I expected anyway, but then 7:00 seemed an odd time. I went with my technical roommate, Will, and we had arrived early enough for good seats. Layton was reading mainly older poems, only two from the new book. We had arranged a secret signal that he would give when he was thinking of me ... it was delicious to know that."

8.

I DID NOT WRITE IN MY JOURNAL AGAIN until the fall of 1977. The summer plans we had made in May of 1976 never came to pass quite the way we had envisioned, and I no longer remember why. We did enjoy a second rendezvous at the Piazza di Spagna in Rome in the summer of '76. We travelled through parts of southern Italy, including Sicily and Sardinia. I remember we went to Taormina in Sicily, and it was gorgeous. There was an outdoor theatre there, and by strange coincidence the Living Theatre was performing. Naturally I wanted to go, and Irving decided he'd come too, as he had never seen them. I recall we argued about the performance, as Irving saw no value to that kind of theatre whatsoever, and I was of course defending it. I made no attempt to contact my former friends from the Theatre, or even see if those I had known were still part of the troupe. As always, Irving and I had a glorious time together, except for the fact that, as always, he could not bring himself to fully commit to our affair or, as committed as he was to our love, he was still unable (or unwilling?) to extricate himself from his other domestic partnership.

Many of the poems he wrote that summer went into what became the next book he published, in 1977, *The Covenant*. "Smoke," "Snowdrift," "Hidden Worlds," "The Presence," "The Tamed Puma," and one of my favourites, "Lady on the Piazza," were written for me or about our relationship. Many of the poems speak to the emotional turmoil and torment that persisted. There are only a couple of letters from him in my file from that year, and they just reveal more of the same conflict, the

78

identical back-and-forth that we had already lived through for the previous year and a half.

I remember one horrible argument that we had during that summer of 1976, somewhere in Sicily or perhaps it was Sardinia. The hotel management actually called up to our room to speak with us about the noise, we were arguing so loudly. Never before or after had I received such a call. I remember afterwards leaving him in our hotel room, walking and walking aimlessly and desolately through the streets in some kind of horrible numb daze, only vaguely aware that children were looking at me with concern and people were staring at me. I didn't care, not about that or anything, tears streaming down my face, as once again I came to the point of no further endurance. I was so frustrated with the situation, so completely exhausted by it all. I resolved, once again, to end our affair. It was impossible for me to continue to allow things to go on in that way, and it was clearly going to have to be my decision to bring things to a final halt. I knew I would have to be very determined, as time and time again we had ended our affair, only for me to be drawn back into his arms when he refused to let me go. I remember one hot night in Italy, when I was so tormented by it all, I thought in my emotionally overwrought state that it would be the perfect end to "the great Layton" for him to die while making love, and I decided with grim humour to actually see if I could kill him with sex. I employed every skill known to woman, everything I knew he loved, everything I loved, and I prolonged the sex, I teased him, and thrilled him until he was jumping out of his skin and roaring with pent-up passion, helpless, begging for release. We were exhausted, and our immense passion culminated with both of us completely spent—and Irving still very much alive. He was a strong man, very strong. I had become his Gypsy Jo, and the only place that felt like home was when we were together, wherever we were did not matter. And I had no choice, I felt, but to leave that "home," because to stay in it would kill me.

Ultimately I did leave, again. I left him in Sardinia. I left for what I believed with all my heart was the last time. Heartbroken, emotionally wrung out, but determined that this torture absolutely had to stop, I left him. I fully believed that he would never ever extricate himself from his long-term relationship, and the tortuous components of our affair had reached the point where I simply could not handle them any longer. I felt that if I truly loved him, I had to let him go. I had to push him away and keep him away. No matter how profound my pain, our pain, I knew that he would make poems out of the pain, and I didn't know how to survive the situation anymore. I didn't care if I never wrote another word again though. I believed I had to sacrifice everything, including our love and any future it might have. I had to be the ultimate muse and walk from him so that he could continue to write though I would no longer be part of his agony. He could not or would not break free and wholly commit to me.

I flew off in a tiny prop plane headed for France. I recall him standing there, watching me go as I walked across the tarmac. I don't know how my legs kept moving away from him. He was desolate but did not say a word. I felt like my heart was going to pound its way out of my body. The flight attendant, observing my distress, thought it was just nerves about the tiny plane, and I remember her reassuring me that it was *"piccolo ma buono"*— small, but good. I flew to Cannes, to the French Riviera where I had previously been on other holidays. I went directly to the Carlton Hotel in Cannes, to hide, to nurse myself back to some form of functionality, and yes to coddle myself and pamper myself with material luxury. Since I was not going to be with Layton—and at that point in time, I was not, that was settled, I believed—I was going to reintroduce myself to the world from which I had come, to some extent. It was a world where the concierge at the Carlton knew my family name, knew my parents after years and years of their staying at the Carlton during the Cannes Film Festival. It was a world where I knew the good restaurants, the good tables and rooms, and how to get them. It was a world I previously never gave a shit about, but now desolately sought refuge in. The values of that world were not the values of Gypsy Jo, but now I was alone. I had once again and—I believed at the time, finally— walked away from Layton. Gypsy Jo was dead. I came to the Carlton to bury her, to bury her under the sand of the beach where the Mediterranean sucked, and under the palm trees of La Croisette. I had to reinvent myself again. I crawled miserably, numb with pain, into the soft zillion-thread count of the tender pink sheets on the large and comfortable bed in the exquisite Carlton Hotel. Sometimes, I slept fitfully, like one who is feverish. Often I sobbed uncontrollably. I don't know how many days passed. From my room, I saw the flow of the Mediterranean, and languid people, the slow meandering of the French who also were seeking refuge, theirs from the Parisian streets, the heat of the city. One day, it was a holiday in France, I didn't know what and I could not have cared less, but there were fireworks and I had always loved fireworks. I watched them, alone in the midst of the people enjoying life all around me. I was intensely miserable, so much so that the misery I felt branded itself so deeply on me that to this day, when I see fireworks I always feel that moment on me again. What I had so loved was gone. Our dreams were dead. I had to remake myself, I had to nurse myself back to health again, and I had to live my life without the man I had hoped to spend the rest of my days with.

9.

WHEN I RETURNED TO TORONTO, I went into immediate and very determined action. There was absolutely no question of my continuing my studies and completing my Masters at York. I could not bear even thinking about the place. My Masters degree was just one more thing that was going to be lost, and in the general picture, it didn't matter to me. It only mattered that I not be at York, that I not be where he could see me or find me and pull me back into his life again. I was no longer the muse and I was no longer Gypsy Jo. I temporarily moved back into my parents' home where their solid house would guard me, I thought, until I found a place of my own. This time, it would be mine and mine alone, I was certain of that.

I soon found an apartment at the Tower Hill East, on Spadina Avenue, and I found work, taking on the job of Publicity and Promotion for Paramount Pictures. Their offices were at One Yonge Street, in the *Toronto Star* building. My office was small but I had a view of Lake Ontario. The Toronto International Film Festival was in its early stages then, a fledgling organization having trouble securing films to show at the festival. One of the pictures Paramount had for upcoming release was the Diane Keaton film, *Looking for Mr. Goodbar*. It was the first picture that Richard Gere broke out in, and his dance scene was pure raw sexual energy. I was friends with the marvellous George Anthony who was the Entertainment Editor of the *Toronto Sun,* and an early supporter of the film festival. I pitched Paramount on offering *Mr. Goodbar* to the festival, but I failed to persuade them. It is ironic in retrospect, now that the Festival is such a major international

82

Paramount screening room, 1978. Harriet, in the back row, last on the right.

event, and studios vie to get their films showcased there. In those days, it was a different story. When we screened *Mr. Goodbar* for the press in the Paramount screening room, I remember the heavy silence at the end of the picture, then Martin Knelman, film critic at *The Globe and Mail*, sarcastically commenting, "Boy, Harriet, you really know how to throw a good time."

I also handled the talent, and again, there was no studio rep giving orders. I nurtured my media relationships, figured out what was appropriate for the movie, arranged the interviews, and usually drove to the airport to pick up the personality, since this was before everyone began using limos.

In addition to George Anthony, my other good friend in the media end of the business was Brian Linehan. Brian hosted a nationally syndicated television show that was an absolute "must-do" for the actors, actresses, producers, and directors doing publicity for their films going into release. Brian's unique style of interviewing included an enormous amount of research, and he was gifted at encouraging an openess not often seen; the talent loved him, not only because he was so good at what he did, but also because he took time with them. These were not sound-bite interviews.

We used to go for lovely long lunches at Mr. Tony's on Cumberland Street. Sometimes George, Brian, and I would meet for lunch at Joe Allen's and get so caught up in talking that before we knew it, it was the cocktail hour, and we'd either stay there, or repair to another spot for dinner, and continue our marathon sessions. Those were such good times. George and Brian were exceptionally smart, witty, knowledgeable, and quick, so it was a sheer delight to be with them. I cherished their friendship and our professional relationship. I could laugh and be fully engaged in the moment when we were together.

Being at Paramount was good; it was a very busy time. I totally threw myself into my work, trying to obliterate my sorrow and pain. Some of the pictures I handled the pub/promo for included *Marathon Man, The Last Tycoon, Black Sunday, Heaven Can Wait, Pretty Baby*, and *Saturday Night Fever*. We were releasing a little picture called *Grease*. Working with the terrific publicist at Polydor Records, who had the soundtrack, we arranged a parade from the foot of Yonge Street right up through the city to the also now non-existent Hollywood Theatre at Yonge and St. Clair. The parade included vintage cars and motorcycles, and everyone was theme-dressed with leather jackets, crinoline skirts with poodles, and pastel sweater sets.

Basically, when the talent arrived in Toronto, from the moment they landed until the moment they got back on the plane to leave, they were "mine." From securing the right suite, usually at the Four Seasons, to putting together the interview schedule, every detail that needed taking care of was my responsibility. My work was a blessing, a refuge from the tumult of my affair with Irving. In my life as a publicist, I could focus on developing my professional skills and nurture the non-Gypsy Jo I was learning to become. I enjoyed the order and discipline demanded of me. Once again I was earning my own living, supporting myself in a nice apartment that was all mine, and enjoying the satisfaction of a career. If I cried in my pillow at night, well that was my choice. Nobody had to know about it.

10.

A T SOME POINT IN ALL OF THIS, Irving returned from his travels, found me somehow, and finally, inevitably persuaded me to see him again. This is the madness that love can be. He was utterly impossible to resist. I loved him still, and was no match against his powers of persuasion, formidable as they were, on so many levels. From the vantage point of my now seventy years, it is tempting to holler as I read these words: "Harriet, what were you thinking? How could you do this?" I hope I never completely forget what it was to love like that, because that is the only answer possible. As Colette said: "Love has never been a question of age. I shall never be so old as to forget what love is."

Irving and I resumed our affair yet again although I continued to work like a fiend and hold onto my space. He often walked from his home on Delavan to my apartment, before returning to his habitual hell. When we were together, we were terrific, as we always had been, although something had definitely shifted in me. My heart was indelibly scarred by the last separation. I loved him, I could not maintain my refusal of him no matter how I tried, however, I no longer had the same patience for his stories of torment and torture, and his inability to break away from that scene. I finally had heard enough.

He would go to a media interview, then come directly to me and we'd watch it on TV, from bed. Then he'd get up and go back to Delavan, making sure he washed my scent off before he left. It sounds sordid and horrible, and looking back I suppose it was. When a woman becomes intimately involved with a married man, especially if that man is still living under the same roof as

Irving Layton, Toronto, 1978.

his common-law partner, that element of sordidness is inevitable. I never had any issue with being his mistress, at any rate. And there is no way to effectually describe how it was with us when we were together. That was what made it all possible to endure, for us to somehow stand it all. The affinity, the bond, the passion, the poetry, the ease, the joy of being together ultimately overcame everything and everyone. Neither of us was willing to accept a life that didn't embrace what we had together.

Louis Malle came to Toronto, to publicize Paramount's *Pretty Baby*. The picture was causing all kinds of disturbance in the political climate of the moment. A young boy had been killed on Yonge Street; it was a tawdry story involving child pornography and child sex trade. *Pretty Baby* arrived in that environment. It was the story of a child, played by a young Brooke Shields, living in a whorehouse at the turn of the century in New Orleans. The Ontario Classification Board had outright banned the movie. There was no question of cuts requested or refused; the picture was banned based on storyline. Louis Malle's purpose in coming to Toronto was to make a personal plea with the Board, in the hope that the film could be released in Ontario. It had passed other Provincial Classification Boards in various provinces.

Because there was such an enormous amount of attention on the picture, I arranged a press conference at the Four Seasons, where I had installed Malle. The press conference was very well attended and he got a tremendous amount of coverage. However, ultimately the Board held firm on their position and Malle was sadly unsuccessful in his attempt. *Pretty Baby* was not released in Ontario.

Irving always loved film, in particular, foreign films. He was a big fan of Fellini, Antonioni, and Malle. So when Irving asked me if it would be possible to arrange a meeting with Malle, of course I agreed to arrange it. Irving always had theories about movies—what they really meant, what the director was doing in this or that scene. Irving would interpret and analyze the films endlessly and his interpretations were always interesting. So, there we were in the suite: Irving, Louis Malle, and me. Irving launched into his lively and engaging interpretation of one of Malle's films, I don't recall which one. Malle listened politely. He was a courteous, professional artist. When Irving had finished, Malle said—politely, respectfully but very distinctly—something along the lines of: "Well, that is very interesting. No such thoughts ever entered my head while I was making that movie. I never intended such meaning or symbolism. However, if that is what you take from it, then that is fine." Irving was a bit deflated. I hugely enjoyed myself.

I worked at Paramount through 1976 until summer 1978. My affair with Irving continued; however, I no longer would travel with him. Even if I had wanted to—which I did not—the business place does not recognize summer holidays like the academic world does. I may have been unable to resist his constant pulling me back to him each time I tried to break away, but at least, by this time, I was able to define some boundaries and keep a part of myself to myself. My work was demanding and I had a high professional standard for myself, so I worked really hard at the job that I felt was in some ways a gift. I kept my apartment and it was all mine.

11.

THE SUMMER OF 1977, I was working, Irving was in Greece. That was the summer of "the break." He said we were going to be together at last; that things were absolutely not resolving in his domestic situation, and there was a new man in his partner's life. Finally, he said, the torture was ending and we would marry our lives. I didn't believe him. Our affair had been so much emotional trauma, for too long, and though I loved him, I did not believe him when he said that this time, for real, we were going to be together. After all, how many times had I heard that? How could I believe him again? I had made peace with the reality of our relationship as a love affair and I was prepared to be his lover and muse for all time, if that was how it had to be. The fabric and texture of our relationship had been woven into a new entity. I paid scant attention to what he said. I continued working, and held protectively onto that part of myself that was not his.

He phoned me, wrote to me, and sent me gifts. I did not respond. When I did reply, but not fast enough for him, he was prompted to compose "Madman on Mithymna Beach": "My love, I can take everything/ the world throws at me/ except your silence/ When I do not hear from you/ the sun's only a distant fireball/ and the sea nothing but an old gossip/ repeating ad nauseam/ her one good story/ to the impassive beachstones at my feet// I try to fill up the silence/ with recollections of your smile/ and perfect mouth/ your humorous melancholy eyes...." etc. Scholars and academics of Layton's work may find it helpful to know that whenever there is reference in his poems to "smiling melancholy eyes," to "the perfect mouth," or to the scent of lilacs, those references are to me.

On August 2, 1977, he wrote to me about the story of the prophet Hosea, with whom he was identifying at that time. "Since we agreed to separate, A. and I are getting along like two doves on the same bough. Since we no longer need to play a role, there's no compulsion to make the other one suffer for imposing it. Hooray! I was able to tell her that I always disliked her and she was able to reply with equal candor and gusto. This morning I summed up my feelings for her. I said: 'I've always admired your character but detested your nature.' Dem's my last words on the matter. Amen."

By the end of August, Layton had composed many new poems. In a letter to me, he writes: "I find myself having the strangest thoughts about sex and death, so it's nothing to marvel at if my new book is titled *The Tightrope Dancer* and is about the poet who dances on a rope strung between the two. Jo, it's probably my best book to date. [Note to the reader: it was one of the more endearing aspects of Layton's genius that he always sustained a childlike exuberance about life in general, and creativity in particular. Every new book was "his best."] I feel I've made the statement I'd always hoped I'd make when time and experience had soaped my head, that I'd really say what living on this beautiful and dangerous planet has meant. Of course, I couldn't have done it without the help of others i.e., wives, girlfriends, and the dictators, schmucks, and assholes who were my contemporaries; nor without the rare and beautiful souls that helped to keep me sane. I'm grateful to the whole lot for whether they willed it or not, they gave me some of the most wonderful moments of my life. Wow!" In closing, he asked me to contact McClelland and Stewart: "...and ask whether they've sent *The Covenant*? Sorry to lay this trip on you but unless someone lights a firecracker under their arse I'll see no copies. Ask for Denise Avery or Anna Porter."

Amazed as I was, that autumn we actually—finally—did move in together, to a lovely main floor flat in a house at 200 Glenn Road in Toronto's Rosedale district. We had a living room, a large eat-in kitchen, a small bathroom and best of all,

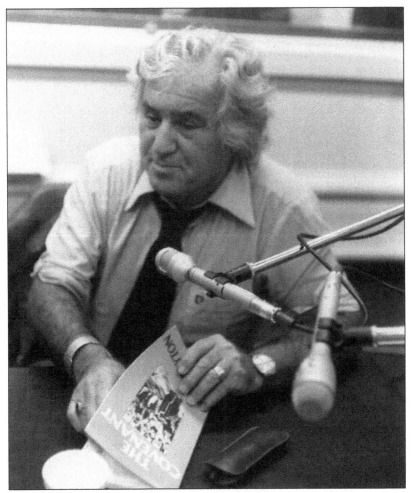

Irving Layton, CBC interview for The Covenant, *1977.*

a working wood-burning fireplace in our bedroom. I continued with my work at Paramount, where I was very busy with another "little" picture called *Saturday Night Fever,* among many others. Paramount was sending the star, John Travolta, on a publicity tour that included Toronto, and it was my responsibility to create his media schedule and ensure that all interviews were handled correctly and well. Mr. Travolta was an absolute delight to work with, entirely professional and charming to all.

The first crisis for Irving and my newly established bliss came when I was offered a job in New York. The man who headed up

Paramount Distribution in New York knew me from his previous stint in Toronto, and he offered me the job. I also had by this time established an excellent relationship with the executives in New York, Gordon Weaver who was President Worldwide Marketing, and Steve Rose, Senior Vice-President, Marketing at Paramount. They must have been agreeable to this offer, as I would be working under them. There is a possibility that my father had a hand in this, although I will never know for certain. He didn't approve of my relationship with Irving—that was easy to understand. I was good at my job, he knew I had always loved New York, so this was possibly a last-ditch attempt on his part to interfere with my life by dangling a carrot he knew I would find tempting, while at the same time getting me away from Irving. My father loved me and meant well; however, interfering with my life was an awful complication and, of course, entirely the wrong thing to do. My father was a little like Victor Newman, the longstanding lead character in the soap opera *The Young and The Restless,* in his desire to control and manipulate everyone around him, all in the name of protecting his family, loving them, and looking out for their best interests.

The New York job was a terrific offer that I had, at least, to seriously consider. Whatever the means by which the offer may or may not have been maneuvered, it would not have been made at all unless it was felt, by those in authority, that I was a good candidate and could handle the responsibilities. I felt that the fates had played a cruel trick on me in presenting this exciting, professional opportunity at the precise time that my lover and I were finally, openly living together. I wanted to be sure of a commitment from Layton. Even though we were now living together, I had been so emotionally bruised by this point that I felt unsure of him. That I would always love him was beyond question. But what did he really want? I needed to hear him say: "Don't go," but of course he would not say those words. Given his age and his checkered domestic history, how could he be expected to say that to a woman at my stage of life? I needed to hear a statement of commitment, and he—whether out of love for me or not—could not give that to me. There is no doubt that in his mind, the fact that we were living together was commitment enough. Unlike others, I never pressed for marriage. I just wanted to hear him say that he did not want me to go; with 20/20 hindsight, of course I realize he would never have been able to say this.

We talked for hours on end about the situation. Ultimately, I declined the New York offer and stayed with Irving in our flat on Glenn Rd. This proved to be another one of those crucial crossroads in my life. Sometimes I say to our daughter, Samantha, that she must have really wanted to incarnate to because it took an awful lot for her to be born!

In November of 1977, while we were living on Glenn Rd., I wrote in my journal: "We spent last weekend in Kingston, for 'Weekend University'—this one with The Irving Layton as special guest. Met Tom Marshall, [poet, critic, novelist and teacher at Queen's University]. Poor Tom, what a nervous, self-conscious guy. He looks to me like he needs a woman. And we met John and Virginia Moss [John was a novelist, critic and professor at Queen's University and then at the University of Ottawa for decades], who were really lovely. They built a fireplace in the middle of nowhere, then built a house around it. Now they sleep there instead of in tents; and there was a three-legged wild cat who slept on their dog, which is ¼ of an inch shorter than the biggest dog of its kind in the world, according to the *Guinness Book of Records*; also a chicken who slept on a horse. It sounds nice. Time to turn out the lights now, here comes Irving to bed."

On November 7th, 1977, I wrote: "L. is in the next room, typing a letter; I've just washed my hair and am drying it in front of the fire. L. finally succeeded in solving the mystery of the fireplace: he'd get a good fire going, then watch in dismay and disbelief as it would die before his eyes. He said it was a suicidal fire. But tonight he figured it out. Apparently the fireplace is built too high. By hanging—temporarily—a piece of wax paper across the top of it, the fire burns on and the apt doesn't become thick with smoke. Now he says it's the perfect symbol of our times, it's an existential fireplace: it had too much freedom and didn't know what to do with it, so it committed suicide. Now it's under control and burning brightly, warmly on. He had a long visit with my mother today; they had a good talk and seem to have gotten on very well indeed. Father stopped by briefly during it—he and L. shook hands and smiled at each other, exchanged greetings. I hope the ice is now beginning to be broken here. I want to be able to go to screenings with L. Maybe this weekend—no, cause Fri night L. has to see Francesca [Valente, of the Italian Cultural Institute in Toronto] about the folio of poems to go with [Aligi] Sassu's paintings.... It's pouring outside, has been all day. It's so wonderful to be in here, this place that feels so good to us, here together. Warm and loving and cosy and the rain outside.... A sad letter from Andrea [my friend from Emerson College days] who has split with Jack [her boyfriend] and is alone again. Goddammit, there's something very wrong with a world where a woman like Andrea has to be alone. She has so much to offer, so much to give."

Journal, December 4th, 1977: "It's hard to believe, so much time has passed—and so quickly. We've been to Montreal, a couple of weeks ago, and I met Bill [Goodwin, Irving's nephew] and Sandra [Bill's wife]; Musia and Leon [Note: Musia was a Holocaust survivor who had met Irving when he was teaching at the Jewish Public Library. She and Leon, her husband and a successful Montreal businessman, remained lifelong dear friends of Irving. His poem 'For Musia's Grandchildren' is a tribute to her]; Gertie and Dora [two of Irving's sisters], and everyone. It was wonderful to meet all of them, after hearing about them for so long. I think we all liked each other. I've been working really really hard. So has L., but he's off for a month now. A week from this Thursday we are going to St. Lucia, in the Caribbean, for ten days of love, sunshine and water, and rest and no phones, and nobody at all to bother with except each other. And are we looking forward to that! We are so very happy together, it's clear to everyone, even my parents. Steve Osterlund has been here this weekend, and he's nice and easy to be with. [Steve was another writer who used to correspond with Irving. He also wrote a book about Irving: *Fumigator: An Outsider's View of Irving Layton*, which was published in 1975; and *Irving Layton: The Poet and His Critics*, published in 1978] Another name becomes a real person for me...."

Irving, with Leon and Musia, ca. 1978

Journal, December 6, 1977: "It's really winter now, and ugh and ugh again. These days L. talks about where should we be—six months in Greece and then what? To buy a house in Montreal, or in Toronto? Real estate in Mtl is down now so a really good house can (supposedly) be purchased at a great bargain price. And Leonard is there, and family and other friends and that's all a big factor for him. Then again, maybe Quebec will split from Canada, or maybe they'll start futzing around with the currency and then what? ...Houses in Toronto are expensive. So maybe, he says, we should rent here. Ah, who knows, and I really don't care one way or the other, here or there. He'll thrash around with it over the next few months and come to something like a decision eventually. A house in Greece seems fairly certain, though.

"L. is funny. He tells me he was talking to some man about doing a talk show, and isn't even sure if it's radio or television ... tells me he's doing an autograph session in 'a book centre in Yorkdale,' which, it eventually is clarified, is really at The Book Cellar in Yorkville. He doesn't know what's going on, in a way.

"*À propos*, yet another writer planning to do a bio of L. He's pleased and excited by the notion; but he also says a biography is relevant to a man's life like his tombstone is.... He's busy working on a letter to some literary rag, attacking a critic's review of *The Covenant*. Not that it was bad, he says—just stupid. I'm eager to hear the letter, which he's working on, revising over and over again, like a poem. It's bound to be another great, humorous harpoon in some unwitting guy's skull.

"L.'s urging me to quit work at Paramount [Note to reader: interesting that only *after* I refused the New York offer did he choose to say these words].... He resents the time and energy it takes. Can't say I blame him there, or feel any differently about it myself. But I'm slow to give up the independence. I've never been supported by any man, other than my father, and it's just strange to me. It means becoming financially dependent on him. It means more trust. Trust is hard for me. Yet I trust his love for me, his wanting to marry me, to be with me. I know that for him, now, it's as if we were. In his heart, the commitment has been made already. As he said last night, I'll just have to adjust, won't I? I am happy to be with him. I want no other man."

Journal, December 16th, 1977: "We are in St. Lucia. It's truly a tropical paradise, where we arrived just last night. The greenery and floral growth are incredibly lush. We've brought two little books with color photos, so we can identify the trees and flowers. There are crazy birdies all over the place, making weird noises. Little bright green lizards. Big crickets. The hotel is built into the midst of it all. We are here for ten days. L. began his first poem on the plane, and is typing a draft of it now." [Note: That poem became 'Sunflight' and it appears in *The Tightrope Dancer*. It's in the Nietzschean spirit Irving so embraced.]

"He's in great humour and so am I. We've decided never to spend another winter in the cold. It's crazy when, as he says, you know that somewhere the sun is shining and it's warm. That first step off the plane last evening was so gorgeous, when that first warm breeze touches you, and you want to hold your face up to it, instead of crouching into yourself, head down, into the freeze.

"I'm really ready for the rest. John Travolta came to Toronto on Tuesday night, for publicity for *Saturday Night Fever*; arrived in his private jet, with an entourage of his manager, his P.R. woman, two secretaries, and a guy from Paramount N.Y. Having spent the last week or two getting ready for them, and then their arrival and all the interviews and the pressure of keeping all those people happy—I was hallucinating last night, from sheer fatigue."

Journal, Saturday, December 17, 1977: "Sitting by the water, rolling in just a few feet from me. Our second day of relaxation and sunshine, it's lovely. L. has been writing poem after poem; he's so happy. The sun is terribly strong—I'm a little red, but not too bad, as I'm watching it and have to take the shade every half hour or so. L. can sit in it for hours, no worry. All the trees and flowers and birds are going into poem after poem—he's turned on like a child, it's beautiful, he's so excited. Soon we are going into the village to explore, and have dinner there. I've been reading an autobiography of Rubenstein, and L. a bio of Dylan Thomas.

"I think he's pretty much exhausted the Jesus theme of his past two books. There's something new simmering in him now, but I don't know just what form it will take. Now it's a return to nature and joy, which pleases the daylights out of me. I think it may have something to do with man-woman relationship: he's talked about it a bit. About woman as nature, providing the inspiration, creativity; man as having twisted it, corrupted it, in a way. I don't know.... He says he keeps waiting for all the old customary tensions to begin. And they don't. And he can hardly believe it."

Journal, Sunday, December 18, 1977: "Bad night sleeping—me, not L.—restless and nightmares. It rained in the early hours. Now it's another glorious day. A funny incident—they bring us toast at breakfast, of white bread. We asked for brown bread, toasted—and they delivered the same white bread, only toasted to a deeper brown color. Now every a.m., they deliver to our table, with some pride, darkly-toasted white bread, saying to us: 'See, yes, you like brown toast,' and we express our delight and appreciation, of course.

"L. barely had time for a few words of 'good morning' to me today, before he plunged once again into the poems he's been working on since yesterday. I read for about an hour while he worked on them, before breakfast, this is. His yelps of 'Hooray' and top-voiced singing indicated his completion of work—for the moment. As his conversation is usually so probing, so intense, and therefore both exciting, exhilarating, and exhausting—I don't mind when he's absorbed with his work. I'm happy to have the time to myself, to read quietly, etc. But it's easy to see how a woman less independent, more possessive, would have a bad time of it with him!

"Last night at dinner, he had tears in his eyes, as he said he wished he were twenty years younger; he felt like a millionaire who'd squandered a fortune. And he rambled on a bit about how you don't know when you're young, how a thing you do, a decision made, may affect your life in the long run. It's amazing to me when I realize how incredibly well prepared I was for him by my parents, especially my mother. Of course, a pity for her, she doesn't have his spirit of joyousness to balance the melancholy and despair. Nor does she—nor do I, for that matter—have his strength, physical I mean, his amazingly healthy constitution. He's strong as ten bulls, and throws off maladies as this dog shakes water from his back, upon emerging from the Caribbean sea at my feet.... He says I *must* give him a daughter.... Sometimes, he says, I look at him in the strangest way, as though I was surprised to see him there and was thinking: 'What are you doing here?' I told him, that's about right. Some moments I have a hard time believing it, after all these years, all the struggles and divisions. But here we are...."

Journal, December 21, 1977: "Frenchmen at one table, Germans at another.... L. is working on another long poem, and having great difficulty with it. He told me today: (1) a man goes mad, a woman just goes hysterical; (2) a man can be divine, a woman can never be divine, she's celestial.

"He also told me I ought to marry a film executive, because I like bad films and would be rich and could feel superior to him, whereas I can never feel superior to him (he says). And, since I can never feel superior to him, I pick on things like my manners being better than his, or my clothes, or his not combing his hair. He said it's the Bernstein in me, that I have to feel superior, but I can't feel so to him. I told him he was being cruel, and he said— 'Cruel, yes of course—I want to be cruel, I like being cruel.' And

I was badly hurt and went away for a couple hours by myself on the beach. I think he doesn't really want to marry me. His misfortune is in needing a woman, as he does. He doesn't really *want* one, but he *needs* one."

Perhaps we were approaching yet another one of those critical crossing points. I was correct in my assessment of him. That dynamic of cruelty was certainly a deeply ingrained habit rearing its ugly head, and I was the new female incarnation on the receiving end of it. In those moments, it was as though I was morphed into non-Harriet to him, I was just the woman he was with, his patterns of behaviour so entrenched, so imbedded into his psyche, that he went into automatic pilot mode. That "tension" he so frequently referred to when speaking of his previous relationship had become something that, whether or not he recognized it as such, was an addiction. Like many an addict, he may have wanted to break free of it, but even in that wanting, he would inevitably lash out at those he loved. Additionally, the creative energy in him had accustomed itself to thriving on the darker side of human relations. Nevertheless, although cerebrally I understood it, I was young, and I was hurt by his words.

Journal, December 22, 1977: "Later in the night, as we were getting ready for bed, he asked me what else he'd said in the afternoon, and when I told him, he gave me to understand that of course he didn't mean those things (about me) but that he has a love of words and how they sound—his use of them not to be taken literally or concretely—why, he asks, should I be restricted in my speech to the realm of truth or reality?—he creates, he says, drama, theatre. One has to, therefore, understand just what one should pay attention to and what not. Above all, he says, I must just let him talk. It's not to matter whether what's being said is true or not, or hurts or not—he reaffirms his love for me, and I'm supposed to be 100% completely sure of that, and know that the other things he says aren't so, and ignore them. But let him talk. Always let him talk. I'm beginning to have this picture of myself as an ear, and a smile.... Over and over again, he refers to himself as a liar, he refuses to 'be restricted ... to the realm of truth,' and the woman with him is supposed to understand that, accept that, not be upset by that."

Had I been older or more mature at that point, I might have been better able to understand his words. I also might have been equipped to more clearly evaluate if that was actually how I wanted to live my life. Was being the muse, being an integral part of his creative process, worth the hurts, the lies, the cruelty? Did they balance out with the passion and the joy? If the woman involved is also an artist, does that help? Although I was working hard at my job, I was also still writing, and Irving was encouraging and helping me. I exalt creativity, and I believe that is one of the things that enabled me to endure the on- and off-again affair over several years. Is the fascination with sensation and creativity a search for meaning and self, or is it a distraction, merely a pushing of boundaries in some futile attempt to define one's own boundaries? I believed that the creative process justifies our existence; I believed it is what exalts us. The issue is only a matter of how much pain one is willing to bear in order to birth the art. Irving's habits of behaviour were so deeply rooted by that point in his life, he was utterly incapable of changing them much, no matter how sincere his intentions or wishes may have been. That, I believe, is part of what caused his eyes to tear up. He knew he was being destructive. He knew he was hurting me, challenging me. He knew he was in peril of losing me because of it, and yet he could not help himself. It fell to me to evaluate his behaviour, to take myself away for "time out" as we tell children, to let him rant and rage and say whatever came out of his mouth, and somehow to understand that he loved me he loved me he loved me and I must learn to forgive and ignore if we were to be together. Now, more than thirty years later, I see with clarity what could not possibly have been seen at that time. As Emerson said, "The field cannot well be seen from within the field."

With the raging passionate emotional landscape that was our history, and given his track record—how could I possibly have understood all he demanded? How was I not to be hurt by his words? He was an AA person: Attack Addict. As much as he wanted peace love and joy, his Achilles heel was to inevitably foul his own nest. His tragedy. And mine. If things were too peaceful, he actually had to create turbulence; that was the truth. His previous partner(s) liked to fight, it was part of what had kept them together. I hated to fight. It was part of what didn't keep us together.

Journal, December 25, 1977: "And a Merry Christmas indeed it is! A little sun, a little read, a little lovin' in the afternoon ... mmmmmmm. L. has written several more poems, including one yesterday, "Yeats in St. Lucia" [Note: this poems appears in *The Tightrope Dancer*] which is great. He calls himself "magnetized" when he's like this—when everything or anything that he says or sees or I say or see or we read can become poetry. It's an astounding process. It has been a terrifically productive vacation. All the new St. Lucia poems are going into *Tightrope Dancer*. I suggested ending with 'Sunflight,' and he thought it's a good idea and says he will. [Note to reader: he didn't; he instead chose to end that book with 'Return to Eden,' which captures the idyllic romance and wonder of our first days together in St. Lucia. He read this poem to me when we got married. It reads: 'You were sent to me/ so that I could make my declaration of love/ beside a Royal Palm/ and kiss your small ears/ under the Chorisia's white floss./ But everything that happened to me/before this/ —what was all that about?']

"It's six p.m. The sky is darkening rapidly, and it's very busy with dragonflies and birds darting in a great rush to who knows what. I'll miss the sound of the sea in the background.

"He's talking more and more about going to settle in the south of France now. It has certain advantages over Greece, and anyways we can still spend a few months Greek island-hopping. But he's inclined to a home in the south of France. That's this week, anyways. We'll see. I'd love it, that's for sure—been a lifelong fantasy of mine. He still says he's the dreamer who makes dreams come true...."

Journal, January 8, 1978: "We began studying French tonight, in 'preparation' for our being there—ah, too sweet a dream, I just can't quite believe it, and I tell him so. And we put a big map of France over the kitchen table (I think we spend more time there than anywhere else)—he calls it the key room, the centre—'the only thing that's important is you and me in this kitchen.'

"I went to Atlantic City this weekend, to see Baba [Note: her name was Minnie Cohen, my maternal grandmother], who had a leg amputated and is recuperating in hospital. She's utterly amazing—her spirit is so beautiful. It was a terribly difficult weekend—very very happy to be back here and happy to have seen her and given her some joy, some smiles, in spite of and over it all."

Journal, January 20, 1978: "Been too busy to write. Just returned from a cocktail party for Lina Wertmuller [Italian director] and Giancarlo Giannini [actor], given by the Italian Consulate. A hell of a night to go out—been snowing steadily since 11:00—but we were keen on meeting her. She's a real character—funny white glasses, twenty lbs. of beads strung around every which-way, sparkly pants tucked into suede boots, hair shoved up on top of her head—but interesting. Didn't talk to G.G., just to her, and I'm so determined to make a movie....

"Last Sat., a party at Anna and Julian Porter's—all the illuminati of the literati: W.O. (Bill) Mitchell, [Earle] Birney. Party was in honour of Sylvia Fraser, just returned from world travels, and whose *Candy Factory* I'm reading. Also there: Charles Templeton."

Journal, Saturday, February 11, 1978: "L. making a fire to Chopin accompaniment (played by Rubenstein, of course)—an evening of some quiet celebration, just L. and me.

"The occasion is (he thinks) the completion of 'Yeats in St. Lucia,' to which he again devoted a day's work. Been listening to him talk about the creative process, which he likens to the birth of a child—how at the beginning 'You are master—but then, at some point, it (the poem), acquires a life of its own and takes over you, won't leave you alone, crying out if something is wrong, wants attention. When I'm tired and can't sleep, I know the poem's not finished.' So saith he, like that....

"And how mystified, amazed he is at how, he says, it starts from nothing, from breath, and becomes so very real, 'more real than these tulips here, because in a few days they'll die, but this poem will be around for a long long time.' What *is* it? he asks me, and I sit silently watching him and listening and I overflow and it comes out of my eyes in wetness.... Also celebrating, tomorrow, with a party for the coming out of *Taking Sides* [edited by Howard Aster]—and Seymour Mayne's book, *Diasporas* [Note: Seymour was a former Layton student, subsequent writer and publisher]. Should be nice, I hope; my parents are even going to come.

"Think I'm going to quit work in a month or so. Get into some screenplay writing, finish my book of poems. L. is urging me to quit. Been a very busy time, as always ... went with L. to Ottawa for a reading there—a resounding success, the Jewish poems to a non-Jewish audience, very favourably rec'd. Then me to work, him to Windsor for another reading, then back for one at U. of T. All in one week, oh Lord, and classes as well. He's amazing. Montreal next week. Looks like maybe the summer in B.C. and a side trip to California; then possibility of Writer-in-Residence at Ottawa U. for Sept-Oct-Nov. Then France, Israel, Greece, India. Says he wants the Taj Mahal to see my beauty. Silly lovely man, says delicious things like that. Everything looking oh so good. Lawyer says everything should be done by beginning of August, and we can get married." [Note to reader: this was in reference to his marriage with Betty, whom he had never legally divorced. However, as Layton now wanted to legally formalize our relationship by marriage, that divorce had become necessary.]

12.

THE NEXT FOUR MONTHS were a time of turmoil, upheaval, unrest. In order to include that period at all in this book, I have to resort to the occasional letter I wrote to my friend Andrea, in Boston. My journal does not contain another entry until July 27, 1978. I have blocked out most of what transpired during the interval. Our survival instincts lead us to forget what is too painful to remember. What I know is, at the time I felt as though I was being manipulated into a role that I absolutely did not want; that I was going to be turned into the "wife" who needed to be escaped from, whether or not that need was connected to me, Harriet, in any actual way. It had become Layton's unfortunate habit to escape from the person he lived with. I categorically, emphatically refused to shoulder that role. If he couldn't break his habit, I was going to have to break it off between us, yet again.

On March 20, 1978, I wrote to Andrea: "Left Layton over the weekend and don't really feel like saying much about it now. Just that, over the past month, some things happened and some doors shut and some feelings died, and sure there was still lots left, but was it enough and I guess I didn't feel it was. The decision was mine. I feel somewhat confused about myself, can't do much by way of explaining my actions to him or me or anyone, just that I moved on guts feelings. Am feeling resigned to being alone, feeling awfully worn out by the whole thing. Am up in the air about my life—have to decide if I'm going to stay in Toronto, or try for N.Y. or L.A. for film business work, or just quit for a while, stay rent-free in the apt. in West Palm and write, or what. Until

I find my legs again and re-locate, am staying at 165 Old Forest Hill Rd. Just wanted to let you know."

Irving, meantime, wrote the short poem "For Another Who Squeezed Back," dated March 18th, 1978, and included in *The Tightrope Dancer*. Dedicated "For Rita," it is about my leaving him, and "Rita" is an anagram of some of the letters in my name. Clearly, he was furious at my leaving, angry and hurt, so he was lashing out the way he knew best: in a poem. This poem is a companion piece, so to speak, with the earlier referenced "Because You Squeezed Back," which is in *The Covenant*.

A note from Layton, dated March 21, 1978, reads: 'To Harriet, with clamorous thanks and whoops of delight for saving me from the folly of my better self. Live to be 120 to render the same great service to other self-deluding poets! Yours ever, Teach.' A copy of "For Another Who Squeezed Back' was attached: "How absurd that because you squeezed back/ your perfume bottles mags etc. are in the hallway/ waiting for you to pick them up at one-thirty"... as well as "For Masha Cohen." Ouch and ouch again. The man was bitter and angry. He could not see or admit that his conditioned behaviour was responsible for my leaving. On the other hand, I—at almost thirty years of age—was asking for a man of sixty-six to accept that, over and above his constant declarations of love for me and commitment to me, he needed to perceive a marital relationship in a new way. I was absolutely not going to be placed in any formerly-established templates, and it would require more than a marriage license for me to stay.

On April 30th, 1978, I received, c/o Paramount, an envelope from Layton. Enclosed were poems: "The Perfect Mouth," "To Blow a Man Down," "Isms," and "Stella." "The Perfect Mouth" is one of the many love poems he wrote for me. I particularly adore this one, entwining the threads of sex and death as it does. The poem, which is in *The Tightrope Dancer*, reads:

Never, I swear,
           in all my travels
did I see lips more perfectly shaped
so yielding, so soft,
the curve of them driving me

out of my mind
as did her chin's roundness

Hear me everyone:
   whole nights I could not sleep
for thinking of her perfect mouth
and in broad daylight
I'd stare at the subtle full lips
   like a blind man
who has just been granted sight

If I can have a last wish fulfilled
   I'll ask to see once more
the carmined orifice
that held me enslaved for so long.
I would forgive all, all,
   lies and mouth honour and deceit
on lips so perfect and beautiful

And watch once more the rose petals
   open on my manhood
to distill the familiar perfume,
making my frame twist with pleasure
as she draws the sperm into her faultless mouth,
   the final spasm
turning into my death quiver

On May 2, 1978, I again wrote to Andrea: "Hello, hello, happy
May. Returned from Los Angeles on Sat. night and found your
note awaiting me. So you won't be living with Jack, aye? Well,
I won't be living with Layton either. The past month has been
bizarre, that's all I can say. I don't seem to have consciously made
a decision, but rather as though I submerged my mind for a while
and just lived, and when some time had passed, I looked and
saw what I had done. We're irrevocably done as far as living
together is concerned; of that I now feel quite certain. In fact, all
of L. seems somehow very far away, as though it happened long
ago. My sense of time has become warped, apparently—among

other things. Admittedly, I'm putting most of it away somewhere; perhaps it's a subconscious instinct for self-preservation; perhaps it's just cowardice. I don't know and to tell you the truth, I don't care. Whatever was, is gone. I'm feeling quite strong. That old antidote, work, has been very helpful. The past week, all week, I was in L.A. for a big Paramount meeting, which was very good. Intensive, exhausting, exhilarating—meetings from 7:30-8:00 a.m. till late late hours of the night. I enjoy the opportunity to be with the "big boys" from head office, New York. I'm trying to get myself into the N.Y. office, in fact. It would be challenging and I need the change, and the room for growth and learning. There's nobody here to learn from anymore, and I'm afraid I'm as good as I can get here. So, all energies now are being directed towards my getting myself transferred to N.Y. I don't know about my chances, though.

"On May 12th I'm supposed to be going to the Cannes Film Festival. It's been a dream of mine for years, and this year Father said he'd make it my 30th birthday present.[Note to reader: My father was undoubtedly so happy that I had broken with Irving, he would have sent me anywhere, done anything to permanently keep me away from him.] Am taking a three-week leave of absence from work. It may be crazy, but what the hell does that mean anymore? I seem to be coping okay, but maybe I'm not looking so hot to others. It seems a brief rest is in order. I feel lucky to be able to take it. Am, obviously, still at the parents' house. It's okay for the time being; they leave me alone. [Note: they were so relieved that I was not with Layton at that point.] If nothing opens up for me in N.Y., I'll have to start looking once again for a new abode. I really want to move to Paramount New York. I feel I need it, and I feel I'm ready for it now. When I was offered a job there last fall, I turned it down, because of living with L. Isn't life funny, ha ha.... Can I have a second chance?

"Feeling mainly not too emotional, quite steeled or is it self-possessed? Am I really okay or not? Who knows? Getting, in some ways, a little hardened I think. Which is okay by me too...." In retrospect, I realize I was in a state of total emotional shock, and whatever self-preservation mechanisms I had, had finally kicked in.

I did indeed go to the Cannes Film Festival with my parents, and my brother, in the first—and only—family vacation to Europe we ever undertook. It was my thirtieth birthday present from my family. We drove a bit around the French Rivier: Gourdon, Nice, the Picasso ceramic museum at Vallauris. Then we went to Israel, for the first time. I adored the French Riviera. But I had never had any particular feeling for Israel, nor any particular desire to go there; it was just a matter of curiosity to scc someplace new. I liked it more than I expected, and I found it emotionally stirring. However, the way we "saw" Israel was not the way I wanted to see any place. It was my parents' trip and I was just along for the ride, and the ride was in the back of a chauffeur- or guide-driven limousine. We saw the country, for the most part, from the air-conditioned luxury of the limo. The trip concluded with London, where we stayed at the Inn on the Park in another suite. This was my parents' way of travel at that point in their lives: they wanted, and paid for, every comfort and luxury available. I was trying, once again to move as far away from Layton as I could, and I truly hoped that this trip would help me, would make me feel I belonged in some world, any world that did not include him, help me lose myself in material things, since the world we had lived in together had vanished. In fact, for the most part, I hated that trip. Instead of finding comfort, it reminded me of everything I did not value; it reminded me of who I was not, and it felt entirely wrong wrong wrong. Emotionally, I felt destitute and ravaged. I had thought I could lose myself in luxury made available to me on that trip so I could forget all I ever wanted, which was to be with Irving. It was a wretched trip.

In June, Irving sent me another envelope, c/o Paramount. This one included "David and Bathsheba," "Man and Woman," "God's Mysterious Ways," "Tickle Tickle," and "The Last Survivor." Clearly, he was pouring his anger and hurt into poem after poem. He inscribed his return address as "100 Damnation Rd., Inferno, Everywhere." So he too was suffering. And he was, of course, not letting me go, again. The poems written at this time were black, bitter, and angry: "Put this down, my sons, as a guiding rule:/ In a woman's eyes every man's a fool;/ He hankers after glory and the tomb,/ She hears his deathknell tolling in her womb." At this time, I no longer was thinking about his ability to create art out of hurt.

On June 30th, 1978, I wrote to Andrea: "God, Andrea, sometimes it all gets so incredibly much. I've turned down going to a screening of a picture I wanted to see, and am going to see Layton, who I want to see even more than the movie! And here I am, alone, in the nice little room [in the back part of my parents' house] called 'mine' when I'm here, after ½ hour solid smoking some light green weed (I've hardly been smoking at all), and listening to 'The Hissing of Summer Lawns.'

"By the way, I hope you're saving some of these letters. In the year 2050, when other parts of the Layton collection are opened, there may be a whole new slew of stuff for folks to get into. Like the Harriet part. So, let's get ours in for posterity, what do you say?

"L. is 'moving' to Montreal tomorrow. All the belongings of everyone are out of what used to be his and Aviva's house. She and Leon [Aviva's new partner, who subsequently became her husband] are supposed to leave for England this coming Wednesday. I met Leon yesterday, for the first time. Would you believe it...? How very bizarre, to do it justice I'll have to perform it for you, re-enact the scene. Not that it was bad or negative. It wasn't. In fact, I like Leon very much. Aviva could hardly wait, after a while, to get him away from me. How absurd.... I'd run to the ends of the earth to avoid loving a married man again. It's another kind of hell. I hope I'll get it down in writing some day....

"I've been working incredibly hard. Today and yesterday, for the first time, I was upset because I did something wrong, I made a mistake, and it was so stupid. I figure it happened because I have so much to do, and I actually am not handling it as well as I feel I should. All of which has distressed me, so I took a tiny bit of valium this afternoon. Layton comes back to Toronto this Wednesday, to go to court on Thurs a.m. about his divorce. From Betty."

13.

A S THERE ARE NO JOURNAL ENTRIES, and memory cannot be relied upon for accuracy, I cannot relate what occurred between us after I returned from Europe. Clearly, Irving once again pulled me back and just as clearly, I was incapable of staying away. The story becomes wearisome, except for this difference: we had been living together in the flat on Glenn Rd., where finally we had set up a home together. What happened to make me leave again? It seems once again I felt I was being forced into a role I refused to accept: his habits of co-habitation were so deeply ingrained that twisted and tortuous as they were, they were familiar to him, and he was unconsciously recreating them, or at least trying to with me. I was not then, nor at any time, prepared to wear that mantle. Was it reasonable to think that at this stage of his life he could change those habits? Clearly, we both thought it was possible this letter to my dear friend, Andrea, indicates.

Letter to Andrea, July 2nd, 1978: "L. left yesterday morning, saying he wished I were going with him. He was crying. How to stand how hard it is?… Today there's a large article in the paper about him and the fact that he's moving back to Montreal. The headline is 'Layton's taking all his love away.' Which really set me up nicely for the interminable day. Went to see the Cuban Ballet last night. It was wonderful. Very dramatic, great scenery and costuming. Alicia Alonso danced. She's amazing, especially for her age. Just finished reading a bio of Colette. What a brave, fantastic woman. One of the truly great writers. I strongly recommend anything she's written, but especially her books *Cheri* or *The Shackle,* or *Break of Day.* She's so sensuous, has such insights into the workings of women. I'm surprised more women, today especially, aren't turned on to her. What an independent, free spirit she was!"

Irving's work at York University had concluded. David and his mother were living with Leon Whiteson, whom she would soon marry; they were in London, England, and Irving wanted to live in Montreal again. He had made the decision when we were not together. This decision made sense considering his people were there, and Montreal was his city more than Toronto had been. We had, in the interim, gotten back together and I was moving to Montreal to live with him. As he had said, this time it has to be forever....

Journal, July 27, 1978: "A fresh page in green ink, green of new life, green of warmth and summer. The book party referred to in the last entry [Feb. 11, 1978] was the beginning of a rapid downhill slide between us. I left L. I think it was at the beginning of April. The past four months have been brutal; nobody will ever begin to understand how difficult—or how necessary. There was an enormous load of shit that had to be worked through. Most of it was in me. [Note: I did feel that at the time, although I do not now, and it makes me cringe to read these words]; things I had put away deep inside myself, resentments and hurts that had been festering for all the years we've been involved. Things I've never dealt with, with him. Always I thought I'd play the martyr, play the role of the Strong One, the I-Can-Handle-It-All one, thinking—oh so wrongly—that he had enough shit to handle, that he didn't need me to dump mine on him too. Fool that I was. I've had to dig—no, gouge deep deep down—and haul everything out and expose it to my eyes, and his. And he's had to work through a lot of stuff too. It was the 'cleansing period' I'd suggested we take last fall, when I felt it was wrong for him to move directly from living with A. to living with me. But we hadn't done it then and it did have to be done, as I felt, somehow, though certainly didn't begin to understand. Now we've done it. And we've come through it. Together.

"I won't go through it here. Nobody will ever know, really. Some of his anger, bitterness, and hurt will be seen in his poems.

My closest, truest friends know more. Maybe it'll go into my book, or my screenplay. Maybe it will remain a mystery.

"This week, on L.'s suggestion, I went into Montreal for the day. I saw the apt. he'd taken (though not fully unpacked in) when we were not together and I agreed with him that it would be too small for us and arranged for a larger one in the same building. In two weeks, I will move to Montreal and move into our new apt. L. is in California now, seeing all the family there. And writing like mad, he says. The he goes to Banff for a week. Then he joins me in Montreal. As he said, while still in Toronto, 'If we go back together, it has to be forever.' And I agree. This time, how much more honest a relationship we share; how much more trust for him I have. Much more belief in his love for me, too. More understanding I have for him, too. A much more mature love. I wrote a poem called 'Commencement,' about a little of it. It feels so good. It was so hard to get here.

"Last Friday I stopped working at Paramount. Told them I was leaving to write—a screenplay, a book ... our personal life is private. Our friends know, that's enough. [Note: How mistaken I was on that score. My life with Irving became a matter of public record!] It's a nice period now. Two weeks before I go and I'm not impatient or restless—for the first damned time in my life! The feeling of peace is extraordinary. Not complete, of course—I have all my writing inside me still—but as far as he and I are concerned, I mean. My gypsy heart—as far as men are concerned—has come to rest, with him. I am enjoying the days so ... a time of construction and very major changes...."

An envelope postmarked July 11, 1978, from California, included copies of 'The Convert,' which is dedicated to me. At the bottom of that page, Irving wrote in his hand: "Dearest H: So you don't think I love you? So how come I can think of nothing else but your eyes, lips and warm embraces?" Also enclosed were copies of 'Male Chauvinist,' and 'Father and Daughter.'"

"The Convert"

Just when my faith is strongest
and I embrace Emptiness

with the fervor of a pill-popping
fanatic of Bay Street;
just when I know
beyond any shadow of confusion
ailing or demented people
are praying to a chimera
and lighting futile candles for him
in hoary churches and cathedrals,
just then he turns his head
to smile goodness and peace at me
with your full perfect lips
and at that instant
I fall down on my knees
an awestruck convert
my eyes two candles glimmering
in the dark.

On July 15, 1978, a postcard from California he sent reads: "Dearest Harriet: Did you get my letter? I mailed it a week ago. I'll write another this evening and post it tomorrow. I've been writing furiously, sixteen poems since I left Toronto, some masterpieces among them. Poems with a different tone—more direct and biting, fierce with insights and honesty. I had a blow-up with Naomi [his daughter, from Betty] the second day we were in Inverness. Am alone once again. Perhaps that's my fate, I dunno. Women seem to be intolerant of my self-absorption, my self-sufficiency. I'm too old to change, alas. Love, Joe." [Note to reader: Irving sometimes used the name Joe. I can't remember precisely how this evolved, but I think it was because—as we seemed destined to be together—he had nicknamed me Jo, so he was also Joe, two parts of one love.]

On July 17, 1978, Irving wrote me another letter. At the top of the page was a drawing, a sketch in red ink of a man, with a balloon saying: "Hi, Jo. Do you really love me?" The letter reads: "A beautiful sunny day for a change! The hills and water just beyond and the green leaves fluttering all around me, since all the walls are largely composed of windows that lets me take in everything with a swivel of my head. For three weeks I'll have the illusion that I'm a millionaire, for I've never been in so luxurious a place in all my life. But I suspect Mrs. Whitney rents this place for the summer because the water's too icy to swim in and medusas abound in it in with terrifying numbers. I counted dozens of them yesterday when I was standing on the wharf. However, as long as I can get in a sunbake every other day I shan't complain. It's peaceful and I'm writing poem after poem. Several masterpieces. 'The Garburetor' is certainly one of them, so are 'Where Was Your Shit-Detector, Pablo' and 'Father and Daughter' which I enclosed in my letter to you. If I can write another three or four as good as these I shall be more than happy with my visit here, despite my row with Naomi. Even the latter may have been a good thing because it's enabled her to get off the grudges she's accumulated all these years and for me to tell her some home truths about herself in a long letter which I mailed off to her yesterday. It will either bring us closer or it will keep us apart for a very long time to come. Either is preferable to a relationship that's based on show and pretense, though of course I'm hoping that it's the first that will come about. The next few days may tell.

"Betty came to see me yesterday and stayed over for the night. And you know what, Harriet? I think for the first time in over thirty years she told me that she was glad to have spent the evening with me—this was over breakfast coffee—because she was going to revise her picture of me in the novel she's writing. I read my new poems to her and she laughed in all the right places, laughed uproariously, and just shook her head in wonder and appreciation at the masterpieces. Her appreciation and regard were so genuine, I wanted to hug her and tell her 'But this is the man I really am, Bets,' but I knew it was unneeded because she'd had a revelation, that she had seen something she had never let herself see before or was incapable of seeing. Whatever, she kissed and embraced me with a tenderness she had never displayed before, and I really think that at last the wall of misunderstanding and pain has come down forever. She's coming to get me on Wednesday to give a reading in Guerneville where, so she says, I have many admirers of my poetry. I am doing it for her sake, though I need a poetry reading like a horse needs a fifth leg. But she says there are some interesting people who'll come to the reading and there will be a reception afterwards so that I can meet them....

"I haven't seen my brothers yet. I'm leaving my visit to them till the last week, for I know that if Hyman got hold of me he'll want to monopolize all my time and there will be no more poems, only hours and hours of listening to him unreel one story after another. I'm allowing myself three or four days of that, and that's about all my eardrums or my nervous system will take. When Hyman is telling one of his stories he demands all your concentration; woe betide if your attention wanders or you don't laugh when he hits you with the punch line. In short, he can be both funny and exhausting. Harry [another of Irving's brothers] doesn't live too far off from Inverness and I'll probably call him when I get back from Guerneville. Betty tells me that his wife, Sara, has a huge stack of poems. This is the first time I've heard of it! The Messiah must certainly be coming, if Sarah also is writing poetry. I'm curious to see what it looks like, though Betty says it's great stuff. Who knows, who knows? Who knows anything these days? Throw a stone and you'll hit a poet. That sentence is not in the imperative mood, it's in the subjunctive." [Note: A poem entitled 'Avantgard' was typed below.] "...I wish you were here with me. I miss all the things that make you so right for me. I always think of you with great tenderness and love." On the back of the letter was another one of his line drawings of a man, with a scrawl to "note the ecstatic expression on his face," below another poem, "Petit Dejeuner."

One day later, July 18th, 1978, he wrote again. This letter included a draft of a poem he wrote during a "sunbake," entitled "The Halo," which appears in the same form in *Droppings From Heaven*. In the letter, after the poem, he wrote these comments: "I think it's a good poem but I'm not sure I have all its meanings. Am I turning away from the peace offered by a religious ordering of one's life? Am I contrasting that life with the all-embracing one which poetry offers, even though I find the former very inviting? What do you make of it? I mailed off a poem to *The Toronto Star*, which I hope they'll run in their letters column. Its [sic] titled 'To The Jewish Dissenters.' I mailed it off today, so perhaps it will appear some time towards the end of next week. I now have 96 poems in the Mss of *Droppings From Heaven*. When I have 100, I'm sealing up the manuscript, otherwise I'll spend the whole summer writing poems and I shan't read a book. I picked up "Born Female" and I've started reading it. I'm also reading Dostoievsky's *The Double*, that is, when I'm not scribbling away. Nothing to do but sunbake, walk to the 'village,' write, make meals and read when I'm not having visions and revisions.... I miss you very much, my dear gypsy. If you were here it would be a repeat of St. Lucia, except for the swimming. Too cold for that and too many jellyfish. Here's another poem that I was awakened at six am to write. It describes something I saw in Molibos several years ago. I've never been able to shake the picture out of my head. Maybe the poem will exorcise it."

The poem that followed was entitled "The Sex Drive"; the first draft was:

> The two cats swooshed past the doorway
> Like greased lightning in fur
>
> And the tom's scratched-out bobbling eye
> I saw raking the white gravel
> swung out wide as they cleared the wall

On July 26, 1978, another letter from Irving, this time with return address marked as the Banff Centre, School of Fine Arts, although he was still in California. It included a fresher draft of "The Sex Drive":

> The two cats are
> eggy bolts from nowhere
>
> The tom's sound eye still on her slit,
> the hanging one
> swings out wide as he clears the wall

The final version of this poem, same title, which appears in *Droppings* went this way:

The two cats are leggy bolts
hurled from nowhere

The tom's unscratched eye still on her slit,
from between his paws
the loosened one
humping the cobblestones
swings out wide as he clears the wall.

On July 26, 1978, he wrote: "Dearest Jo: Got your letter and poem yesterday. Both moved me greatly by their wonderful simplicity and truth. There's something solid about you, and I don't mean you're overweight. You're upfront, generous and sensitive. You're okay, and you even write good poems! I miss you, Jo. When anxieties and doubts assail me, I think of your love and how constant it's been despite some shattering ups and downs. I wish you were here so that I could talk some of these things out of me. It's all clear skies now but the blow-up with my daughter threw me, as they say, for a loop. It seemed to prove to me once again that *there's something in my nature that makes a woman want to start screaming or taking a knife to my throat* [emphasis mine]. I've no doubt that Naomi was absolutely in the wrong, one hundred percent, and yet I know the thing goes beyond right and wrong, that subterranean forces are at work; what the Russian scientists call 'biofields.' Maybe there are lots of hidden mines in my biofields and when a woman steps on them she blows up, to make a bad pun. Look at all the women that have walked out on me: Boschke, Aviva, yourself, and now Naomi. Some record, eh? Maybe someone is trying to tell me something! Well, there are things and things we must talk about. Staying here by myself is great for introspection—what else is there to do but tear at all the psychic scabs? Of course, I've accomplished a whole lot more than that. I've written some of the best poems in my life and put together a book that even surpasses *The Tightrope Dancer*. This morning I typed out my 105th poem. I wrote a great poem for Musia and another one for Aviva ... both of them coming from that region where all good poems come: straight from the heart. I'm doing things, Jo, I've never been able to do before. There's a suppleness and simplicity in these new poems that only rarely was I able to achieve formerly. Like the poem on the other side of this page which I finished last night."

The poem is this one below; also on the page was "The Sex Drive."

"The Black Tom"

Someone had dragged the dead cat
off the road
and she lay in the rough grass
as though she had fallen asleep in it.
I saw no wheelmarks on her,
no blood on her white and black fur.

The next morning when I came by
she was still lying
curled up in the grass, her head
buried in her forepaws
and looking as if nothing
could ever wake her from her deep slumber.

And today two weeks and thousands
of cars later
the cat's still resting peacefully
on her side,
but now there's some grass between her paws
and the black tom has made her pregnant.

The letter continues: "Does that last line give you a frisson? It's grotesque the way a dead body bloats up, as if Death were making some kind of black joke. I seem to be inexhaustible, and I know that if my spirit is not weighed down by *anxiety-producing* responsibilities, the next ten or fifteen years could be my crowning ones. Can you or God or anyone give me that assurance? I'm not like other men, Jo. Because I've two eyes in my head and a nose and use human speech I fool people into thinking I'm 'normal.' My passions are not normal! What

117

I'm trying to say is that anyone living with me will have to love me very much and have the understanding that comes with wisdom, great wisdom. At thirty, do you think you have it? Ah, why aren't you here so that I could find re-assurance in your laugh and wonderful eyes?

"I've also finished the Foreword, three pages long, very mordant, very lively, very witty. The long knives will be out for me when it's read. But Truth is my master, and I say it like it is. So now if I'm sensible I'll seal up the Mss and start reading a couple of books. I've written a book that's going to be around a long, long time. In a way it's my last will and testament, my legacy to the world. Anyone in the next century wanting to know what it was to be alive in this one, I mean the 'psychic feel' of it, will find it in the pages of *Droppings.* Now other things are beckoning and I hear new sounds.

"Dear Jo, will you please collect my mail at York? Put aside the unimportant things and mail the rest to the Banff Centre. Make sure you insure it. Put it all in a large manila envelope. And mail me anything else that you think I should see. And enclose lots of hugs and kisses."

On July 31, 1978, he wrote me again: "My lovely Harriet: Yesterday my daughter took me to a lake, really a large swimming hole, where I had my first swim of the summer. Everyone there seemed to be a nudist though there were a few eccentrics that wore trunks or bikinis. Wherever you looked around the rim of the swimming hole you saw cocks and cunts and sufficient pubic hair to have made dozens of mattresses. Imagine sleeping on one of them! Who would sleep? Yes the whole spectacle, this display of cocks, cunts, breasts after awhile began to sadden me for it robbed the sexual attraction of all its magnetism and romance. The electricity was all gone, the creative tension that exists when male and female are clothed. My final thought before I plunged into the water was that, alas, the genitals were only for pissing! Another five minutes of viewing and I'd have wanted to tear up all my love poems: in the glare/ of all that pubic hair/ I almost wished they weren't there. They seemed false and pretentious. However, instead of tearing up my love poems I left the place resolved never again to go to a nudist swimming hole.

"And this morning, though it's not yet ten the sun is strong and bright. I haven't seen the sun in the morning ever since I came to Inverness—not once. July I've since learned is the month for fog and mist and that's what I've had for the two-and-a-half weeks I've been here. Usually the sun would make a brief appearance around noon, disappearing after an hour or so. Very infuriating, such tactics, not at all the way he conducts himself in Greece. No wonder Ms. Whitney rents her place for the month of July and comes here only after her last disgruntled guest has left. Of course, it would have been different had Naomi and I not had a blow-out. We could have driven a couple of miles from here to a higher altitude and gotten as much sun as we wanted. I could also have gone swimming every day. But God works in mysterious ways to help poets like myself. I'd never have been as creative with Naomi and me thrown together in that sort of mutual dependency. The blow-up was the best, the very best, thing that happened. [Note: it was part of Irving's irrepressibly joyous nature to always convince himself that whatever happened was for the very best; the other side of him, the irrepressibly dark one, having created the horrible situation in the first place.] A couple of days ago I finished my 110th poem and added a paragraph to my Foreword. The book is ready for sealing. I've written Lucinda about it to alert her to the possibilities of marketing the book in the U.S.A. Quite a number of poems are about California. Lu ought to be able to negotiate a good deal for the Love Poems because there's no such book anywhere, nor will another like it ever be written again. I'm the last of the great erotics!" [Note to reader: The reference is to Lucinda Vardey, Irving's agent at that time. He had never had an agent, and Lucinda was a friend of mine. We had met when we worked together on a film project, she representing the publisher of the book on which the film was based. When I learned Irving did not have an agent, I called Lucinda and she agreed to represent him.]

"In another two weeks I shall be kissing you all over your desirable body. I'm excited thinking about you in the apartment. We're going to be very happy in it. My head is full of wonderful plans for the future. I'd like to go to India with you and also to Sri Lanka (Ceylon). I'd like to spend some time with you in

Israel and, of course, Greece. Travel very, very light and have adventures. Hitchhike, take busses, caravels. And then, one night, find ourselves in Paris where we go to the snootiest restaurant and stay in the snootiest hotel. And from Paris to slide down the Italian boot and land on your ass in Rome. On your ass I'd be willing to land anywhere. Even in Hades, where Satan seeing it would have something other on his mind than to roast it and me with it for I wouldn't be far behind your behind. No, he'd torture the denizens of those gloomy pits with sight of your body, so that even Tantalus would forget his craving for water in his longing to embrace it. No, I'm definitely going to keep you out of Hades. The poor bastards suffer enough without you adding to their torments.

"I shall be going to San Francisco tomorrow. I hope there's one more letter from you before I leave. Your handwriting does queer things to me, completes me with the love it brings me. It always, always makes me happy to think of you. Look after yourself, my love."

Journal, Thursday, August 17, 1978: "We are in West Palm Beach, in my parents' apt. at 1200 South Flagler. I write the address down so that some day people who are interested can make the pilgrimage here and look at the building and see where we were and where he wrote some of the best poems in *Droppings From Heaven*. L. came back from Banff on Sun. night. We spent three days in Tor. taking care of a number of matters and arrived here today. Two poems already—more, many more brewing. We've been up since six. I'm exhausted, he's on the porch, typing.... We are happy, we are good."

Journal, Sunday, August 27, 1978: "Sitting in the sun, by the pool of the apt. We've had a lovely time here. L. has written about a half dozen fine poems and is beside me now, shaking his straw-hatted head, writing another. I've written a prose poem to Colette. L. says it's good. I've been cooking good meals every night and there's a poem called 'Gazpacho.'"

Journal, Wednesday, August 30, 1978: "So far, it's been the same every day. I should like to put it down, for posterity and future interested readers, what the process is like. L. is out of bed before me. He goes through his current book, every day, several times. Sometimes a poem is taken out, a small change is made, perhaps only one word. When he's repeated this process an infinite number of times and made no changes, the poem is done. While he goes through it, or works on one, I prepare breakfast (he loves his strong cup of Colombian coffee). We have breakfast and while I clean up, he's back at it again. We descend then for sun and swim. His nose is usually buried in a book, a magazine, a paper.

"So far, each day while we've been out here, he has suddenly gotten up and with the most pleasure-filled, excited, mischievous gleam in his eye, has reached for book and pen and begun a new poem. For the next couple of hours he sits, scribbling, muttering, shaking his head. I never ever bother him during this time, or afterwards during the next stages of the poem's birth. After he has his swim, we return up to the apt. The first sheet goes in the typewriter, the first of many drafts. While I dress and prepare dinner, the typewriter is my constant, clacking accompaniment. Usually by dinnertime, or coffee later, I am read the poem. Sometimes he asks me to read it, so he can 'hear what it sounds like.' Sometimes it's a good poem. Sometimes it doesn't work at all. This has happened twice this week, in which case he works on it all evening.

"Last night, after I fell asleep warming my cold feet on his hot body (he's like a furnace, really, he generates such intense heat), he was out of bed and sat on the porch working and thinking till around five a.m. Before breakfast this morning, he read me another great poem, 'The New Piety.' It may have gone through fifty drafts since last night and I see again his genius at work. What was last night has been transformed—there's now a different form to it, a core, a tension, an intensity of meaning. And so the process goes. He's obsessive and completely self-absorbed with it. Past women have found this hard to take and it's easy to see why, as the woman is left out and must fill her time in her own ways.

"For me, far from resenting it, or finding it a problem, I am fascinated to observe the process and excited to be the very first person in the whole world to hear each new poem. There are many moments in between the beginning and completion, and these are filled with hugs and kisses on the back of my neck and what he laughingly calls 'pussy feels and titty feels.' He must have lots and lots of affection and love. Given that and good meals, he's a happy man, who wakes up each day singing.

"The sun and water and quiet here have been marvellous. He's written about a dozen poems for the book and says it's been the best holiday of his life. I should add, every book that's being written is 'the greatest one yet.' I first heard that over *For My Brother Jesus*, then *The Covenant* was 'the best, the greatest book I've done yet.' Then, *The Tightrope Dancer* assumed the position. Now, of course, it's *Droppings From Heaven*. He was saying that he'd like to bring it out in March or April, he can't wait until next fall. However, I said, that's because you're excited now, at this moment. But when we return, *The Tightrope Dancer* will just be coming out and there'll be all the excitement about that. Then there'll be *The Love Poems,* and the Sassu book [Note to reader: This portfolio was titled, *There Were No Signs, Fifteen Poems by Irving Layton, Fifteen Etchings by Aligi Sassu,* published by the Madison Gallery in Toronto and Trentadue Editions in Milan; coordinated with the help of Francesca Valente of the Italian Cultural Institute in Toronto]. And the portfolio with other Italian artist, Carlo Mattioli [Note: *Irving Layton/ Carlo Mattioli,* fourteen poems translated by Francesca Valente, and seven etchings by the the artist, also published by Trentadue Editions in Milan. Both books were released in 1979], and so much, it's too much, he'll have to wait with this one. And he agreed, of course. When he's not writing he does involve me, in everything.

"We have spent hours and hours and hours just talking. I occasionally feel inadequate, especially compared to the intensity of his brainpower and knowledge, the vastness of reading he is armed with. It's a good thing I have a strong sense of myself and a fairly healthy ego. These I see as essential qualities for his wife. Also an intense love of poetry, and the entire creative process. Also the acceptance of everything the world offers, the ability, guts, courage, curiosity to take it all in, the ugly with the beautiful, for all the ingredients are needed, and they all go into his garburator. Also patience, humour, wisdom, and unfailing love for him.

"But, what I was saying about his involving me in everything, when he's not writing..... Even as I've been writing this, he has a few times stopped me to read an excerpt from an article in the newspaper he was reading. If he's reading a book, I am read passages from it. A few days ago, he read a book by Bertrand Russell's daughter, about her father, and nothing would do but I must read it too, to talk about it with him and understand, more importantly, what he has to say about it. Truly it's exciting to be with him."

14.

JOURNAL, OCTOBER 2, 1978: "Cannot believe the passage of time—it doesn't seem possible that so much time has passed since the last entry. Naturally, lots has happened. We were in Tor. the beginning of Sept. for a couple days, then moved to Montreal. It was chaos at the beginning, all my things and Irving's to be sorted out—we worked all day every day for a week and made great progress. Now it's quite comfortable, tho there's still some doing to be done. We've begun to go out a bit, doing some socializing and some entertaining. Last night, for the [Jewish] New Year holiday dinner, we were at Bill and Sandra's [Irving's nephew and his wife]. David Solway [young Montreal poet] was there too, with his Karen. It was the first time I'd met him. He impressed me as being very bright and fast-talking, but also very nervous and fucked up. Irving says he's a truly good poet, and is very fond of him—and concerned about him. This morning he came over for coffee and counseling. He spoke a lot about Karen and their relationship, which is fraught with difficulties and tensions. They've been living together for two years, now—and she's just taken a place of her own and nobody knows what's going to be. Of their love there is no doubt—but we all know how much more is necessary, beyond love. Much of the time, he sounds like a tape recording of Irving.... So Irving sits and listens to him, and tells him what he can, from his own hard-earned wisdom. Also, Leonard [Cohen] has been over a couple of times this week."

Journal, October 9, 1978: "Must have gotten busy in the middle of that entry and here it is a week later, already....The first time Leonard came with another man, Milton Rosengarten, who Irving tells me is a life-long friend of Leonard's and a very fine sculptor. He was pretty quiet all the time he was here, but he has a very nice, warm smile. Leonard looked sort of grim. Irving started off talking by telling Leonard that we had been listening to his album the previous evening and how we had both been moved to tears."

Journal, October 26, 1978: "Just returned from Chicago—the Encyclopedia Brittanica gave Irving and eight other people an "Achievement in Life Award"—his for Achievement in Literature. First class airplane ride, beautiful room in the Ritz Carlton Hotel—a black tie gala. Dinner last night and the awards ceremony. Met Pearl Bailey [the actress and singer who won a Tony for the title role in the first all-Black production of *Hello Dolly*] and Steve Allen [comedian and TV personality, who hosted *Tonight with Steve Allen*, the precursor to Johnny Carson's *The Tonight Show*], who gave a brilliantly witty speech, and Jim Bishop [journalist and author], and Hank Aaron, baseball champ. We were treated royally and it was fun and interesting. We composed some doggerel, which Irving read at the close of his little thank you speech. He was a big hit. The only two little things that went wrong were that the bowtie to his tux wouldn't stay clipped onto his shirt and I broke a tooth during the dinner. Nothing that can't be fixed. Oh, and Irving lost his hat on the plane to Chicago. We tried valiantly to get it back, but somebody must have just walked off with it. But he bought two new ones in Chicago (in Saks, no less) and as long as I'm with him, he won't lose them. It's remarkable, he's always buying and losing hats. Upon landing back in Montreal, he forgot his tux onboard—fortunately, we remembered while we were getting the luggage and an agent came off the plane and gave it to us. Then he was funny, sitting in the cab and formulating the most psychologically complex reasons for why he forgets things like that—not for him the too-simple 'explanation' of absentmindedness—I suggested pre-occupation and he liked that better, but carried it on a bit, offering various theories and psychoanalytical explanations. He's funny. Anything to make life more confusing. As a publicist, I've been frustrated with the E.B. people and with M.&S.—neither of them are alive when it comes to P.R. A major publishing house like M.&S. and do you think they do anything about this award? *Nada*. And the same goes for E.B. They had some coverage last night—but for Chicago. Period. The Canadian so-called president [of E.B. Canada], who looks like a junior clerk, is a real asshole and a tight-assed one at that. The intro he gave Irving was the worst one anybody gave anybody last night. And he's done nothing about publicizing the thing here. It's so dumb, they could do themselves so much good, get such mileage out of it here. I mentioned it to them—but really, what's the use? Who's interested in old news? ...We had wanted to do a few things in Chicago and I got some suggestions on where to go and what to do from Gerry [my longtime friend from Forest Hill Collegiate, Gerry Mandel]—but it was pouring all day and blowy and nasty and Irving is still fighting a cold, so we didn't get around at all.

"The same thing happened a couple of weeks ago, when we were in Buffalo. [Robert] Creeley [prolific Black Mountain poet] is at the U. of Buffalo, and he asked Irving down to read to his class. While there, he also read at the Allentown Community Centre, with Leslie Fiedler and Allen Ginsberg. I didn't like Fiedler at all—not the man and not his so-called poetry—but Ginsberg was nice and warm and put on a good show.... He performed one long piece (including a song) ranting on and on about 'Plutonium.' As I say, it was a good show, but the best poetry was Irving's. Afterwards there was a party and it was utterly bizarre and strange, for me, to be there with Irving, sitting by Ginsberg and his 'wife,' Peter Orlovsky (all of them past heroes etc.) and watching the young people dance to the blaring sounds of—of all things—*Saturday Night Fever*. It was the mingling of so many of my worlds, so many of my lives, yet somehow there was no real fusion.

"I dispensed some 222s [an aspirin/codeine pill sold over the counter in Canada] to Ginsberg and I enjoyed that. Ginsberg had been complaining of a headache, so I gave him the 222s for which he was most grateful. He thought it was very cool that a pill with codeine was an over-the-counter item here. He seemed to hold Irving in great esteem. He also asked about Leonard and we told him, yes, we'd seen him recently and that he was okay.

Allan Ginsberg, to the left of Irving Layton, 1978.

Meantime Leonard's book *Death of a Lady's Man* has come out. Irving has found reading it a somewhat frustrating experience. He says it's brilliant, but has no focus, no centre and though it doesn't make much sense to him, he says it doesn't have to.... Leonard's supposed to be in town now, just back from L.A., so maybe we'll see him and hear some news about how he is and what's happening."

Journal, October 31, 1978: "Happy Hallowe'en. Bought goodies but there hasn't been one trick or treater yet. Irving is at class, it's 8:49 and we've just returned from his weekly Ottawa trip and in addition to the usual there, he gave two readings and we met Natalia Babel, yes Isaac Babel's [the great Jewish Russian short story writer] daughter. She's teaching at the Slavic Studies Dept. at Ottawa U. When she and Irving met, it was one of those times when there's an immediate bond. She told him she felt she'd known him all her life, and she wrote a beautiful inscription in a book she wrote on *Crime and Punishment* (which I'm just reading now) and *Les Miserables*. She was charming, dark, and with high colour in her cheeks, very rosy."

Journal, November 9, 1978: "We are to be married two weeks from today, in Toronto, in a rabbi's study, with a party afterwards at my parents' house. It will be a small affair, but should be very lovely. From here, Irving has asked Musia and Leon [Irving's lifelong close friends], Bill and Sandra,[Irving's nephew and wife] and Leonard [Cohen, of course]. Also his sisters by way of courtesy, but they won't be coming. Leonard may or may not—things like this with him are very iffy. Francesca Valente [from the Italian Cultural Institute in Toronto and a great supporter of Irving's; she also translated some of his poetry and helped facilitate readings in Italy] is to come and Lucinda Vardey [my friend/his agent]. For me, Gerry [my friend, Gerry Mandel] will come and my friend Andrea [Andrea Gilbert] is coming from Cambridge. Uncle and some of the parents' friends, thirty or so in all. I am excited about it and happy and just a little scared. Irving seems to be happy about it, though perhaps not entirely without trepidations. He keeps asking if I'm sure I won't change I keep telling him, only for the better! [Note to reader: Even though we had been through so much over all the years, Irving had a need to hear over and over again that I wouldn't change—that who I was would remain the same. I often wondered about his experiences with other women that had made him so fearful that I would somehow morph into another form.] Lucinda just returned from Europe....

"Irving wrote two new poems this week—he's very excited about 'Shlemiel.' He also revised about four from *Droppings* this morning. He was very pleased. He keeps saying how he needs Canada, how the schmuckiness of the people here is such wonderful fodder for him, fuel. Where else, he asks, would he get such good fuel, see such stupidity and blandness and obtuseness?

"He also says I'm 'ruining a great erotic poet' because he has not any of the desire he used to have for other women, which means he doesn't get the stories and poems he used to get, along with all the attendant tensions and conflicts. I daresay he'll manage one way or another. He's been incredibly busy. Media people are constantly after him, people for readings too. Tomorrow he's got three interviews in the morning, followed by a reading. And tonight we have the symphony ball. Good Lord, I tell him, he *has* to slow down—I can't keep up with him!"

Journal, November 20, 1978: "It's the usual solitary, quiet Monday evening for me, as Irving is making his weekly trip to Ottawa. My mother called this evening to tell me that *Macleans Magazine, and* Zena Cherry [the society columnist] from the *Globe and Mail* called and want to cover the wedding on Thursday. I had already arranged w/ Edie [Edie Frankel, who was a journalist for various publications and television, and a close family friend] for *Macleans* to do something, but Zena Cherry really gave me a laugh. Zena of the society column, of 'the Lieut-Gov and kings and queens of WASPdom,' my lord, what a joke. I'll check with Irving and let her know. Myself, I think it's pretty funny, but okay.

"…Instead of Irving going to London in Dec., David is going to come here. Apparently, he's lonely for Toronto and Montreal and wants to see his friends. It's much nicer than Irving going there, as far as I'm concerned. His last conversation with his mother, on Sat., was a distressing one—for him, and consequently for me. She laid one of her misery trips on him and he told me she said (besides God knows what else) that 'he might have waited.' Waited for what? I asked and he told me, for her to get over her *mishagas;* that her being in London is temporary and she probably will stay neither in London nor with Leon. Who knows? With her, one time it's okay, the next time it's awful—it's blow hot, blow cold. I wish the day would come—will it ever?—when she leaves him alone—or, better, when he stops being so affected by it all. Other than that, everything is okay. Amazingly, Irving has been writing poems. Considering his schedule, that is really remarkable. It's a good thing that there's only another couple weeks of this term left—he's really driving himself.

"He's entering a new phase now in his poems—a critical look at the underside of society, the other side of Dionysianism, the destructive, negative and brutal parts of man. Since these poems are rounding out *Droppings*, he may incorporate his new thoughts into a play or short stories. So he says, anyway….

"I am more determined than ever to begin soon on the screenplay. I just need to feel more certain about how to begin."

Journal, December 4, 1978: "Supposed to be the last Monday night for Irving to be in Ottawa, and are we glad. It's almost a little frightening, how emotionally dependent I feel on him sometimes. When he's away, I really miss him; it's so quiet without him.... I feel that I just want to grab all the time I can. I don't want to regret not having done things. It's always been that way for me, I've lived that way, but now I feel it more than ever....

"This morning as Irving was leaving, he was saying how happy he was that this was the last Monday for Ottawa, that he wouldn't do it again, for any money, it wasn't worth it. But then, most of the time, he says he enjoys it. He says different things most of the time, so it's sometimes hard to know which of the things he's saying he really means. I went out on the porch, as I always do, to wave goodbye and watched him running down the street to catch the bus to the train station. It was just past seven a.m. and still dark and cold and wet, and as I watched him running I just thought shit, he's sixty-six years old and why is he knocking himself out like that?

"He got a letter from A. the past week and talking about it all a day or two after, it made him cry. Such a lot of heartbreak there. I think it's pretty awful of her to always make things harder for him, keep making him—or trying to make him—feel so terribly guilty and responsible for such unhappiness. How can such selfishness and twisting manipulation have been so effective for so long on a man who says he loves and admires and respects generosity so much? But then, he admits that he can't handle tears, says that when a woman cries, he falls apart, he'll do and give anything.... Also, I understand that, as he says, he mistook hysteria for vibrancy. Enough. We are happy, we are in love, and I hope we have a long time to be happy together. We're so looking forward to going to West Palm and then Mexico. In about a month now, we should be on our way. We both need the sun.

"Meantime the days are busy. Aside from the usual chores, I'm sending thank you notes to people for wedding gifts and also starting on New Year's/Seasons Greetings cards.

"It was a lovely wedding. The ceremony was short and very sweet, the rabbi did what he was there to do, Irving read 'Return to Eden,' and we had a great party after at my parents' house.

Irving and Harriet, wedding day, November 23, 1978.

The champagne and caviar flowed and a splendid time was had by all, as they say..... The *Globe* sent a photographer and next day it appeared not just in Toronto, but was sent on the wire service and ran all over the place! *Macleans* is out, with a big colour photo. It's great, and funny, looks like Irving is taking a bite out of my face. We keep getting congratulated everywhere, it's funny."

Looking back on that page from *Maclean's* these years later, one of the things that is amusing about it is that Irving and I are the main attraction with the large photo, and then there is a smaller article about a young comedian called Jim Carrey, who was just beginning to make a name for himself. I showed the article to Samantha, when she was an adult, and she was quite astonished that we were bigger news than Carrey at that time; it provided a perspective for her, and a laugh.

Journal, January 13, 1979: "We arrived in W. Palm on Wed. afternoon and are we happy to be here—happy, no, that's too mild—we keep doing little ecstatic dances across the room. I love this place and so does Irving. One of the best things is that nobody has the telephone number. Just the freedom from the constant phone ringing is such delight. Irving, fortunately, didn't know it, or the address, so he couldn't give it to anyone—and I just kept quiet. The only one we gave it to was Leonard, who we saw our last week in Montreal. We were at Bill and Sandra's for a little New Year's party and all of a sudden in walks Leonard—it was a nice surprise. He came over the next day, and when we said goodbye, he was supposed to be on his way to Hydra for a month. This morning guess who calls from N.Y.? Good old Leonard. We told him how beautiful it is here and urged him to come down and he said he would. But will he really? What Leonard says and what Leonard does are not usually the same thing.... There's something so impossibly sad and vulnerable about him, he makes you want to offer shelter and comfort, somehow, and you know you can't. There's also something very aristocratic about him and magical. Irving says he's [Leonard] lonely and thinks he'll come....

"Irving has been invited to attend the Fourth World Congress of Poetry in Korea, July 2-9, all expenses paid. After much deliberation, he sent a letter of acceptance. We have revised plans for the summer now. Irving has decided that he doesn't want to go to Europe in the summer, because there are all the crowds and everything is more expensive, and it's really a lot of hassle. He's thinking, instead, of coming back here and from here, exploring some of the S. American countries. Sounds good to me—Ecuador, Guatemala, Peru—love to see those places. Meanwhile, who knows, Irving has different thoughts on a daily basis. But he has sent a 'yes' to the folks in Korea.... He decided that it's yet another step towards his Nobel prize and it might be important for him to make himself visible there."

Journal, Sunday, January 14, 1979: "Leonard phoned again this morning, asking about a hotel. I told him he could stay here, but he said he was coming with someone and it could get crowded. We agree, Irving and me, if Leonard comes with someone, it's better they not stay here with us. Leonard said, 'I'll be down one of these days. I have reservations to fly down tonight, but I don't know if I'll take them any more than I've taken any of the other reservations I've made.' He likes to be really indefinite and evasive and independent obviously.

"Irving has begun to write—a poem, this afternoon. I wondered how long it would take before he started. Up until now, his nose has been constantly buried in one book after another. He's really so excited and happy about having all this time to read—I think that's largely what has led—or is leading him—to decide against continuing to teach. He seems to be thinking that if he were not teaching, he'd have the time and energy not just to immerse himself in reading, as he longs to do, but to start working on some new things—specifically, short stories and perhaps some plays, or his memoirs. And, of course, there's our screenplay, which we are to begin writing tomorrow.

"Also, re: teaching—he has determined that it's certainly not for the money he'd continue, because after taxes, considering the bracket he's in, there's not enough left to mean anything much at all. Also, we're hoping very much that he'll get the Canada Council grant for three years, which would mean about 17,000 for each of the three years, and which would really be helpful.

"The next item up for consideration, then, is where do we live? Toronto or Montreal. Up until now, he's been firm on staying in Montreal, claiming that it's uncertain and unpredictable and therefore more interesting a place for him. And he's gone on at length about learning French and whenever he'd have an encounter with [David] Solway [Montreal writer] or any of the other writers there, he'd come back bellowing about how *that's the kind of thing that never happened to him in all his years in Toronto*, and that's why he's happier in Quebec.... And when I'd say how it's like a ghost city there, how deserted the streets are, how the air is somehow disconcerting, how eerily quiet it is, he mutters 'that's the way I like it' and claim it was like a *shtetl*, like a village and he liked it like that.

"But this past week, when we were in Toronto for a couple days before coming here, I got a good one in: we were staying at the Park Plaza and as we were going out one afternoon, who do we run into, but Jack McClelland and Scott Symonds! It was a grand surprise and we went into the bar for a drink and chat. (Aside from the nice surprise of it, it was a lucky thing, as we were planning on going to Mexico to visit with Scott—but he'd just quit Mexico and had come to Toronto, planning to stay a couple of years, as he's doing a series of articles for the *Globe*. Also, he's apparently finished his novel, which we guess is why he was meeting with Jack.) Anyways, it was very nice and as Irving and I were leaving, he was saying what nice a surprise it was to run into them like that and I said *yes, that's the kind of thing that could only happen in Toronto*. He had to admit it was true. He has also admitted that the air in Toronto does have an energy and dynamism that Montreal certainly does not have. Until now, we've been planning on staying in Montreal mainly because of Concordia—but if he decides not to stay on teaching, we have to, as he says, rethink the matter....

"When we were in Toronto, we spent some time with Max [Irving's eldest son] and Stephanie [Max's girlfriend]. Max had the copies of *The Love Poems* (sans cover) ready for signing and he and Steph arrived at the hotel with an enormous mountain of boxes of books. We spent the evening working. We had a really fine assembly line worked out, as L. was signing with a fountain pen and so the pages had to be kept open until the ink dried. It was a chore, but it's done now. There were a couple of no-goods and Irving brought one down here and he keeps looking through it and it gives him enormous pleasure."

Harriet's parents, Mary and Jack Bernstein, in their West Palm Beach condo, 1979.

On February 24, 1979, I wrote to Andrea: "My dear Andrea—a quiet Saturday night in good ole West Palm. I really like being here so much—the weather has been pretty lovely, and even when it's not so lovely, it's lovely compared to Montreal. Somehow 'the livin is easy' here and in my old age I do appreciate it so.... Actually, we've been hard at work on our screenplay—at least three hours every day. I think it's coming along beautifully (Irving thinks it's magnificent)—and we ought to have it done by the time we return next month. It's a psychological drama about a young woman who wants to be an actress but has grave problems and becomes involved with a cult. I think it's a very commercial story and plan on sending it to Paramount when it's done. Can you imagine if it actually was approved and went into production? My dear, what a celebration we'd make then! The tentative title is *Amber Savage,* which is our young woman's name. How does it strike you?

"My father was here about a week ago and read as much as we'd done; he started snorting around, you know how he does,

Irving, Worth Avenue, Palm Beach, 1979.

which means he's excited. He had some valid critical suggestions to make but seemed on the whole to think we had a pretty good project under way. Perhaps if you're not impossibly busy, I could send it to you to read when it's done.... Aside from that, have been reading a lot and cooking good things, and trying to get in some swimming every day, for the exercise. Irving and I have been together almost constantly, with virtually no outside associations. We get on amazingly well, especially taking that into consideration. He has been writing poems like mad—quite different from his previous work. These have a power and intensity that's truly extraordinary, even for him, and they deal with humanity in a deeply psychological way. He's been invited to go to Korea and represent Canada at the Fourth World Congress of Poetry. It's the beginning of July and I'd love to go. They pay his expenses, but his only and it's too expensive for me to go. Unless I can convince somebody that I'm an invaluable publicist ... which ain't too likely....

"Meantime, we keep talking about all kinds of alternative plans. Our latest is, instead of settling in Montreal or Toronto, to take off for some extensive travelling come the fall. IF Irving gets the Canada Council grant he's applied for, then things will be easier financially; and if he gets it, he says he won't return to teaching at Concordia. Which means we could leave after *Droppings From Heaven* (his next book) comes out, in September. In this dream, we go to Paris and then Rome (our city, for old times' sake), and then Greece. By winter we'd be in Israel and then India. We'd be away at least six months, and, except for initially getting overseas, would do all journeying possible by boat rather than plane. I'm very fond of this particular dream.... Then we'd come back, and get a house someplace, and make a baby. Nice dream.... Barring that, as an alternative dream, if he decides to teach again in Montreal, we'll probably come here in the summer and from here take off for a trip to either Mexico—especially the Yucatan—and/or Colombia and Ecuador, and who knows where else in Latin America ... which would be nice too.... I'd rather settle in Toronto than Montreal, but I won't be miserable if he decides on Montreal. Anyway, I'm suggesting, if it *is* to be Toronto for us, someplace more like the country, in the area surrounding Toronto rather than right in it. I like the idea of more space and air and quiet, anyways ... there are nice places maybe ½ hour from the city, where it looks like we could have the best of both worlds.

"When we return next month, I'm to look around and see what's available for renting. May as well get an idea anyway...."

Included with my letter to Andrea was a photocopy of an article that appeared in the *Montreal Gazette*, for a Valentine's Day story. It ran a picture of Irving and me, from our wedding, with a heart imposed between us as we gaze affectionately into each other's faces. The line under the picture read "Harriet Bernstein and her husband, poet Irving Layton, are working on a film together."

In retrospect, what a delicious and privileged time that was. Time to read, to write, to soak in the sun, swim, walk on the beach, nap or make love in the afternoons, whatever we wanted, and without the phone ringing off the hook every minute. A golden time. All too brief, but precious and fantastic. We felt hidden away from all the people always wanting, wanting, wanting a piece of him, or of me. We were so peaceful and happy together, so completely compatible. How could I possibly have imagined that precisely this kind of peace—as much as Irving wanted it, and believe me he did—was also going to be impossible for him? When someone is addicted to tumult, can they embrace peace, even though it seems—is—desired and idyllic? Those were truly halcyon days.

15.

JOURNAL, APRIL 25, 1979: "...Today is a special date—today we sent off our screenplay to Frank Mancuso [then head of film distribution] at Paramount in New York. We celebrated with some wine and poached eggs and dreamed for a while.... Then Musia stopped by and we had some cognac over that, and over her very successful meeting with the chairman of the Dept., who was very positive and encouraging and approving of her PhD thesis. Then I drove Irving to the airport and he's on his way all the way to Vancouver, to give a reading for the Committee for the Holocaust. Goodbyes are not my forte and I cried, as usual. Irving is stronger, he didn't cry, but he did look a little queer. We've gotten awfully attached to each other.

"We've bought a house, in Niagara-on-the-Lake, Ontario—gracious and spacious, seventy years old, white wood and on a corner and a good buy. Irving got the Canada Council grant. The day the letter arrived, I was unpacking groceries (we were in W. Palm) and Irving said—'Well, it's from the Canada Council; here, read this and weep'—and looked so solemn. I read it and it turned out to be an acceptance! And he laughed at me and we laughed together and hugged and jumped around a lot. So that decided him not to go on teaching. We began looking for a house, outside of Toronto. Everything was expensive and ugly. One day we saw an ad in the paper for a place in Niagara-on-the-Lake. Irving had never been there! I always liked the place—it's very small and charming, so we took a drive (it's only an hour and a half from Toronto) and Irving saw it and loved it. We looked at a few places there, then found this one. We're supposed to drive

Toronto this Sunday and settle the finances on the house on Mon-Tues. As of May 1st, it's supposed to be ours. We're planning to move on May 31st.

"Naturally, we're excited about the possibilities and naturally Irving has very mixed feelings about leaving Montreal. Meantime, this night is somewhat desolate and lonely with Irving's absence. We spend so much time together, even a short separation is a big one. I know that the quality of our relationship is unlike any others he's had. He sometimes mentions the tenderness and concern he feels for me, that he was not so before—sometimes adding that if he had been, perhaps things might have been different. Which always brings him full circle to—if things had been different, *he* could have been different. Still, just this afternoon, he was saying how really extraordinary it is how well we get on together.

"We were in Toronto a couple of weeks before, for the launching of the Layton-Sassu portfolio. The opening was packed all evening—the press coverage was okay, but I was disappointed I couldn't get more. The CBC was not there to cover it and we were pretty angry at that, especially following the controversy in the Italian community over their *Connections* series [Note to reader: this was a two-part documentary series for CBC television investigating organized crime in Toronto, Montreal, and Vancouver]. Coverage of the portfolio would have been the perfect opportunity for them to balance out the picture the series presented of Italian = Mafia. Irving wrote a splendid letter and it was printed in the *Toronto Star.* He was also a little disappointed that Max couldn't find a half hour or so just to come to the gallery and say hi."

Journal, April 26, 1979: "Irving called from Vancouver this evening—said the reading was a huge success and he'd met some beautiful people and the weather was beautiful—all in all, the trip was a great one. I told him I'd be at the airport to pick him up tomorrow afternoon, and that if, on the plane back, he again got one of those middle seats he hates and was sandwiched in between two people—may they at least be attractive ladies. Which made him laugh and say I was really a devoted wife....

"We went to see Altman's new picture this weekend—*A Perfect Couple*—and liked it very much. It was good to see Altman back on track, especially after the disappointment of his last film, *Quintet*. But, as Irving says, Altman—like all great talents—make their great disasters. Only the mediocrities don't; the greats, when they're good, are very very good and when they're bad, they're terrible; but it's because they take chances and have their visions. We're eager to see Woody Allen's *Manhattan*. My parents say it's great—his best yet. We're also eager to write more screenplays. We've been talking about the idea for the next one already. As soon as we get settled, I hope we'll get into a program of writing and reading more, away from the time-demands in the city. I'm still plugging away at getting Irving started on his memoirs. He has so many wonderful stories to tell. I think it's really important that he write them. No biography could come near his telling the tale himself."

On May 20, 1979, I wrote to Andrea: "Many thanks for the card and the beautiful cookbook. I've been reading the recipes and they look so good—am eager to get into it in my new BIG kitchen. We're scheduled to move out on May 30th and into the house on June 1. The address, until we get a P.O. Box, is just General Delivery, Niagara-on-the-Lake, Ontario. Apparently mail isn't delivered to one's house there. I mean, it's *really* a teeny tiny town.... We returned here last Thursday p.m., after 2½ hectic weeks in Toronto, during which time I did a lot of running around, trying to organize everything so that the place will be live-able by the end of the month. It's a shitload of work— but very exciting, all the same. I've counted five maple trees on one side of the house (four green, one red) and a walnut tree and the silver birch and we think maybe the big gnarled one in front is apple, but we're not sure yet. The apartment here is chaos right now, as we're in the midst of packing about 5,000 lbs. of books (no exaggeration—that's the mover's estimate!) and the rest of our things. Boxes everywhere, etc. At times like this there's the urge to set a torch to it all, or sell it, or give it away or something, anything not to have to cope with it all. But we're working through it all okay and are really looking forward to being there. Meantime, the sweat pours on.... A family of pigeons has adopted us! I discovered, behind the chairs on the balcony, two baby pigeons huddled in their little nest. Mama seemingly abandoned them, so I've been seeing that they don't starve. Then this morning Irving came and said 'There's a pigeon in my room' and sure enough, there it was, strutting around in a very familiar manner. I think it's very nice—and amazing—to have the new life of the babies on the balcony, in the middle of the city and all....

"The elections are on Tuesday and Irving's been obsessed with them to the point where I've sort of had to become interested too. [Note to reader: At that point in my life, I was not highly politicized, beyond some peace marches in the sixties and campaigning for legalized marijuana. I had, however, become interested in politics when John Kennedy was campaigning and, of course, being in Boston when Robert Kennedy and Martin Luther King Jr. were killed was inescapably involving. And, like most people, I had become enchanted with the young brilliant Trudeau.] We watched a debate on TV between [Pierre] Trudeau, the Tory leader [Joe] Clark, and the NDP man [Ed] Broadbent, and when it was over there was no question in our minds that Trudeau is the only man with the brains and balls enough to handle this country. However, there's a serious chance of Clark being elected ... and if he is, Irving predicts big trouble in *la belle province*—maybe a return to the terrorist tactics of the FLQ a few years back, who knows? Maybe civil war...."

The rest of the letter referred to the bad car accident Sandra B. [a female admirer of Irving's] had been in, as well as another accident that had happened one car away from me while I was driving back from shopping, plus two more car accidents that Irving and I had passed on our way home. All of these made me somewhat nervous about driving, though normally I was a good and confident driver.

Journal, May 22, 1979: "Been busy packing as we move out this coming Wed. Surrounded by boxes, all this packing away of our things—aside from the hard work it is, it's somehow unsettling, depressing maybe. Irving's been helping—with his books—and been busy with wrap-up sessions with Musia and Vennie [a former student and friend of Irving's] and Bill and Sandra. And would have been with the other Sandra too, except that she's in bad shape, recovering from a car accident. Lousy luck. I'm more nervous than ever now, about driving in this city.

If we ever live here again, I don't want to have a car here. Aside from all this moving stuff, Irving's been working on the book of light verse—now entitled *For My Neighbours in Hell* instead of *Let There Be Light Verse.*

"Tomorrow we're having a 'garage sale' and hoping to sell a lot of stuff. Irving watched in dismay this week as Joe Clark was elected the new PM. Election night was a little like a wake. Now, true to form—that trick L. has for turning things around—he's saying that Clark must have something to have gotten where he is; that electing him indicates exactly where this country is—they don't want a man with passion, big brains, and balls—they want a Joe Clark, a servant of the money boys, a mediocrity. He also said that the outcome of the elections are exactly what [René] Lévesque hoped for—that now Lévesque will say how the country is truly polarized, how Quebec should separate. Myself, I'm glad the elections are finally over as Irving was obsessed with them to such a point that I, at first, had to tune into them and get involved and then, subsequently, had to get turned off.

"I'll also be very happy when our move is over. I suppose I'm more eager than Irving is—I haven't the attachment to Montreal; it's my first house; and he doesn't have to cope with the kitchen here, dishes, etc.... Leonard is, as usual, in silent absence. David Solway apparently left for Greece and Irving didn't get a call to say goodbye. He's even more miffed because Bill told him that Solway said Irving was responsible for Henry Moscovitch [a Montreal poet and friend of Leonard and Irving, who suffered from depression and possible mental illness] becoming the way he did...."

Journal, Saturday, May 26, 1979: "Observations on Irving: frequently, he is busy reading—himself! Gets tremendous pleasure out of reading his own books. Often—like today—he re-discovers a poem he's written and carries on about how great, what a masterpiece it is and gets very excited as though it were new—today it was the 'Catacombe dei Cappucine' poem. Says he'd like—no, *love* to relax, but is driven like a madman. *Has* to run here, run there, see this one, that one, because he can never tell where an image, a metaphor, an epiphany will pop from, like a mouse from a hole. Describes himself as a cat running around,

143

trying to cover all the holes in case a mouse pops out. Says it's no wonder he gets exhausted since he's always transforming the ordinary into the extraordinary."

Journal, Sunday, May 27, 1979: "Irving's on one of his super-wound-up cycles. Revising a thousand times, and writing new too, for *Neighbours*. Sleeping restlessly, waking up in the middle of the night, early in the morning—like this morning. A *line of a poem* wakes him up and that's it, he must leave bed and go to the typewriter."

Journal, Wednesday, June 6, 1979: "9 Castlereagh, Niagara-on-the-Lake, Ont. Our first night in the house was last Friday, June 1. Come hell or high water, we were determined to stay here and hell sure came! Not really, just unbelievable chaos. Workmen all over the place, a fine film of dust all over from the floor-sanding, the smell of wet paint and the movers and carpet men arriving at the same time. Irving lost behind mountains of boxes of books. It's getting better now—the kitchen is done—cabinets in, handles on them, floor down—and it's beautiful. Irving's library is pretty much set up and so's the bedroom. We can bathe (shower's not ready yet) so we're managing okay, tho the furniture from the living room is still piled in the hallway, so we have to creep sideways to get by, and the phones still haven't been installed. We've been working outside, too. The vegetable garden is planted, and I've been working on the flowers in the front of the house. It's hard to describe how happy we are here, how delightful it is, how sweet the air smells, how peaceful we are. Irving said he thinks maybe he died and went to heaven. He's been sleeping better, he says, than he has in years."

Journal, Tuesday, June 12, 1979: "We are finally getting ourselves in order here. Every day we are hard at work, every day I'm on the phone (now that they're in!) chasing after somebody to do something they said they would, but haven't: the TV man, the plumber, the painter, the electrician, the carpet man—finally the rugs are in and there's an end to the dust floating over everything. I unpacked the last of the suitcases today, hooray. Still a few more boxes to go. Lord, I hope we don't have to move for a long time. Working over the weekend was rough, because it was suddenly uncommonly hot and humid—the sweat was pouring off of us.

Then it suddenly got uncommonly cold and Irving's been wearing his heavy warm shirts and I've pulled out my socks. Weird. Irving wrote his first poem today: 'Painted Bird,' dedicated to Jerzy Kosinsky." [Note to reader: Kosinsky was the Jewish Polish-American novelist who, having survived the Holocaust under a false identity, came to America where he taught at Yale among other universities, and is well known for his novels *The Painted Bird* and *Being There*.]

"Irving came into the kitchen singing away at the top of his lungs, happy as a baby. I said, 'you're singing so much, the poem must be really deadly,' and he laughed and sang our song 'Getting to Know You,' and said, yes, I was right. It's a very strong poem, a further development of his current theme of Jew vs Gentile, going beyond religion. He said it came to him when he was sitting in the garden. And he laughed and said, the more beautiful his surroundings and the happier he is, the more vicious are the poems he writes.

"The vegetable garden is all little green sprouts and I can't believe they came up so quickly. Irving laughs at me and is quite smug and proud and says he has a green thumb, that's all. He's been invited to read at the festival in Skopja, Yugoslavia, the end of August. He said okay, he'll go and take me. Maybe after the week in Yugoslavia, we'll go to Italy, do a three-week excursion thing. We're also going to Banff, the beginning of August, for a week. The days go by so quickly...."

When Irving said: "The more beautiful his surroundings and the happier he is, the more vicious are the poems he writes," it should have been a warning to me. Maybe not a warning precisely—after all, we were in the first year of our marriage, the fifth year of our love affair, and the first month in our new home, and we were very happy. I guess what I mean to say is something about the poet and the man: the fact that beautiful surroundings and happiness propelled him to expunge venom from his being is an indicator of the part of himself that proved ultimately to have a fatal hand in the undoing of us. The need to foul his own nest, to create mess and mayhem, an inability to allow happiness to infuse too many days, and why was that? Is it so much more difficult to create poetry out of happiness than out of turmoil?

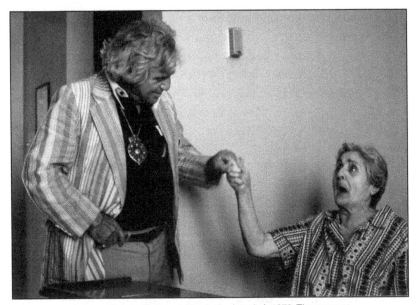

*Irving and sister Esther visiting in the hospital, 1979. The moment
that inspired "Senile, My Sister Sings."*

Was it so much his deeply ingrained habit to be in domestic
distress that he truly did not know what to do with domestic
delight? What was that darkness in him that had to muddy the
waters? I continue to wonder about that today.

Journal, Monday, June 25, 1979: "Went to Montreal for a few
days, stayed at Bill and Sandra's. Irving was busy—one day with
Musia, one afternoon with Sandra B., and Leonard. While I sat
and listened to Sandra.... [Harry] Rasky [journalist and Emmy-
award winning documentary film-maker] was doing a film on
Leonard, which Irving unknowingly walked into, so they used
him in it. He was excited and happy and called to tell me about it.
Leonard got on the phone and said lots of beautiful words about
how wonderful Irving was. Irving said he heard Leonard's new
album ... that Leonard seemed pleased enough about it.

"However, the main reason for going to Montreal was because
Irving's brother Harry was there, from California. So we spent
some time with him. He's nothing like Irving. Doesn't look like
him, as Dora [Irving's sister] does, or have the spirit of Dora or
Gertie [also Irving's sister]. He was nice, but didn't seem to be
interested in anything much, other than Russia. Kept trying to

Irving and sister, Gertie, 1979.

draw Irving into a heated political discussion. Unsuccessfully.

"We went to visit Esther [another Irving's sister] in the hospital and at one point every one of us was in tears. The picture in my head of Irving leaning over her, holding her hand, and singing to her, and her face—there's no way to describe it. The heartbreak is sometimes overwhelming. I took a lot of pictures. I hope something comes out! [Note: This visit resulted in the poem 'Senile, My Sister Sings' that is in *Droppings from Heaven*.] Then we were in Toronto for a day, while I ran around doing chores, stocking up on fresh fish and other things we can't get here. It was nice to be there. My parents have developed a real fondness for Irving and he for them too."

Journal, June 27, 1979: "A dull, rainy day. Irving wrote poems, I cleaned. Last night on TV we watched a fascinating and very well done show about the discovery of Tuthankhamen's tomb and today Irving wrote two poems inspired by it! The mind reels at the thought of what would happen if he ever actually visited there—which he's already said he would love to do and probably will, if there's peace. The days just go by too quickly, that's all. No word yet from Korea, so we sent another cable to First Violet today. [She was an acolyte and advocate in Korea for Irving.] It's very weird not to have heard from her yet. I wrote to Clara Thomas [Professor of Literature, Margaret Laurence specialist, and one of my favourite teachers at York], thanking her for the loan of the tape of Irving and Margaret Laurence, and also for taking care of us at the convocation [Note to reader: Irving received an Honourary Doctorate from York in 1979, and it was Professor Clara Thomas who nominated him.]. She's really an okay lady. Irving's been dipping into *Gulliver's Travels* and some critical writings of Swift, with whom he has been identifying the past couple of days. Has a couple of quotes from *G Travels* for the beginning and end of *For My Neighbours in Hell*, which he says he absolutely must give to Howard [Aster, who with Seymour Mayne owned Mosaic Press], so he'll stop working on it. A few days ago, he had 101 poems in it—today he announced he had 110! Once he gets going, there's no stopping him. He's been planting in the garden every day too and really enjoying that. We may have quite a crop—carrots, potatoes, lettuce, cucumber, tomatoes, celery, peas, radishes, beets, squash and onions— amazing, really.

"Frank Mancuso [then head of Paramount Pictures distribution in New York] is in Toronto and tomorrow my father is going to see him and ask him about our screenplay. I'm a little—what's the word—anxious? Hoping he's not going to say no go. If he doesn't and it's a yes, or maybe even a good maybe, Irving and I may drive in and accept his invitation to join him and my parents for dinner on Friday. I think Irving wants to meet him—I think he should—but then again, Irving says he's so perfectly content and comfortable here, he's reluctant to go anywhere! We'll see tomorrow....

"Everything is looking so beautiful in our house. We both wander from room to room, admiring it all and looking around with such delight. Irving will come downstairs and say, 'You know, I just love my den. It's the nicest one I've ever had. I just love it.' Then, later, we'll be sitting in the kitchen and he says, 'I love this kitchen. It's just exactly the way a kitchen should be. I love to sit here and look out there and see those trees and the sky.' And so on. As for me, I just feel the days go too quickly, and there's not enough time for me to get my fill of it all. In the mornings, I love to just walk around the house, once, check out the roses and the trees and the beauty of it all. We wake up in the morning to the birds singing. And there are loads of birds. The car is covered with bird shit to prove it!"

July 2, 1979, I wrote to Andrea: "No matter how many pens I buy, I can seldom find a pen when I want one. This is no excuse for not writing prior to this, just an observation. Irving is always lifting them. Pens, not obs. We are pretty much settled now and I am happy. What a lot it took—a lot of energy, a lot of time, a lot of money, a lot of aggravation, etc. However, here we are and it's really lovely. Inside is nice, outside is nice. We have a flourishing garden of (hopefully) veggies: lettuce, tomatoes, cucumbers, celery, squash, cauliflower, peas, beets, radishes, potatoes, onions, carrots. Do you believe it? You should see Irving with his hoe…. We haven't explored the area yet, but it looks beautiful and we should be able to start getting into it now. The little shops here are so adorable, the whole place is quaint and unreal. The grocery store I shop in is historical, there is a great homemade Ice Cream Shoppe and two great fudge places—see it made, take a free sample. A shop with things for children in it that's so charming it makes me wish I had a child (I don't go in there).

"We are going to Banff on Aug. 5th for one week. Irving has to go to work and I'm going too. Then, the end of Aug, he's been invited to read his poems at a festival in Yugoslavia, for one week and I'm going with too. Goody! We'll probably do a three-week excursion thing, maybe go to Italy from Yugoslavia….

"Drove into Toronto last weekend, had dinner with Frank Mancuso who was in for an opening. He was very encouraging about our screenplay. It's in L.A. now. After it's been read, it'll come back to us for some more work, then back to N.Y. and we'll see if we get a green light. Looks encouraging, but a little way off yet. Irving told him the idea for another one, which he liked and immediately said it sounded like a film for Louis Malle and we should send him a treatment…. Lots to do…. Am keeping very busy and finding life interesting, challenging, and sweet…."

Journal, July 4, 1979: "How is it that a week has gone by already? I don't believe it, that's all. We drove into Toronto last Friday and had dinner with the Mancusos. Frank was encouraging. The screenplay is in L.A., with one of Paramount's readers. Then it will be sent back to Frank, hopefully by the end of this week, so he can see what direction they (that's 'they' in L.A.) think it should go in. Then he'll send it back to us and we'll have to work on it some more and fill in the things as we discussed with him. Then back to N.Y. and we'll see if they decide to assign a writer to it, to work with us. Meantime, Irving told him another story idea and he seemed to like it very much, immediately saying it was a project for Louis Malle and he asked us to send him the treatment. Which we will do, before the week is over. We stayed in Toronto over Sat. too. Went to a screening Sat. night, and came back here on Sunday. My father came up with a plan to launch *Droppings*—involving a reading here, with money from it donated to the Shaw, and the mayor proclaiming Irving Layton Day, and a reception at one of the estates here, and media and Shaw people to come, etc. etc. It's a really good idea. So yesterday we called Jack McClelland and I told him the plan and he sounded very interested and said he thought it was good and he would talk to his people at M.&S. and get back to us and we would all have a meeting and talk it out. A photographer came yesterday to take pictures of Irving for *Weekend Magazine*— they're finally supposed to be publishing the article, for 'A Day in the Life.' They'll have to do the story over again, tho, because it must be nearly a year since it was originally done and everything is different now.

"Irving's latest letter from A. came last Friday and he says it was a good letter, that she sounds happy and is very busy writing articles and her novel, and that the Marx thing is being made for TV, and that David is flourishing and gets on better with Leon than he ever did with either of them, and that they're all going to Greece for a month in the summer and that they'll be staying in London till November and not returning here in Aug. as originally stated. And that she really likes London now, finds it very exciting. I asked Irving why she doesn't stay there, then and he said because of how expensive it is to live there and how hard it is to earn enough. Or something. Anyways, happy we are for a cheerful, chatty letter."

Journal, July 18, 1979: "Having lunch today with the M.&S. publicist, the Shaw publicist, and director to flesh out all the details of Irving's reading and launching to benefit the Shaw. They thought it was a good idea, obviously and why not!" [Note: Later the same day I added:] "Reading set for Aug. 26, two p.m., Courthouse Theatre. People at lunch nice enough, but not terribly interesting—no curiosity at all. Want to speak to Jack McClelland next time I see him about his publicist.... Irving is putting the finishing touches on his latest poem, 'Dracula.' We saw the film last week in Toronto, and were both in raptures over it. Irving has one of his interesting interpretations; he wrote a letter to the *Globe* about it, then decided that a letter wasn't enough, and wrote the poem today. It's great. He has it the modern Faust, the modern Oedipus Rex, and concludes with Dracula being Everyman.

"We wrote a treatment over the weekend, the story we told Frank at dinner, about the woman and the poem and her trying to guess who wrote it and going through all her men. We're calling it 'A Thing of Beauty,' from the first line of Keats' 'Endymion'; Keats-Shelley-Byron figure in the story. That night at dinner with Frank, he seemed really enthusiastic about the story and immediately saw it [again] as a vehicle for Louis Malle. Now let's see what happens with *this* one.

"I can hardly keep my eyes open, I'm so sleepy. And there are still things I didn't get to finish today. The days are not long enough, that's all."

Journal, July 23, 1979: " Was just looking through a Gertrude Stein book and came across a line I'd underlined a long time ago: '...*and if you write not long but practically every day, you do get a great deal written.*' I'm gonna try to remember that every day. Boschka [Betty Sutherland, Irving's second legal wife, with whom he had Max and Naomi] called tonight to say she's coming. As we have to go into Toronto on Thursday, we'll meet her there on Sat. and drive here with her on Sun. and she'll stay with us a couple of days.

"Somehow we got on to talking about what we'd name a girl

child—Clara Layton maybe—and what we'd name a boy child—Samuel Moses Layton, maybe.

"I guess because Boschka called and then Irving spoke to Stephanie [Max's girlfriend] and then he called his brother Harry—we got on to talking about his family—his parents and brothers and sisters and so on. Thinking about them always makes him sad, he said, because not one of them was mediocre and they all deserved better and their mother did a job on all of them. I asked him what he thought his parents would think of him now, being the poet he is, and he said that it wouldn't mean anything to his father, because he was of another world and only concerned with (the bigoted prejudiced narrow old sense) religion; but that his mother—curiously enough, it would mean something to her. Yet of all the children, Irving says he is the only one in whom the father lives—in that Irving is a deeply religious man—in the true sense, the only sense in which we really mean religion. Also he's like him, he says, in his having to force himself to believe in, or be aware of, what we call the real world, things material."

Journal, August 2, 1979: "Lots going on, as always. Boschka was here with us for a couple of days. It was okay her being here—no tensions.... Boschka is very artsy, casual and bohemian. She showed us some slides of her work and there were two or three I especially liked. We're taking one of them—a very large thing, the head of a gypsy woman; it's very powerful and really touched something in me. Boschka was very warm, very nice, with lots of humour and life in her. As Irving had to spend almost all the time reading her novel, she and I were together alone a lot. I'm not crazy about his disappearing and leaving me alone with someone I don't know well—but it was necessary this time and it was okay actually. I wouldn't mind her coming again.

"Went into Toronto last weekend. Celebrated my mama's birthday, dinner at Napoleon's was gorgeous and we had three bottles of glorious wine and got a little high. Musia was in, on her way to Japan, and she came by and Irving spent a couple hours on her PhD, while I went shopping with Mama and bought two much-needed dresses. Mona Adilman [the poet] was also over—bringing her manuscript for Irving to read; it's being published and Irving has to write the introduction for it. Then we got Boschka and came here with her. So, Irving has been busy with Mona and Musia and Boschka and the Mss of all of them. I'm busy reading H. G. Wells' *The Outline of History*. Irving got a copy for Mama too and has given her an assignment and says he's going to test her on her reading. I think that's great—she *has* to have something to do and she just might do it, for Irving. Scott Symonds called this afternoon, he was in town filming a segment for a series on Ontario, being done for TV Ontario. He came by this evening, with a lady from the crew and the producer. They stayed for a little while and Irving was happy to see them go. He's funny—they are his friends, his guests sitting here, and he gets up and disappears—goes upstairs, or goes out to look at his vegetables all of a sudden. Funny man.

"And Gerry [my old friend from high school, Gerry Mandel] is coming out tomorrow afternoon. He's gonna stay the night and we'll drive into Toronto with him on Sat., because we leave for Banff on Sun. morning. Be there 5th to 12th, return to Toronto and then Irving is leaving for Athens on the 14th. Since the Canada Council pays his expenses and it won't cost him anything, he's decided to go to Greece for ten days, stay with Leonard in Hydra, and see him and A. and David, who have taken a house there for the month. (They, who are always crying 'broke'—must be nice....) This all started out as being tied in with Yugoslavia and the reading there—but that, in the meantime, has fallen by the wayside and he's not going there at all, but only to Greece. I will take the opportunity to go to N.J. with Mama and visit Baba, whom I haven't seen in about 1½ yrs, which is really too long already. I'll be there just a couple of days and divide the rest of the time Irving is away between here and my parents' house. He comes back on the 24th.

"Tad Jaworski called today, asking Irving if he'd host the series on Marx. He probably will, but said he'd like to see it first, so that should happen some time next month. There are interviews with all the leading Marxian scholars, so Irving is very excited about that. Our vegetable garden is growing like crazy. There are a couple of big green zucchinis hanging down like fat penises and some tomatoes, still green, but getting bigger, the lettuce is getting very large and little peppers are hanging. The broccoli has lovely flowers and so does the cucumber. It's very impressive and Irving is very proud. It's been incredibly hot and humid—we are more or less getting used to being wet all the time. The worst part is how it wipes you out, just sort of saps your strength. The only bad news is I can't find my manuscript of poems and I'm upset about it, and Irving maybe even more so. Other than that, everything is lovely. We are getting on beautifully and very happy indeed. It's really extraordinary to spend so much time together and get on so well, without arguments or tensions. We're so lucky and what's more, we know it."

Journal, August 6, 1979: "Arrived in Banff yesterday, late afternoon. The flight to Calgary was nice, had a hassle with Budget Rent a Car, gave the manager shit, got the car, and drove here. We're in what they call a chalet—it's a nice little cottage, all woodsy and rustic, with a kitchenette so we can eat breakfast here. The best part is the name—all the cottages are named—and this one is called 'Ho-Ho.' Really. The mountains are indeed magnificent and we were just talking about when we can make time to go around a bit and see some of the area. Tomorrow morning Irving gives his spiel; every day at 1:30 is the workshop session; then he's meeting them privately at 4:00. SO, he's been very busy (wants to earn his thousand bucks). I may have to see some things on my own. Irving says the students are much better this year than last; more mature, very well-read, with good critical insights. So far as first impressions go, he's very pleased with them. He takes the workshop with another guy, Richard Lemm [poet and professor at UPEI], who seems very nice though somewhat nervous. But NOBODY deals with a poem like Irving. When he tackles it and offers criticism and suggestions, he brings the whole session up a few levels. And I can see it in the faces of the students—when Irving is talking, a keenness comes into their faces and they're so clearly enjoying themselves so very much."

Journal, August 9, 1979: "Afternoon rest in Chalet Ho-Ho. The people involved in the writing program—Ruth Fraser, Sandra Jones, Len Sokul, and Richard Lemm—are a nice bunch of people. None of them know an overwhelming amount

Irving in Banff, 1979.

about poetry, but they all have an appetite, appreciation, and enthusiasm. They also have a lovely warm camaraderie between them and of course seem eager to include us in their circle of friendship. Last evening Ruth made dinner for us all and we spent an enjoyable evening in her apartment. Jack McClelland flew in today, spoke to the group about publishing—a very realistic, hard-nosed, no-bullshit talk. We've invited Jack and the others, plus Jim de Felice (screenplay writer—did *Why Shoot the Teacher*) over after supper tonight for some wine and conversation. Irving has been so busy with sessions and private interviews and I've been sitting in on the group sessions with him—that we haven't been anywhere yet, haven't explored the area at all. But we have some time tomorrow and most of Saturday to go and see Lake Louise and wander over a few mountains." [Dear Reader, it should be noted that as brilliant a publisher as Jack McClelland was, he was an awful driver. We went out with him one night while there, which was not a good idea because wine had been consumed and these were mountainous roads. Jack drove like a madman. It was terrifying, as well as exhilarating, to be that close to death, and I recall having visions of the headlines: "Publisher Jack McClelland, poet Irving Layton and his wife, killed in auto crash near Banff."]

"Irving, finally, been letting them have it, on the amount of garbage that passes for poetry today. We got [David] McFadden's book [another Toronto poet and teacher] and Irving has been able to point to specifics and show the class how it's not poetry at all, but prose in vertical form; that it's journalism, reportage. The kids (some of whom were McFadden fans until today) are good listeners and seem very open to Irving's criticisms, which they take in a very constructive way. The state of poetry in Canada today is like the old 'Emperor and His New Clothes' story—everybody is afraid to call it like it is and say 'hey—this just is not poetry.' Irving's is the one voice that stands a chance of setting them straight. I do enjoy the reverence with which everyone listens to him—and bloody well so they should! [Dear Reader: I was nothing if not loyal!] No matter how often I hear Irving speak, I still always delight in it. There's nobody who can come near to touching him."

Journal, Sunday, August 19, 1979: "Well, we finished up in Banff with a reading, very well received. Afterwards, there was yet another party—one too many for me, as I could hardly wait to make my escape. A week of so much close contact with so many new people became too much for me. The need to be off alone was irresistible. I took time out to have a smoke and solitary stroll around the dark grounds, listening outside for a while to some very fine jazz, live. Irving, when we found each other, seemed as eager to escape as I was. And we did. We had a nice flight home, got back to Toronto on Sun. night. Monday, Irving did an interview ('the best ever', as always), for the *Montreal Star*, we met Francesca [Valente] and discussed the reading tour in Italy that she's organizing. I did laundry and got Irving ready to go away again. On Tues., I took him to the airport and bade him a slightly tearful farewell, as he left for Greece for nine days, to stay at Hydra with Leonard and visit with him and David and A. and Leon. He says it's important for him to spend some time alone with David and since Leonard's house is available for him to stay in and since the Can Council pays for the airfare, he took the opportunity; besides, he misses Greece."

In retrospect, I observe how somewhat inappropriate this trip seems. We had been married only nine months before—why was I not going to Greece with him? Was it only a question of finances? Or was it more likely that he was beginning to cast me in the 'Aviva' role, the 'wife' who stays in one place while he goes off to Greece, as had become his habit. I don't even remember discussing it with him much. I recall having at least one conversation about going with him, but as I recall, what mostly was the impetus for this trip was his desire to spend time alone with David. It was important for Irving—in his mind anyway—that David understand that although they were not a family unit anymore, he was still a very involved and loving father. I could probably have insisted on going with him, and if I had pushed it, I would have gone. However, pushing things was not my way and had never been that way throughout our relationship. Maybe that was part of the problem.

The journal entry continues: "On Wed., Mama and I left for New Jersey to visit Baba. She was as okay as can be, but that's not too good after all and I think she'd be happy to be dead. She can't speak well at all, she sits all alone, an amputee in her wheelchair all the time and what kind of a life is that, after all. She wets her pants and can't express herself well to anyone and for a woman with her pride, it must be a ghastly hell. Still, she was delighted to see us, and she still has her spirit and ability to laugh. It was pretty gruesome for me, hating to be in New Jersey as I do. Going there is like putting yourself on hold! I found, in Philadelphia, a marvellous bookstore and brought back several new things to read, including—best of all—a book by Colette that I haven't read! Magnificent find—I thought I'd read everything she wrote—at least, everything she wrote that's translated in English and available. So, it was worth the trip, just for that. Irving is supposed to return to Toronto on Friday, and I'm supposed to spend the week here, except that I'll drive to our house on Wed. and come back to Toronto on Thurs. afternoon, so I can pick up mail, water the plants, check out the growth of our garden and have the house cleaned. I miss Irving."

16.

JOURNAL, SEPTEMBER 4, 1979: "It's the end of a day, I'm at the kitchen table. The room is large and bright, warm and secure. Fresh bouquet of flowers in front of me. It's quiet. Irving is upstairs in his study, probably re-reading his poems, or perhaps dipping into a book. The typewriter isn't clicking away, so he's not doing correspondence. Last Friday I was rushed into the hospital and into the operating room. A possible ectopic pregnancy, the doctor said. He performed a laparoscopy and found it wasn't an ectopic after all. Just an ornery ovary or something. After-effect of being on the pill. I got out on Saturday and we came home. Everything is so especially beautiful, after being in hospital. Just to be able to sit in the garden and read, to move my hand without an I.V. tube attached.

"After Irving came back from Greece, he slept a lot. It seems he didn't get much rest there.... The pity of the trip was that, after all, he didn't even see David, which was the main reason, presumably, for his going. When he got to Hydra, he learned that David had gone to Molibos to be with friends. And he just left him there. So he spent his time with Leonard and A. and some attractive ladies. I don't really understand going all the way to Greece for nine days to see David, then not even letting him know he was there, when he was only on another island. However, he'll do just what he wants to do and there's nothing to be gained by my questioning it.

"Irving has dismantled all of the vegetable garden, except for the tomatoes, celery and peppers. One kind of lettuce was dying and the other was growing as tall as me, with flowers on top—

but no edible lettuce leaves. The peas shrivelled and died and the squash produced two zucchinis and lots of orange flowers. The cabbage had large, marvellous leaves—but no cabbages, and the broccoli and cauliflower didn't grow at all, but did produce flowers. It was insane—a flower garden not a vegetable garden. Irving said he couldn't stand it all there, a reproach to him—so he went at it one afternoon and cleaned it all out. He says he can't understand what happened, he'd never seen a garden like it. Well, it was fun and good exercise anyways. We may yet have some tomatoes, peppers and celery from it all!

"I've been helping Irving with making the selection for *The Collected Poems*. It feels almost impossible to me. I mean, how presumptuous for me to tick off poems I don't think should be in. The only way I can do it at all is to offer my pure gut reaction, to say which poems don't leap off the page for me; and besides, I know he'll do what he wants pretty much anyway. It's been a labour of love, I'm not yet tired of reading his poems....

"Just finished *A Captive of Time*, Olga Ivinskaya's memorable book of her years with Pasternak. I wept for quite a while when I'd finished. It's a great book, a great love story and a tribute to creativity under the most horrible, oppressive circumstances. How she went on, in spite of being sent—twice—to work camps; in spite of being spied on and harassed; in spite of all the emotional manipulations she suffered. The book gives an intensely vivid picture of what it is to live there—especially for the artist, the free-thinker, the creative individual. There's nothing too base, too devious for those vermin to stoop to. Irving and I were talking about it, I was pouring out my emotional reaction to it, and what really surprised and puzzled me was Irving's saying that I'm the only one he can talk to about it. I'm the only one who reacts in that way. I don't understand how it's possible for anyone to read about what goes on there and not react. He says he doesn't understand it either. It is scary. Are people just so apathetic or determined to remain ignorant, or do they really think they're so safe? Irving just came in and said I must put down that he loves my nipples—that people will want to know that he loved sucking my responsive nipples! He says that's very important...."

159

As I read that entry, I am embarrassed to have included the part about my nipples. However, that was part of how we were together, it was his humour and his passion, so how can I edit it out and still maintain the honesty of this memoir? I'd also like to delete the part about his going to Greece to see David, and then David not even being there. I want to say, now, that I was really angry about that at the time. For whatever reasons, I sublimated that anger, or swallowed it. Maybe after all the years of on again/ off again, I was happy to be married and in our lovely home, and felt I had to weigh carefully what fights I was gong to take on and what I was going to let go. I do recall telling Irving that I thought it was absurd, but when it came to his doing what he wanted, you could go whistle Dixie if you thought he should do otherwise, most of the time. In all likelihood, he saw it as a nice opportunity to visit his beloved Greece for a short while, see Leonard, and David ... and why spend so much money to bring me along, for only nine days? Me, his wife of only nine months.

Journal, September 6, 1979: "Yesterday Morton Rosengarten arrived to do a (litho) portrait of Irving. There's a book being put together, edited by D. Jones—fourteen top poets, a poem by each and a portrait of each by Mort. He's still working at it today. The study is covered with attempts, most of them awful, a couple pretty good. He said it's been taking him an average of three days to get an acceptable one done. So poor Irving has to sit still for all these hours, can't type, can't read. In addition to Mort, last night Joan Sutton [columnist for the *Toronto Star* and the *Toronto Sun*] came for supper and to talk to Irving. She's doing a column for the *Sunday Star* on him. And my incision has gotten an infection, and my stomach is still bruised and sore. Not the best timing for all this guest activity. BUT we manage. What else was I to do but manage? Mort seems a nice guy—but awfully nervous and we don't know about what. He keeps saying how he's really crazy now. Irving says maybe he's right! Irving says this is the first time Mort's stood a chance of really making some money from his work; that he's been living pretty much of a hand-to-mouth existence up until now. Mort said he's finally decided to get married, have kids and all that—only he can't find a woman! Irving suggested Sandra, itemizing all her fine qualities and Mort said yeah, maybe he'll check it out when he's back in Mtl. Mind you, he was drunk at the time...."

Journal, September 9, 1979: "Well, here we were, just sitting in the garden, reading the Sunday papers and now there's a little crowd of five people hanging over our fence and Irving is standing in the remains of what was our veggie garden, autographing books. That's the second big laugh of the day. The first one was the article in the *Sunday Star* that Joan Sutton wrote—about Irving and me! I laughed and laughed reading about our home and my meals and the description of me—very flattering it was too. This proves beyond any doubt that we'll have to plant some shrubbery here next year to get some privacy from people.

"Just spoke to my parents. They could have been happier about the article. My father just kept saying 'Joan Sutton is full of shit'; my mother said, 'As your parents, we're not pleased to read "she's a worthy successor" etc.' Irving said he agrees with them, matter of fact ... doesn't know why she had to put it like that. Poisonally, I don't care.... We have to go to Toronto tomorrow and we'll probably have to stay there a week, until Irving is okay enough to come home. He's supposed to go in the hospital Wed., have the sore on his chest cut out on Thurs and come out on Friday."

Irving had scar tissue on his chest, from where he had set himself on fire as a boy. Fascinated by a candle flame, he had carelessly held it too close, and his nightshirt had caught fire. It had burned off one of his nipples. He had gotten a sore on that scar tissue, and it was not healing, so the docs said it should be excised. The operation was to cut out the sore and graft a piece of skin from his leg onto his chest. Although the infection was quite deep, there was no cancer found.

Journal, September 13, 1979: "They just took Irving down to the operating room (it was up to it, actually, but it feels like down). About an hour ago, the nurse gave him a pre-operative needle, to make him drowsy, which it did. We read some Catullus for a while, then his mouth got too dry to read and I read to him about Wagner from the new *Encounter*. Just as the elevator door closed and they were taking him away, he called out to me— 'I don't wanna go' ... not a happy moment. I'm concerned, of course, and will be a little anxious until I see him safely back in his room. I promised him that tonight I'll bring him chicken soup and *Commentary* [the intellectual magazine], and he liked that, it gave him a laugh.

"He read at Harbourfront on Tuesday night and it was a good evening. The place was full—about 250-300 people there. Harry Rasky [documentary filmmaker] came and Len Gasparini [poet] and Ron Hambleton [writer and Journalist], and Gerry [my friend, Gerry Mandel]. We decided (Irving and me) that what everybody has against Greg Gatenby [writer, editor, and then Artistic Director of the Harbourfront Reading Series and the International Festival of Authors] is: he has too much on the ball. One writer after another has said nasty things about him (they're a malicious bunch altogether) and he seems to me to be bright and affable, enthusiastic, fast, hardworking—and doing a lot of good work at Harbourfront. Who can (under)stand it? So much brains, energy, drive, focus and success.... Certainly not the run of the mill dullard and apathetic passive commoner.... Then again (part of me says) maybe he really is a louse and I just haven't found it out yet.... It's true I am not trusting, I am suspicious—and I'm sad I was made that way by experiences with people.

"Irving is saying more now that I'm to buy some blank tapes, that he wants to get to work on his autobiog. Great. Finally. He's going to talk it into our tape recorder, then I'll type it out, then he'll work from that transcription. I keep after him about it (how long is it now?) and it looks like he's coming close to starting. It seems to me high time; and certainly Brebner's [Canadian writer] plans for a critical study doesn't have anything to do with it. It will be nice if Brebner does the book—he has a good name. As a matter of fact, Irving just finished reading Alfred Kazin's *New York Jew* (one of the books I got in Philly) and Kazin mentions Brebner as one of a group of bright, talented minds, I don't know the exact context. It pleased Irving. Gatenby says he's going to start a movement for Irving to get the Nobel Prize. Now we're talking. I know that's something Irving wants ... he's mentioned it frequently—jokingly and all, but still....

"Last night we were watching *Holocaust* on TV. We've

discussed it and agree that it's a good show, soap opera of course, that's inevitable, but all in all a good thing that it's being shown. For thousands of people, it's a revelation, an eye-opener—an introduction to something about which they are totally ignorant. Yet, last night, after a while Irving got aggravated and said: 'You know, beyond a certain point, I get so that in a way, I wish it weren't shown. I hate to give the goyim the satisfaction of seeing how the Jews were slaughtered. From now on, I just want to see Jews with guns in their hands, with bombs.' Horrifying to me, to have to write it, but it is what he said...."

Journal, September 18, 1979: "Back in Niagara-on-the-Lake since Sunday, but we go back to Toronto tomorrow. The operation went okay—it took hours for Irving to completely come out of the anesthetic, during which time he'd float in, take hold of my hand, and float out again, still holding on. He got out of the hospital on Friday. When I went to pick him up, I'd just had a 2½ hour session in the dentist's chair (two crowns) and I think I was in worse shape than he was! He rested up Fri and Sat, and Sat night we went to a party—after seeing ...*And Justice for All,* Norman Jewison's new film, which closed the Toronto Film Festival. We met Jewison and saw a few people we hadn't seen for a long while—Brian Linehan [broadcast journalist and my dear friend] and Sid Adilman [entertainment columnist for *The Toronto Star*], and Adrienne Clarkson [journalist for many years with CTV, writer, and eventually Governor-General of Canada], John Weinzweig [esteemed Canadian composer] (I guess Dan [John's son] brought him), and John Basset [journalist and media mogul, founder of CTV]. Maybe we'll send our *Amber* to Basset ... perhaps it's better for TV than for film.... [Note to reader: John Weinzweig, one of Canada's foremost and esteemed composers, had been a friend of my parent's forever; he had in fact composed his marvellous work, *Wine of Peace,* with my mother (professional name Mary Simmons) in mind, and she had performed the World Premiere at Massey Hall, and subsequently on several other occasions. John's sweet wife, Helen, was a writer, who had let Irving and me use her little study on Markham Street near Honest Ed's when, in the early days of our burgeoning affair, we had needed a place where we could be together, alone. Their son, Dan Weinzweig, had gotten his start in the film business, thanks to my father. They were lovely people.]

"It's so beautiful here now. The trees have that end-of-the-summer slightly dishevelled look, the maples have the first touch of red. We're eating lots of corn, tomatoes and peaches—we'll soon be into the apples. Then it'll be all over. I can't believe the summer is gone. It's been much too fast.

"Irving got a letter from A. today—she and Leon got married. I think that's great news, and I think Irving thinks so too (he encouraged her to do it, he says), although he looked a little queer when he told me. I guess he'll never remember her without some pain—but definitely no regrets, he says.

"Tomorrow, on the way to Toronto, we're supposed to stop off at Howard Aster's, pick up the manuscript for *An Unlikely Affair*, and give it to Adrienne Clarkson to write an intro. Tomorrow night we're going to a party in honour of John Irving (author of *The World According to Garp*); Greg Gatenby invited us. He said there'll be lots of interesting people there. Thursday I'm giving an interview to a woman who's doing an article for *Chatelaine* on what it's like to live with an older man.... Thurs night we're meeting with Francesca [Valente] and the Italian publisher, Alfredo Rizzoli; he wants to bring out a book of Irving's poems in Italian. He translated [Ezra] Pound, and he said he'll submit Irving to the Nobel Prize Committee, on behalf of Italy. He has plans to ask Irving to Taormina in '81, and we'll discuss the tour in Italy for this April. He's a Jew, and the author of *The Garden of the Finzi-Continis* (I think he's the guy). If he is, my parents offered to invite him for dinner on Friday, as it's Rosh Hashanah; a Jew alone in a foreign country and all.... I think the offer is beautiful, we'll make sure he's the guy and see on Thursday.

"Irving these days is carrying on about Russia and the threat to North America. He finds it sickening that the Americans don't seem to see or comprehend how serious and threatening the situation is. He says how can it be, that all they seem to want is distraction, entertainment?... That America is in no way capable of handling the Russians—and the Russians know it. And how about the Non-Aligned Nations meeting and all of them with Soviet backing and all of them attacking Israel. It's grim to listen to him, since he's usually right with his prophesies. About two to three years in advance of the rest of the world, that's all.

"We had a lovely fuck today, the first since the operation. Irving said it was a different kind, it was a 'spiritual come'; it wasn't like an ejaculation, it was 'spiritual dew.'…It's true, we seem to be coming closer and closer…. It's sometimes just a teeny bit frightening to feel myself becoming so dependent on him. A part of me wants to hold back, keep to myself. But I think it's been too late for that for a long time now. I know what we have, what we are, is new for both of us."

It's painful to read those words I wrote in September of 1979. Painful because Irving's politics, which I accepted unquestioningly at the time, never having been highly politicized myself, now seem to me to be so extremely inappropriate. Painful because I was not yet a mature enough woman to question more, challenge more. I was his muse, his publicist, his lover, his protector, and then his wife, making a home for us, tending to our physical needs, to the daily business of living—the tedium of routine chores that he for the most part did not want to be bothered with at all—but still I was his student, still mesmerized by the power of him, the seduction of his words. I did not feel up to the task of challenging his political beliefs, particularly as I believed he was so much more learned and steeped in politics and history than I was. If he had known Samantha as an adult, they would have enjoyed some magnificently heated and informed discussions, since she is very politically aware and every bit as articulate and impassioned as her father was.

On September 18th, I wrote to Andrea, telling her the news about our operations and about our trip to Banff, among other things: "…We didn't have too much free time, but one day we went exploring and it was so beautiful. Not a soul around, just us and the mountains and wild raspberries that we picked and ate, and the friendly mountain goats that climb down and amble along the road. Really nice trip…. We're supposed to be here until after the 1st of Jan. Then we're planning on Mexico: the Yucatan part…. If $$ allows, we'd love to go to Peru or Guatemala—have to check about fares etc…. I am feeling very good—life was never so sweetly arranged as it is now. I love my life, I love Irving, I

165

love where and how we live and I sometimes can't believe it's happening...."

Journal, September 23, 1979: "A glorious autumn day. We went for a long walk, explored the old graveyard—some wonderful stories to be made up from there—stopped by St. Andrews Presbyterian Church and met Rev. Gillespie, who recognized Irving and shook hands warmly, called him 'Irving' and wished us a happy Rosh Hashanah. Then, been working hard all day and evening on the definitive selection for the *Poems of Irving Layton*—the new collection of all-time biggies, the greats—taking time out only to make dinner, including baba ganoush, which Irving loved, said his mother used to make it and he hadn't had it for maybe fifty years. Didn't even get to read the *Sunday New York Times*, or *Variety*. The day went too quickly for me to do all the things I wanted to and now I'm sleepy and want to go to bed, but will I get to sleep, or will I think about all there is to do?

"Irving read the *Times*, wrote some letters, and read some poems, and mowed the lawn.

"I told him part of the problem in my going through his poems like this is that I have to look up a lot of them, because I don't know *everything* so well just by the title and when I look it up, sometimes I get so caught up in the poem, so carried away by it, that I read it all through, even if I know it; so it's taking me a long time, because there are so many great things. He said he understood, he feels the same way. That's why I see him so often reading his own books; he says he re-reads them for the charge they give him (all with a smile). He's irresistible.

"In Toronto last week, 'Rizzoli' was wrong; it was Rizzardi and he was not the Finzi-Contini guy. We're supposed to meet *him* this coming Sat., in Toronto. But we did discuss with Rizzardi (and Francesca of course) the reading-lecture tour in Italy in April, and the bringing out of a book of poems he'll translate, as he did with Pound.

"The party for John Irving was nice, though we didn't meet him till we were all leaving. Saw lots of people we hadn't seen for a while—[Margaret] Atwood, Sylvia Fraser [novelist], Bronwyn Drainie [arts journalist, editor, and sister of my friend Jocelyn], [Earle] Birney [esteemed poet], and lots lots more—Columbo

[John Robert, prolific writer and editor], strange [Harry] Pollock [writer, editor and Joyce scholar; Harry established the James Joyce Society in Toronto].... It was crowded and there was food, but we didn't somehow get around to eating, so we had a bowl of soup when we got back to the house. Irving enjoyed himself."

Journal, October 1, 1979: "At the house in Toronto still, since last Tues evening. Been, as usual, an incredibly busy week. Irving read some of his 'Italian' poems at the ROM [Royal Ontario Museum] part of their fund-raising ROM Carnival two-day event. Had dinner another evening with Greg Gatenby, Francesca and [her husband] Branco, [Giorgio] Bassani (author of *The Garden of the Finzi-Continis*), Susan Musgrave [poet], then on to Harbourfront, where Bassani read some poems of his, and Irving read some translations and Greg read some translations. Bassani is a very boring reader—reads everything in this pretentious, heavy-handed monolithic voice that's terrific—for going to sleep to. When Irving read the translations I woke up; but then, Irving could read the phone book and make it sound good....

"Francesca has done a lot of good for Irving, even if it's for her own aggrandizement more than anything; BUT she *does* tend to take advantage of the friendship a bit and she is very manipulative and shrewd. She went a bit too far this week—sucking too much time from Irving. Also, at Harbourfront, we told her we had to be somewhere by 9:30 and so asked if Irving could read his translations first, and when the time came, she'd paid no attention and Irving had to wait and we were stuck there till 10:15. *She* (and what's good for *her*) comes first and there's no doubt about it. But, after all, she has been helpful and I know we'll continue to see her and be involved.

"I like Susan Musgrave; it was nice to see her again. The vibes between us are good. When I talk to her, I don't get any sense of all that gothic weirdness that's in her poetry—she seems very unaffected and sensible. Irving says that's because the gothic crap is all fake, and comes as a result of the influence of her mentor, Robin Skelton, who hasn't got much to say himself.

"Met with Lucinda [Vardey, Irving's agent at that time; she went on to become an author and theologian] for lunch, and she tried to placate me, ease my impatience with regard to getting Irving a good publisher in the States. She's working on it, but it takes such a long time. We do have confidence in her, though—besides really liking her a lot. She's off to Europe for a month now—book fairs in London and Frankfurt, business all over. When she returns, we've planned to take a trip to New York with her, so Irving can present himself at some of the publishers. I'm a great believer in personal contact. I also believe that there's a great market for Irving's poetry in the States and they would really go for him. There's nobody like him, or near his talent and I can't stand that he's not known as well there as he is here. According to Lucinda, the poetry market is dwindling, some publishers have completely closed their poetry line, others are cut way back. But there *must* be a way and we'll find it. I think a personal visit would be a great idea—who but a complete asshole stiff could help but respond to him.... So we're planning to go in to N.Y. some time in Nov. with her.

"Tonight we're going to see *Apocalypse Now* (for the second time), with Max and Stephanie. We've (L. and me) been talking about it so much—Irving convincing himself more and more that it's corny, empty Hollywood pyrotechnics and nothing else and me maintaining that it's a great picture. [Note to reader: film was clearly one of the areas where I stood my ground, felt capable of arguing my points, etc.] Now Max and Steph have seen it and they think it's a great picture too. So, Irving wants to see it again and we'll talk more about it; he says he's open-minded, and would be happy if we can show him why it's great, because he just doesn't see it. He's funny—he starts off playing the role of devil's advocate—and winds up convincing himself! His immediate reaction after we saw it was somewhat overwhelmed and an instant desire to see it again, since he felt he hadn't been able to take it all in. Since then, the more he talks, the more he convinces himself that it's no good and he didn't like it!"

Journal, October 3, 1979: "Well, Irving came out of *Apocalypse Now* raving about what a great picture it is. He really missed a lot of the dialogue the first time, he said. Now it's a magnificent, great picture, an epic of the twentieth century. He sees it as a great anti-communist film, the first and only film to show the actual truth about Vietnam. Also showing 'the horror, the horror'—(there are several)—Kurtz is a genius and has to be sacrificed; we (twentieth century western civilization) humanitarians and tolerant people will be doomed by those very two characteristics—our only chance for survival lies in being utterly and purely ruthless. And how can we—romantics, humanists, etc.—acquire purity of action and live with ourselves, continuing to read poetry and books while ruthlessly murdering? Because that's what Kurtz (Marlon Brando is magnificent) had become—a genius moving in his own realm, beyond the accepted norm (therefore they—the generals—ordered his murder)—yet the only man with vision to see what had to be done—and he did it. And even so, all that awaits us at the end is flies and maggots. To become the mythical figure he wanted to remain, he knew he had to be sacrificed."

Journal, October 12, 1979: "I'll never get what happens to time.... We returned to our home here on Tuesday and [author and professor] Howard Aster and a friend came for dinner and an evening of talk with Irving, which he seems to have enjoyed enormously. It's been continuing cold and rainy and there's something wrong with the heating in our house, so only the downstairs is getting any heat and upstairs it's bloody cold.... Irving is discovering the delight and comfort of my hot water bottle in bed....

"Today we mailed off another of Irving's infamous 'letters to the editor'—to the *Globe and Mail*—his analysis of *Apocalypse Now*. I called United Artists this week and got sent a press kit and a gift besides—the soundtrack LP. Also called Famous Players and got Don Watts [a senior advertising executive at Famous Players, then the largest circuit of theatres in Canada, and my father was President. It was later swallowed by Cineplex] to send the reviews from the Toronto papers, which Irving termed 'abysmally off the track.' I sent a copy of the letter to George Heiber [then the Canadian General Manager of United Artists in Toronto] and to Dan Hall [then the marketing rep. at UA in Toronto] and hope that it will get to Coppola."

In retrospect, this was an absurd notion of mine. Had I known the players better, I would have realized that these people were in no way likely to pass along Irving's letter to the people at United Artists in California. Nobody in the film industry here would initiate something like that. Intimidation from Los Angeles runs high.

When I worked for Disney, my situation was unique. I was the first woman to be appointed Canadian General Manager of a major film distribution company. I was also the only Canadian General Manager—then, and to date—to shoulder responsibility for both the Sales and Marketing sides. I was fortunate to enjoy an excellent relationship with the people in Burbank to whom I reported: at that time, Richard Cook was heading up the distribution arm of Buena Vista Pictures, and Phil Barlow was his brilliant VP and daily hands-on man. They not only listened when I had something to say, they welcomed the input. They backed me up on my decisions, and if any exhibitor in Canada ever called them in Burbank with a complaint about me, Cook or Barlow would calmly inform them that if they had a problem, they'd better sort it out with me, because I was their person in Canada. This being a highly contentious business, arguments were inevitable, and sometimes if they were particularly heated, the person complaining might go over the Canadian GM's head, and call the bosses in California. But Cook and Barlow both had my back. I was very lucky to have that level of solid support, which I think is rare in the business today. [Note to reader: It was truly a privilege to work with those outstanding men, and some of the other studio executives, a few of whom I am friends with to this day]. I think that while I was living with Irving Layton, I came to believe that anything was, in fact, possible. The power of his convictions was so strong that I was seduced into believing that people might actually mobilize, get off their asses, and DO something. It was a nice delusion.

Journal, October 12, 1979 continued: "Two of my poems have been taken by *Poetry Canada Poesie*, which was nice. I wrote another one this week, called 'Superstar'—it's about the Pope. At this rate, I'm sure to have a book out in the next decade or so.... No, Irving is determined I'll have a book ready within the year."

Journal, October 13, 1979: "Still grey, cold, and no heat upstairs. Irving wrote today a great poem, called 'Comedian,' about Sandra B.—no, rather, about the unconscious, but inspired by Sandra B. Or, as Irving is wont to say, 'given to him' by

Sandra. He returned from Montreal last week quite browned off, especially with Sandra. She had apparently done a couple of things (I don't know what) that he felt were too much using him and were devious besides. So he's decided not to be part of her *mishegas* any longer. But today, after he'd read me the poem, he said, 'You see, I would not have written this poem if not for Sandra, so I'll always be grateful to her, because it's a great poem.' Other observations of his today: 'That's the worst part of being a writer—the constant moral pulse-taking.' Also, 'It's not that I don't see what people are, or what things they do; I just ignore—or repress—those things that are unpleasant, or that I don't want to know.' And more: 'The poet is generosity and joy. And by generous I don't mean being able to give; I mean being able to receive, being open, open to experiences, open to everything. Only those who can take, can give.'

"Part of our kitchen dialogue today:

I: 'How come I'm so happy here with you?'

H: 'I just stay out of your way.'

I: (laughing) 'How come you know all the right answers?'

H: 'I have a good teacher.'"

Journal, Monday, October 15, 1979: "Hooray, we can get heat upstairs now! Other major achievements of the day: a huge pot of applesauce, a pot of compote, a letter off to Andrea, marketing done, laundry, etc. Irving busy working on the revising of poems, beginning to make the weave of *For My Neighbours in Hell*. I'm exhausted—haven't even had my 'read' for the day. Have a premonition of something bad happening—can it be just that everything is going so nicely, I'm afraid it can't last? Feel like a young girl, I mean the 'now-I've-said-it-so-it-won't-happen' syndrome; some kind of primitive warding off of evil, or something, I suppose."

In a letter to Andrea, dated October 15th, 1979, I wrote: "Met a couple of interesting Italian men: Rizzardi, who is *the* Italian translator for Ezra Pound and is going to do the same for Irving Layton—plans to work on a large edition, both hardcover and soft. He's also head of the Institute for Canadian Studies over there, so we began arrangements for the reading-lecture tour in Italy this April. It's very exciting. Also met Bassani, the fellow who wrote *The Garden of the Finzi-Continis*—remember that one? It was mildly interesting—we had to attend a reading of his and he was quite Bor-ing and pompous.... Irving read Eng translation of some of B's poems and they sounded much better.... Have been working on my poems. At Irving's urgings, I sent some off to a new literary paper called *Poetry Canada Poesie*—and surprise, they're going to publish two of 'em! I'm loathe to send my stuff out, but teacher says it's important for my work to be seen and my name to start being known around (when I write, my name is Bernstein).... Reading a number of interesting books—*The Conquest of Death* by Benjamin Constant, a superior psychological study of a love affair that (so far) seems to be doomed. Also *The Russians*— been dipping into that for two months now. Also the poems of Catullus, raunch and smut in translation from the original Latin, from around 65 BC, Rome; things really haven't changed much since those days. People then and now carrying on their little games, intrigues, and manipulations.... There's a chestnut tree down the street and Irving just couldn't resist the 'gift from nature,' so he brought me a huge bowl with about fifteen pounds of chestnuts, which I proceeded to fart around with for hours—I boiled 'em, I baked 'em, I mashed 'em with cognac and sugar— all to no avail. I finally determined that these are definitely not the edible variety you get nice and warm from the street vendors. Now for the walnuts I've harvested from the garden. Irving tried to eat them, and discovered some juice from them—walnut stain I suppose—doesn't come off the hands. We've tried turpentine, alcohol and nail polish remover—*nada*. Irving has lovely walnut hands now ... ah, country living!"

Journal, October 18, 1979: " Still grey and damp and cold and miserable. But inside it's nice and cozy. I like to stay inside most all the time. Have to find gloves, scarves, hats, warm coats, and all the rest now, so that going outside doesn't have to be a freeze. Went to the Pen Centre for shopping today, didn't get the main things I went for and was thoroughly discombobulated, if not depressed, by the time I got home. All the people look old—most of them are, but even the young ones look the same, you can see their fates on their faces."

Journal, October 20, 1979: "Was too blue the other day to

continue—but I put it in a poem instead, which is even better, I suppose. I'll never go shopping there again, except for essential groceries or household things I can't get here. The rest will have to be in Toronto—it's just too awful there.

"We've spent the past few days putting together the mss. of *The Love Poems of Irving Layton,* and now it's ready. I asked Irving and he admitted I'm the only woman to help him like that—from selection to typing. It's a little strange, typing out all these love poems for other women; but let's face it, he was sixty-two when we met and had a lot of living and loving behind him. I'm just totally (or as nearly as can be) objective about it. Now we're working on *The Poems of Irving Layton*—the biggie, the definitive collection. Irving's been asked by the Korean Cultural Institute to go to Korea. There's an impressive list of others who've been asked before him and he's going to go. The other morning over tea we were dreaming up the following plan: mid-Jan., we go to Mexico. Return after about six weeks, say the end of Feb. Then Irving to Korea and a couple of days later, me to India. We meet in India, say the second week of March or so and then do India-Nepal-Israel. April 10 or so, to Greece for ten days. Then to Italy for the three-week reading and lecture tour. Then to France. I really want to rendezvous with my parents at Cannes and show Irving the film festival and be there for my birthday. Then home. It's a beautiful dream, except I don't much love not going to Korea with Irving and going to India by myself. He, plainly, doesn't want me to go to Korea with him. Makes excuses, like: they'll want their money's worth (they pay his way) and will keep him busy and wouldn't want to be bothered with a wife. I think that sucks shit, but I'm leaving it alone for the moment. It'll mean an argument if I bring it up again and he's awfully obstinate and I hate arguments. But—we'll see."

This is yet another example of how young and inexperienced I still was in some ways throughout the course of our marriage. Given a similar situation today, I would welcome with open arms a plan to travel such as the one he laid out for me. I would also understand that a little time alone would be a good thing; two people, I think, should have time away from each other. They should each have their own adventures, then come together and share. On the other hand, I also was painfully aware of a pattern beginning: what I saw as the template of Irving's previous relationships and his attempt to overlay that template onto our life at that time.

Journal, October 20, 1979 continued: "Right now, he's sitting with some student who's at Queens and doing a paper on him, and wrote him asking if he'd spare her some time to talk about himself. As I've told him, his generosity, plus his vanity, is a fatal combination. He admits it, cheerfully or ruefully, as the mood strikes! He was disappointed at seeing her, as she's tall, skinny and blonde—not at all his type. Pity."

Journal, October 22, 1979: "On Sunday morning, Irving had a reading and talk at a synagogue in St. Catharines. He did it for free, because, he said, they're a poor congregation. They received him very enthusiastically and a nice little thank-you speech was made by a new member—a Scottish man, who had recently converted—and his whole family—to Judaism. Irving was pleased, and moved.

"Meantime, we've finished the mss. for *The Love Poems,* and done the selection for *The Poems of,* and given Howard the mss. for *For My Neighbours In Hell.* Irving is sort of at loose ends today, adjusting to not having a book to work on. He said he feels amputated. Like he's given birth, and his children—the poems—are now out in the world. And how he really looks at them quite objectively and knows that some are better-favoured than other, and will always be well-received, while others—the ugly ducklings, so to speak—will only get a polite passing nod. He really talks about them like they're people, with their own, independent lives. He wants, I think, to be always pregnant.

"The other evening—Sat. to be precise—he was sipping some fine old Scotch we have—a gift, of course—and carrying on about how good it was. So I said, 'Why don't you buy it for yourself, then?' Because the only time we have good things to drink are when someone gives them to us. When Irving goes out and buys something, it's always cheap-o crap. And he reacted very badly, and angrily said to me, 'Oh shut up.' Then said, 'Sorry, but I can't afford this.' I was very upset at his anger towards me and his telling me to shut up like that. He'll tell me all about how much money he's making from his readings and his investments and how well-off we are—then remind me again how I should try to save every penny. I have $500 a month to run the house—all the food, drink, cleaning, and housekeeper once a week—plus all the bills and, if I need anything for myself, that too. But he's happy to send A. $400 a month—guilt money I call it. Supposedly support for David money, though honestly speaking, half that amount would suffice. But that's okay and I'm not to say a word about it. I have to understand how 'grateful' he is to her, for the poems she inspired—and understand how money means nothing to him, it's just a way for him to appease his conscience. But if, God help me, I need a couple of new pairs of pants, or a new pair of shoes, I have to get the money from him for it—blood from a rock—and I have to scrounge for bargains. I'm angry and I won't listen any more to how much money he has coming in, and how bloody well-off we are. If I say anything, he'll just call me a 'bourgeois middle-class merchant's daughter'—again. I think sometimes I ought to get a job again—but he doesn't want that. And besides, how can I, when in the next few months we'll be moving around such a lot. Perhaps after our travels, when we're more settled down, I'll take some part-time work.

"I despise having to ask him for money all the time. But I have to. If I never asked, I'd never get. It's an ugly business, totally odious to me. But, when it comes to the bucks, he's tight—and that's a new one for me to adjust to. He'll give it to others—to anyone at all. But me, I'm called 'bourgeois and spoiled,' reduced to the mass of 'ordinary women, who need new clothes, new baubles to make them happy.' Nice.... On Sunday, I suppose he felt sorry, so on the way back from the reading (where he'd sold some books and picked up $125 or so), he magnanimously offered me $10: 'Here, go buy yourself something!'—which I refused to take. As though $10 could actually buy me anything, other than some cigarettes or a couple of pairs of stockings. He's back half a century, when it comes to the prices of things. What a drag it is.... But I do love him, money matters aside. He always asks me, 'How much do you love me?' and I always answer, 'Too much.' And it's true...."

When I re-read this entry, it was a shocking reminder of how much I had blocked over the years. I chose not to remember the money issues with Irving. They provoked ugly words and feelings. However, the journal told it like it was—he did use those words, and often. When it came to material things, he was tight, that was the long and the short of it. I had been used to making my own money and doing what I wanted with it. I had never in my life been in a situation where I was financially dependent on a man—other than my father and he was an extremely generous man. However, Irving and I lived in a very nice house, and he had planned a lot of travel for the two of us, which had to be budgeted for. And what was that about a housekeeper once a week? I don't remember that and I don't know why I had a housekeeper. It seems indulgent, but the journal has this for the record, so it must have been. I do remember, prompted by having re-read this entry, that Irving never wanted to go out to eat. He always said that he loved my cooking and so he never wanted to go out and pay a lot of money for food that was not as good as what he got at home. And I would say to him that it was fine and that I was happy that he loved my cooking so much, but it was also nice for me to have a break once in a while and get taken out to eat. This he did not appear to understand, though once in a while he'd take me out—to one cheap place or another—and he'd order the cheapest thing on the menu and he'd complain about how much it cost and that it was not as good as my home cooking. The grumbling would pretty much take the joy out of the experience. He liked fine things well enough, but only if he didn't have to pay for them.

This was a reality that I had never known. My father had worked his way up the corporate ladder. I was not born a princess in one of those big Forest Hill Houses; we lived in an apartment on Eglinton Avenue and subsequently in a small house on Mayfair Avenue. It was not until I had left home in 1966 that my family moved into the big house on Old Forest Hill Rd. Nonetheless, my father was generous, and while I was not spoiled, neither did I want for anything in the material realm. He bought me beautiful things: jewellery and clothes, and he did it because it gave him pleasure to do so, never because I asked for it. My values were not those of material riches. Even though I had grown up in Forest Hill, I was always the outsider. I thought it was absurd to hear the girls in high school having contests to see who could go the longest without wearing the same thing twice. These were not my values at all.

After I left my parents' home, I had worked and supported myself, and bought myself what I wanted or needed. And yet, there I was, happily married to Layton, but in a situation where I was financially dependent on a man who, while he would spend money on some things, did not ever consider indulging himself or us in the smaller luxuries he so enjoyed, like a good bottle of scotch. His streak of cruelty would emerge when he'd call me 'bourgeoise,' or 'a merchant's daughter,' and I think the anger or cruelty were his way of gong on the attack rather than just admitting that he didn't enjoy spending the dough. I find a lack of generosity distasteful, the financial tightness that was another part of Layton. Worst of all was the money he continued to give to A. at that point. She was married to Leon! I wouldn't have cared if he had also been considerate of me, and my needs. But, when it came to buying things for me, he was not considerate at all. This was an ongoing bone of contention. For a woman used to making her own money, supporting herself, and buying what she wanted (or could afford), being dependent on a man, my husband, was uncomfortable and unpleasant.

Journal, Sunday, November 4, 1979: "Just returned from Toronto. Went on Thursday, had a meeting at the house first with Tad [Jaworski, documentary filmmaker. He brought Irving into the project "The Challenge of Karl Marx", which is what these meetings were about], then with Howard [Aster, of Mosaic Press] and Ludwig Zeller [Chilean Surrealist poet], and his Suzanna Wald [surrealist visual artist and Ludwig's wife], and Howard's friend, the nice Irish teacher from Sheridan whose name I never remember, maybe Ken. Tad came in depressed and disgusted and angry—they're stalling him on the Marx thing. Irving and I read the script and felt it was poorly done. Irving found it totally unacceptable on a scholarly and intellectual level—a sentimental and inaccurate picture of Marx. And I found it very shaky on a filmic, dramatic level—some dialogue so bad it is a parody of itself and some scenes that I can't see working. Irving felt himself to be in a moral dilemma—he felt he should say what he thought but the situation makes it a bit 'sticky.' [Note: Tad wanted Irving to host this series on Marx that TVO was developing. I don't recall how Aviva and Leon were involved.] 'As far as the outside world is concerned,' he said, 'Leon went off with my woman' [Note: this doesn't make much sense, as Irving and I had been married for a year, and been together for longer, but it may be more a hint of how Irving felt than anything else.] So, maybe, he was afraid what he'd say would be taken for sour grapes. But aside from that, which really isn't important, he doesn't want to say or do anything to foul up the plans for the show or the present or future prospects for Leon. How Leon would react is another thing, again. Apparently, A. thinks it's superb. Apparently, one's critical abilities are severely endangered when exercised over the one with whom one lives. Funny, I said, they sure seemed to work overtime when she was living with you, end quote. A wry grimace from Irving.... So in walks Tad and I pour him a very stiff screwdriver and he tells us TV Ontario has decided they want a marketing analysis before shooting. It sounds like a stall, but who knows what's really behind it. Meantime, plans are rolling along as usual. Irving told Tad what he thinks of the screenplay as diplomatically as possible.

"The other meeting was about *Neighbours in Hell*—Zeller and Wald are going to do pictures for (yet another) deluxe limited edition. Irving loves them; he gets so excited telling about it. They're also doing a portrait of him (first sitting planned for the twentieth) and a cover for the M.&S. book. All of this in the talking stages, anyway.

"Irving today said he wants to teach for one semester, next Sept. A course at Sheridan, blending politics, poetry, and film. He told Howard, who's going to talk about it with whomever at Sheridan and arrange a meeting. Irving obviously misses teaching, for all his talk of time to read and write. It's partly that he misses the talking (and, I suppose, the captive audience, the admiration and adoration), and partly that he really feels the responsibility of teaching—that most students are in such poor shape and most teachers are so lousy, that if *he* doesn't help them, show them, enlighten them—*who will?* A kind of messianic mission. The point is, it's true. There are so piss-poor few good teachers around—and he's the best I ever had, that's for sure. It's marvellous to watch how the students watch him."

Journal, Monday, November 12, 1979: "An incredibly busy week, last week, with Irving reading at Niagara College on Mon, U. of Guelph on Tues., Ridley College on Wed., and Glendon on Thurs., plus lunches and dinners and lots and lots of *blah blah blah*. At Niagara, two very good women teachers, the kind of people I'd like to see again, spend some time with—very warm and open, somewhat witchy. Guelph was a lively bunch of students, relatively speaking, which really doesn't mean much. An asshole of an Eng Dept. guy, who was a lesson in superficiality and bullshit breeziness. Also met Dean Baker there—one of Irving's long-term perennials [a young poet seeking Irving's help]—who seems a nice guy, albeit terribly nervous and full of problems. Ridley was a trip—suddenly we were back a century or two, in England, rolling through the iron gates onto the grounds of this big old classy private school. And the Headmaster and his wife— oh so very English, so very proper … marmite sandwiches, blue ceilings and pink walls, and blue and pink flowered floors, and oh gawd. Actually, we rather liked them—tried to guess their story one evening and found out we were dead on the next day. A previous marriage, a scandal, 'the usual rot,' as somebody'd say. Also there—Robin Mathews [another poet]. I didn't much like him. A few others, nobody particularly interesting or worth mentioning. All so WASP-ish, so reserved, restrained, repressive.

"We came home with a craving for salami and spiced olives, something smelly and sharp. The students were pretty dull and we all said what a good group they were. Glendon—another bunch of stiffs. Irving got very hot and was thundering away at them. Reaction? A few squirms, some uncomfortable looks, or embarrassment at so much outpouring of emotion on Irving's part. Only one student with any questions or comments at the end and he—not surprisingly—a Chinese exchange student. Spent Friday in Toronto, chores as usual—a visit to Tad and TV Ont. to sign a contract for the Marx thing and discuss the format.

"Came home Sat. Sat night Len Gasparini [poet, novelist] called, asked if we were here, I said yes, he said he thought he'd take a drive down. I said sure. He and his wife arrived around 1:30-2:00. Irving and I thought they'd visit a couple of hours and go. No. Six came and went (and with it, our favourite show, *60 Minutes*. At eight, I prepared dinner, thinking surely when they see that and since we haven't asked them to stay, they would go. No. Finally, it was after eight and we were starving so I said, okay, let's eat, and all four of us did. Then, we thought, well now surely after dinner, they'll go. No. It was going on to midnight when we finally got them out. Unbelievable! How can people do that? We were aghast, appalled. But they were nice. Mary Anne, Len's wife, is a lawyer—very bright, a nice straightforward no-bullshit way about her. We liked her. Len—well, he's nice too, but a funny sort of guy. She seems brighter than him, but Irving says he's no fool either."

17.

JOURNAL, THURSDAY JANUARY 3, 1980: "Brought in the new year—the new decade—on Monday. This year it was my turn. We were at the family homestead, with my parents and Marc—and Bonnie and Thor [relatives from the U.S.], who'd been here with us visiting for a week. It was very cozy and warm and I was happy to be surrounded by people who care about me and vice-versa, for a change. Last year we were at a party at Sandra's and that was no delight for me. The year before, we were at a party at Delavan [Delavan St. was where Irving and Aviva had their last house, before parting ways], and new lows were reached in that one, one of the all time miserable nights in my life. So, as I said, this year was my turn."

Since the last entry: "Irving's been to Nanaimo, BC, for a reading, which he says was one of those very special, great evenings. He came back enraptured with the community there and for a few days I thought we'd be moving! He also gave a reading for the Italians, in Montreal, organized of course by our dearly beloved Francesca, who, by the way, in the interim has gotten *married* to Branko! Yup, another twosome gone legit. They've also left Toronto now. Francesca's gone off to be head of the Italian Cultural Institute in San Francisco—and Branko's trying to get into Berkeley. Of course, first thing on her agenda was arranging a reading for Irving in San Fran next fall! We just found out from her too that apparently Irving starts reading in Italy on April 21, so I guess we'll be leaving here around the 18th.

"Francesca's gone—and A.'s back. Arrived last Thurs. night and could not wait to call here, which she did late Thurs. Friday we went into Toronto. Sat. evening Irving went to see them. And Sunday, all evening. My parents were not thrilled with her calling every day. It got a bit testy. However, Irving and I had a long talk about it, in fact all the drive back here we were working through it and I hope, maybe, it will be a little nicer now, but it seems I just have to live with it. They're apparently going to be in very close contact. Irving will continue to be more involved than I see need for and what I feel about it really doesn't matter. Irving will do what he wants to do. Period. But with our talk, at least I got it all out of me and I think he is more aware of—and concerned for—my feelings than before. So long as me, my feelings, my needs, come first, it's okay. But it is, from time to time, necessary to assert myself."

Reading these words thirty-five years later, it is so obvious that this was a critical event in our marriage. Irving saw nothing at all amiss with his spending both nights on a weekend with A., while I remained in my parents' home. I fully understood—and understand—that his and A.'s ties were deep, and they shared a child in whom Irving was deeply interested and to whom he was committed. But after all, our marriage was still young, and I was young; surely he must have realized that he was playing with fire, spending so much time with them. I felt that I was being cast in the role of "the wife," and Aviva had, in a way, become "the other woman." In fact, Irving did not think anything at all about the situation.

Intuitively, instinctively, I hated what was happening, but I could not find a way to take a stronger stand or deal with it in any way other than telling him how I felt. He knew how I felt, but he ridiculed how I felt. He did not want to hear any of it. His response was to repeatedly tell me that how I felt was ridiculous. He was dismissive of my feelings, and that ultimately put one more nail in the coffin of our marriage. The writer in him—and the dark side of him—enjoyed the tension, and he wanted to see what would emerge from the stirred up waters.

Now I ask myself why I didn't accompany Irving when he went to visit David and his mother. I was his wife and it seemed to me that we could have avoided a lot of tension and hurt feelings if he had included me instead of being exclusionary. On the one hand, he'd speak to me about his vision of one big happy extended family; on the other hand, he'd go off to see them by himself, leaving me alone. Why he thought that was okay was beyond me. In retrospect, why I did not assert myself more was also absurd. While Irving was probably enjoying having it all, so to speak, I was frustrated that he seemingly did not respect my viewpoint enough to adjust his behaviour. He was clearly was pushing things—spending most of the weekend with Aviva and allegedly David. Why was just a part of the weekend not enough? I simply wanted Irving to honour my feelings and act accordingly. Now I see that that was like asking a zebra to change its stripes.

Irving always wanted to come and go as he pleased, when he wanted, where he wanted and with whom he wanted. Considering our history, this ought to have been abundantly obvious. If I didn't want him to go somewhere, it was my problem, not his. When a new woman would begin to appear in his poems, I had the choice of believing it was simply a "coffee romance," as he called them, or a new affair. And by affair, I do not mean a sexual affair, although that was commonly the desire of the woman involved. Irving had attained legendary status as a "lover" or "ladies' man," and my marriage to him had helped further delineate that image. Many women saw this as a challenge. They wanted to see for themselves what the fuss was about. Maybe they wanted to have a poem written about them. For Irving, it was mostly about the chase. Irving loved women, loved the look of them, the smell of them, loved their stories, loved their come-ons; but he was not one to jump into the sack quickly, as I have already detailed. If a woman bared her breasts for him and placed his hands on her nipples, he'd enjoy that moment, of course. But that's where it would end, most of the time anyway, depending on the temperature of his marriage at the time. Given our relatively new marriage, and considering the amount of lovemaking we still enjoyed, it was highly improbable that he was going to fall into another woman's bed.

To Irving, if he loved you—whatever that meant to him, not you—married you, lived with you or had a child with you, you were to some measure always together—even if not in a physical sense. His soul, once touched, was ever a part of yours. That's the way he felt. He was, in that sense, a Romantic. Not for nothing did he love Shelley, Keats, and especially Byron, and he'd refer to them frequently, as well as Lawrence of course.

Irving loved the idea of his extended family, his harem of wives, his assorted children of various mothers, all playing together. In a darkly comic scenario, I think he might have liked to have had all his women at the same time and let them fight it out between them as to which one was Wife Number One, which one he would share the bed with that night. While the women fought it out, he would be in his study or sitting on a rock somewhere, writing poetry, oblivious to it all on some level, yet using it on another. He loved all of his women and he would create art out of their anguish and that would be sublime for him. The art always more than justified the turmoil and torture felt by either the women or him. He would rationalize that the anguish was temporary, but the poems were eternal. As he said to me on more than one occasion, "I never leave my wives, they always leave me." And that was true. Had Betty been willing to live with him while he had his affair with Aviva, he and Betty would likely have remained together. Had Aviva stuck with him while his affair with me continued year after year, he probably would have let the tatters of their life drag on and on forever. Had I been willing to accept the role he inexorably cast me in, we would most definitely have remained married. He absolutely would not have left me, ever. It was the same with his lovers and other friends—Musia for example—the women he did not marry but also loved and who remained part of his life for decades.... He loved all of us in his own inimitable way and we all continued to love him even after we sadly accepted that living with him was no longer possible.

This touches on the crux of the matter. Beyond the superficial and obvious interpretation of Irving as misogynist and womanizer—the role in which he cast himself, or was cast, or both, I no longer know for certain—he was ultimately deserving of compassion. He was unable to step outside this persona, unable to make the kind of emotional commitment he so desperately and continuously sought and yearned for from his women, a commitment I believe he himself equally wanted to make. An emotional disability was part of his make up. Sometimes he would say to me, jokingly, that I was going to ruin him as a poet because he was far too happy with me. It is possible that in my heart I knew those words had a ring of truth to them, although of course in our years together, I could not have allowed the thought to take shape, or how could we have been married? A woman in love wants to be with her man, period; she will not believe for one instant that his love for her will ruin those very parts of him that drew her to him in the first place, and that formed the foundation of their initial relationship. Irving was a tragic figure in the true sense, because he was irrevocably doomed to destroy that which he most loved. His joyfulness and exuberance was a basic part of him that no woman could claim responsibility for. She could enhance it, or she could dilute it, that is all. She could not destroy it because it was who he was—it was the core of his soul. The flip side of his joy was, of course, the pull to darkness, the chaos out of which he also wrote. The two are inextricably tied. He needed both, like air and water. Any woman had to be willing—had to understand, to embrace with her heart, her legs, her belly, her breasts, her cunt—the fact that she could participate in the joy, up to a point, but she would also be pulled into that darkness; she could not have one without the other. And he, no matter how much he loved his woman—and I believe he loved me as much if not more than he ever loved any woman, or had the capacity to love any woman—could not and would not stop himself from entering that darkness and taking the woman with him because, ultimately, art was his greatest love, the poems were his First Wives, the creative process was life, lover, child, friend, everything; poetry was in every breath he drew, the place from which his energy came, and the first place his energy went. Everything else—love, sex, desire, fantasy—all served as fuel for that fire. So when he wrote: "They dance best who dance with desire/ who lifting feet of fire from fire...," it was not only a metaphorical or poetic fire, it was the true burning flesh fire that was him, that lived in him.

In a poem I wrote that first year at York in his poetry workshop, which marked the beginning of our life together, I wrote: "the fire within you inspires me, and many;.../ ten years, twenty years after you are buried, the grass over your grave will scorch/ and the flowers will burst into flames." To be a student of his was to be touched by that fire. To hear him read was to feel that fire. To be his woman was to become part of that fire. The fire could warm you, and could kill you. It was mesmerizing, even as you felt your flesh singe and the stink of your burnt hair filled your nostrils, you inhaled it because the magic and power and passion of an Irving Layton comes only once in your lifetime, if you are so blessed. This was why his women put up with so much from him. This was why his women left him. This was why he inevitably fouled his own nest.

Journal, January 3, 1980 continued: "I've had a cold for the past few days and I'd been ignoring it completely, going out and around and doing everything. When we got back here, I fell into bed and have pretty much been here. I feel okay now, not 100% but better than I was; it's just this awful sounding cough that's settled deep in my chest. Irving has been very sweet—yesterday morning and this morning, he woke me up with a cup of tea in bed. My God....

"Also, in the interim—the really important thing: Irving and I went to New York, met Lucinda there and went to see some publishers about bringing out a book of Irving's. We met David Godine of Godine Press. He was nice, but was in a great rush, didn't have much time for us, but seemed interested and enthusiastic. Then we saw Bob Bender of Morrow Press. It's a larger house, which apparently can work to our advantage or disadvantage. He was nice too, listened to Irving read some poems and seemed very sold. Next step, supposedly, is for him to 'talk to the money people' and tell them why they simply must bring out Irving. There's one more publisher who's interested; he's supposed to be coming to Toronto next week so Irving can meet with him. Surely something will jell with one of them. They all look at his work and ask the same question—where've you been till now? They all can't understand why all this hasn't happened before. Hooray for me, for getting him to understand he needed an agent and for getting him Lucinda and for chasing after her till she set all this up. If I hadn't gotten after him, it might just have gone on and on in the frog pond here, as it always had. I'm also working on getting some readings for him in the U.S. Been in touch with a Judy Drucker some sort of Sol Hurok of the South—she brings in Isaac Stern and Luciano Pavarotti and Beverly Sills and Mstislav Rostropovich—all kinds of greats, to perform at the Beth Shalom synagogue, for which she is Cultural Director, in Miami Beach. She wants to start some readings as part of her program and someone—Mrs. Woll. from fellows of Brandeis, with whom I've been in touch— put her on to Irving's work. She's said she wants him to come, but we're awaiting further communication. Meantime, cousin Ken [my first cousin], at the University of Miami, has jumped into the ring and has taken it upon himself to see if he can't also line up some readings in the States. I had a long talk with him a couple of weeks ago, sent him off a bunch of press on Irving, and now we'll see what happens. He says U. of Miami and another U. in Florida are interested, so is U. of Penn. We'll see what works out. When in N.Y., we also met a lady-friend of Howard's—who's going to be agent for Irving in N.Y.— her name is Alyss Dorese. She was very enthusiastic about the Layton-Roth correspondence, thinks it might be a good book for now. Also another couple of things—this aside from what Lucinda is doing. I want to see Irving as well known in the U.S. as he is in Canada. I want to see him on Cavett and Carson and doing readings at all the important schools.

"What else?… Jocelyn was here for a short visit and it was sweet and easy to be with her again. Then, as I said, Bonnie and Thor came. Irving didn't sit with us too much—a little chat over and after dinner and then away he went to his study, where he spends most of his time. I would have liked it if he would have sat with us a little more. I am a little uncomfortable, the way he goes away all the time. But, too bad! That's the way it is, can't do anything about it. Just wait till the next time some of his friends are here and I get bored or tired of their pseudo-lit *blah blah blah*—watch me hi-tail it upstairs! After all, it's not really so important to me. I do love him, too much as I always say and it is fascinating to live with him, watch him closely as I do. Just every now and then, I have to make sure I don't get lost.

"As Russia plows into Afghanistan, Irving's predictions grow dimmer and dimmer. He shouts and rants on about the naïve, stupid Americans and how they are not seeing the danger—how great or imminent it is....

"Just finished reading Fania Fenelon's book, *Playing for Time,* about her experiences as part of the women's orchestra in the concentration camp at Auschwitz-Birkenau, then subsequent interment at Bergen-Belsen. It's a book that will stay with me as long as I live. And there's being a film made of it now, with Vanessa Redgrave up to play Fania."

Journal, January 5, 1980: "I was feeling well enough to go out briefly today. Went down the street into The Little Prince and told the woman there that tomorrow's *New York Times* would be our last for ten weeks or so, so not to order for us; that's the first active move I've made with regard to our upcoming Yucatan trip. Are we really leaving a week Monday? We go into Toronto on Thurs. to have time for a few chores, visits, etc. Have to see Lucinda, have to stock up on medications, and I want to get to the travel shop on Cumberland and maybe get a new very light suitcase and an immersion coil and travel cups for tea in the room—things like that. Maybe see Joss in her new apt. Irving will see A. and David and so on. Have to start planning what to take, by way of clothes and books. Irving's already been going on about how light we're going to travel, what few items of clothing he's going to take—he's been making the all-important Selection of Books To Take. He nudges me about too many clothes, I nudge him about too many books ... been studying some Spanish too ... an ad in today's *Globe* for *Neighbours in Hell* and *An Unlikely Affair*....

"We had some more conversation about moving back to Toronto. I think it's too quiet here for Irving; he needs people too much. We'll see. I won't mind, really, if we do, tho I'll be a bit sorry to leave this nice house and garden—we sure won't be able to afford a similar place in the city. However, it would have advantages too, I s'pose—and I'd probably look for some part-time work if we live there. It's a ways off yet, but I won't be surprised if it happens. Irving needs more action. Me—I can do without it and without the people—but I think he can't. Maybe when he's ninety or so…. Maybe. According to Irving, World War is likely…."

Journal, January 9, 1980: "Merida. Hotel Delores Alba. Toronto-Miami flight okay; upon arrival Miami, discovered that Fisher Freemont [Travel Agency] made a mistake—we had to wait from 2:30 till 8:30 for the plane to Merida. First confirmation of my weird feelings of anxiety, feelings of something being not so good. Second confirmation: after trying a half-dozen times at the Aero Mexico desk to get confirmation of our luggage having been successfully transferred from Air Canada, I found out it wasn't. Air Canada was closed; there was nobody to talk to. The plane was a narrow and awful DC-9 that kept making pulsing sounds, plus occasional flashes of light on the wing, the most awful food ever on a plane and jiggles all the way. Somewhat to my surprise, we arrived safely. No bags, though."

Journal, January 17, 1980: "Had to go to sleep last night. Slept till about 6:30 this morning—I think it was the mosquito bites and not the noise that awoke me. To continue: we did go out to the airport again yesterday and we did get our bags—hooray! Merida seems to be a pretty fair city—a couple of nice squares—with flowering trees and fountains. The women mostly wear a cotton sack, which is white except for a very beautiful and colourful floral embroidery across the bodice and at the hem. At the bottom, an extra piece hangs down; it looks sort of like a slip hanging out, only it's part of the dress. Sometimes they also wear a long scarf around their shoulders as part of the costume—it sure isn't to keep them warm as it's plenty hot here. There is a breeze though and it's not too terribly humid. So far the food is horrendous and I have eaten nearly nothing, except for some delicious red snapper (*huachinango*) yesterday afternoon. For dinner, I had a cheese sandwich, which was made with onions and very hot peppers…. What I don't eat, Irving does … he'll eat anything. So far, we're okay, stomach-wise…. The hotel Delores Alba is a little dark and dingy, but there *is* a private toilet and shower and a sweet teeny pool, by which we are now sitting, with our rum and cokes. Not bad. Spent the a.m. finding out about getting to Isla Mujeres, where we're going tomorrow. Got our bus tickets today—it's a four-hour ride to Puerto Juarez

Irving, arriving at Isla Mujeres, 1980.

from where we take the ferry. We walked about three hours so far today. Irving bravely marches on, sweat pouring down his reddened face, saying from time to time what a great way to see a place, and how good it is for us, and how much weight we'll lose. He said we should have no trouble taking off about twenty pounds and I said, no trouble for sure—but I don't want to lose it all in the first week! One of the best things is a freshly squeezed orange juice—they use about five to six oranges per person. It's a huge glass and costs about 12 pesos. Cokes are 6 or 8 pesos— cheaper than at home. Last night we checked out the university of Yucatan—quite nice-looking and watched the girl's volleyball team have a game, which was played *con mucho gusto* and with much yelling from the stands. Naturally, Irving went on for a while about how he'd like to teach here and live here for a few months, and how he feels a closeness to the people here.... After our swim and siesta, we're off to the archeological museum, supposed to be a must-see. After dinner, there's some mariachi band performing in the square; might be fun. There are lots of beggars around. Irving gave some money to one yesterday, said she reminded him of his mother. Didn't give money to another one today, but said she reminded him of his mother too. He was all eaten up with bites this morning and that, plus the aggravation of having had his belt, razor blades, and hairbrush stolen from his suitcase when it was lost, didn't put him in the greatest mood. But we walked it off, you might say, and he was soon okay. Took the bus yesterday to the airport. The bus was at least fifty years old and had no shock absorbers and when we got on it was so full, Irving had to stand on the steps and hold on as the doors couldn't shut. Lively, it was. As we drove by the homes, I looked inside and saw they all have two things: a crucifix and a TV!"

Journal, January 18, 1980: "Here we are in Isla Mujeres and I wish we were happier about it. The trip here was a trip. Took the bus at 9:00 a.m. It wasn't too bad, but it was already first class! It took about 4½ hours to get to Puerto Juarez. The boat was supposed to leave at 2:00. Two, 2:30, 3:00 came and went while we waited with about sixty other people. The ferry was there all right, but I was told it had *muchos problemas*. Indeed, all the while we waited, we watched them bailing water out of the boat and the engine was dismantled. Finally, another little boat arrived, maybe a little less than half the size of the ferry. There were six lifejackets and that's probably all the people the boat was meant to take, but all sixty-odd of us clambered aboard and away we went. We were jammed in like the proverbial sardines and had to stand all the way; there was no place to sit, no room even on the floor. After about an hour we arrived at Isla Mujeres. A man and a kid about nine or ten put our suitcases on their heads and led us to the Hotel Berny. We have a nice-sized room— white stucco walls and brick-red tiled floor, a toilet and shower with—thank God—hot water. There's a swimming pool in the courtyard around which the rooms are laid out. A ceiling fan keeps us comfortable, as it's quite sultry. We have a balcony and can see the sea from it. We unpacked some things, showered, and fell asleep immediately. Woke up, went downstairs to the hotel

Irving in the Yucatan, 1980.

restaurant. I don't think I want to describe the meal—enough to say it was ghastly and I hardly ate anything and even Irving didn't do too much better. We took a walk after and then I had to rush back and get to the toilet, with cramps and bad runs. I took a couple of pills and feel better now. Maybe it's that we're tired, maybe also because the food was such a turn-off—but whatever, the place looks pretty dismal. We're desperately hoping that tomorrow the sun shines and we can go swimming, check out the beach, and also the pool here. There's a 10% tax on food that really hurts. Apparently it used to be 4% and this year the government upped it to ten. It's lunacy. It's got to severely cut into their tourism. Seems nothing is really cheap anymore. We're thinking we're not gonna last six weeks here."

Journal, January 19, 1980: "Well, the cock-a-doodle-doo woke us up about five this morning, then the dogs' barking took over, just to make sure we didn't get back to sleep. The bed was so soft and lumpy anyway, it's a wonder we slept at all. Having not eaten much last night, we were hungry and decided to have 'a good breakfast.' Better not to describe that either. Eggs *can* be made inedible. So we began to explore—looking for another hotel. We looked at a couple, each one as awful as the other. Finally found Hotel Posada del Mar. What they call luxury accommodations is what we have now. A very large room, with a carpet and drapes that really close and air conditioning and a fairly sleepable bed and a nice bathroom, with pretty flowered towels and a shower and hot water. The lights are blue globes and outside there are blue lanterns, which remind me of Colette and so it is very lovely. This place is right on the beach and the room is set back from the road, so no traffic noise will bother us. They don't know about mufflers here. There's a real pool—good size—and the place is beautifully landscaped. Coconut trees and flowering shrubs and flowers lining the walkways—it's truly beautiful, reminds us of St. Lucia. Irving told them we want to stay for a month and made a deal and got the room and continental breakfast for about $30 a night.

"After we moved, we went to the market and got some oranges and bananas and peanut butter and tostada, so we won't starve. Then—at last—to the beach. And it was gorgeous—Irving settling into the sand, muttering 'I don't believe it,' then dozing off, having a swim. The water is very clear and salty, nice white sand, no rocks in the water. It was really good. Then we came back here and wrote some postcards while sitting around the pool. I phoned my parents to let them know where and how we are, then took the loveliest swim in the big green pool, which I had all to myself. Came up, took a nap. We were going to get dressed and go out now, but we both feel a little queer. So we've taken a couple of lomatil. I've had the runs again and Irving has been gagging and throwing up a bit. Nice. So this is Mexico. Undoubtedly the line for today comes from Irving: 'You can't judge a shit by its smell.' I think we won't go out for dinner tonight. The less, the better, anyway.

"A couple hours later—well, the pills are helping. My runs have stopped and Irving isn't heaving anymore, though he's still not right. It'll be a sad day when the liquor candies we brought

Irving's favourite positon on the beach in the Yucatan, 1980.

are all gone. I've just taken a picture of Irving scratching his bug bites on his back against the brick wall. Cute. We take turns spreading insect repellant lotion on each other's bodies and then antihistamine cream on the bites of any parts we'd missed. Irving sits and wryly says, 'Some holiday; if we get out of here alive, I'll be happy.' We amused ourselves for a while discussing various optional courses of action should we become more seriously ill.... My right eyelid is swollen almost shut from some insect's bite.... It's terribly attractive."

This was the 1980 version of what is now known as "The Mayan Riviera." I laugh whenever I hear that name, recalling our experiences there. I guess we were trailblazers of sorts. We had gone there because it looked beautiful and primitive, remote and cheap, and neither of us had ever been there. The fact that even Irving got sick—he had the constitution of a bull, a stomach of steel—says something. When I had nearly died of food poisoning in Greece back in '75 with him, he had had only a little bit of the runs. But here he was, throwing up! Feeling really queasy! Having runs! I never saw him like that before, or afterwards.

Journal, January 20, 1980: "Considerable improvement over yesterday. Had our toast and tea/coffee downstairs, took a little stroll, got some mineral water and bug spray for the room, tried to recover Irving's nose stuff [an ointment he used to prevent burns] in the other hotel (didn't) and went to the beautiful beach for a couple hours of sun and swim. It was a magnificent day. Took a swim in the terrific pool here. After a nap, Irving went out for a walk and I wrote some postcards and got cramps and runs again, took a couple lomatil, and got better again. We went downstairs for dinner, decided to keep it very light and I just had an omelette. Seems to be sitting okay so far. Irving called Howard, who said he'd gotten—at last—the intro from Adrienne [Clarkson] and Irving gave him the address here to send goodies along as they come. We were invited for a drink by an American couple, Mary and Terry.... They were pretty drunk and totally bizarre. From Texas and quite screwy. Terry wants terribly to just be a liver, an eater, and a fucker—but he has a mind and his thoughts haunt him: or, as he put it, 'thinking just rots my brain all to hell.' A colourful talker, he kept repeating the line from Zorba: "Boss, you think too much," obviously feeling himself suffering from the same curse. Mary had lots of pleading in her eyes and seems to be in her own very private hell. She doesn't have much respect or regard for him. As Irving said, it was very [Who's Afraid of] Virginia Woolf-ish, she telling him he only thinks of himself, telling him to shut up, he calling her a bitch, putting her down for thinking she's so superior to him. It was interesting—we couldn't make up people like that, that's for sure.

"Then we went for a walk, thinking if we went to the luxury hotel, Zazil-La, we'd be able to pick up some newspapers or magazines. No such luck. The info we have is that such items are not available on this island, only in Cancun. Too bad. We wonder if the rumour we heard is true, that China invaded Russia. We are so totally isolated here, the world could be at war and we wouldn't know. Irving has been busily thinking and talking a lot about wanting to not think so much anymore. So far he hasn't been able to find the off switch. He says he'd like to turn away from the whole literary scene and live a healthy outdoor life. Up till now, of course, he hasn't had any choice—he's been compelled to write. Now he says, he wonders if he has that choice. Personally, I don't think so."

Journal, January 21, 1980: "I'm feeling fairly shitty today, and I do mean that literally. Crampy and diarrhea; the weakness I suppose is just lack of food. Irving is fine though, and in fact has begun work—on a poem. He's very happy here now and says it's the best place he's ever come to. The fact that I'm not well doesn't seem to enter much. Never mind, I'll either get better or I'll leave. Didn't want to wander as far as the beach, so I sat by the pool most of the day and read. When Irving isn't reading himself (he does a fair bit of that), he's reading a book called *The Age of Atrocity*, which he's very excited about—says the author is the only other person he's ever come across who shares his visions. And since Irving is a genius (he so proclaims several times a day), this man must be too!"

Journal, January 22, 1980: "Much better today, can abandon thoughts of having to leave. Irving writing poems like mad—I think it's three so far. I've got down a first draft of one too. Delicious lobster for dinner...."

Journal, January 23, 1980: "What do ya' know, it rained, it poured today. I went to the pool and had a good long swim, watched the little German brother and sister play; a few drops fell, then stopped. I felt restless. So up I got and in I came and then down came the pour and I watched everybody else run for cover. Irving was here all day working—struggling—with a poem. It's 10:15 p.m. now and he's still there on the porch, banging away on the typewriter. We went to the market this morning for a pineapple and some bananas, had a good glass of freshly-squeezed orange juice while we were at it. I wrote to Mike at Fisher-Freemont and a long letter to my parents. Finished reading the book about the Mayans, began the one on Islam, and of course dipped into Colette a bit. Finished re-reading *My Apprenticeships*. This evening after dinner I read some of her to Irving, who agrees she is a superb prose writer, an absolute delight. He's into poems again now and is really hesitant and I think having some anxieties about beginning his memoirs. I think listening to Colette was a discouragement, the opposite of what I'd intended; she has such a mastery of style.

Irving sighed 'What a lot of work it is to perfect such a style.' Then he reminded himself that Pasternak's or Mandelstam's prose isn't like that, either—that, after all, hers is the style of the novelist ... slight consolation? At least we were feeling better today, though we're both still taking the lomatil. I hope we can stop it in a day or so. My mind says our bodies really ought to be adjusted by now; now, if only our stomachs would agree. Had a 'typical' Yucatan dish for dinner tonight—*padazules*, or something like that: a tortilla with chopped hard-boiled egg inside and a bit of a tomato sauce. Unfortunately, I really don't much like the taste of tortillas. But I put a lot of hot chili sauce all over it, pretty much killed the taste and left a lot of burn. Now I can't quench my thirst. Looking down, I see little Gina, the hotel doggie, chasing after first one leg, then the other; she clearly thought that walking, my walking, was a game invented for her delight."

Journal, Friday, January 25 1980: "Don't know what happened to yesterday. Except I remember it wasn't good for sitting in the sun and we found a truly good restaurant—there is one, hooray, and we ate like mad and didn't get sick feeling at all and went back again for dinner tonight. Today was nice half the day—at least we got some sun. Irving finally wrestled out his poem—it's a strong one and I wrote another one too. Am reading a collection of Chekhov stories and really enjoying them. Irving's dipping into the prose of Mandelstam and a book by William James on *Varieties of Religious Experience*."

Journal, Monday, January 28, 1980: "Spent some time over the last couple of days talking to Terry, a helluva nice guy who's trying to be a writer and has involved himself with a real mess of a female. I mean she's so sick, you can't talk to her—she's beyond layman's help, maybe beyond any help. A real neurotic who's draining him, and he's so vital and alive and curious, full of thoughts and ambitions. So we talked to him and talked to him, and Irving told him some down home truths and maybe he'll extricate himself and maybe he won't. Anyways it was an interesting encounter and Irving got a poem out of it. We exchanged addresses and I won't be surprised at all if we hear from him.

Harriet, Yucatan, 1980.

"The weather has been very spotty. The other day we were on the beach and the sun was shining and it was beautiful and the next minute it was pouring. Today, it got cloudy, so we decided to be tourists and see the things you're supposed to see—the Mayan ruin, the giant turtles, the coloured fishes. So we asked about a boat, only they wanted 300 pesos—that's too much for two people, it's okay if you're a group, but we are not. So we found a taxi and tried to harangue with the driver but couldn't bargain him down, so we agreed to the price—150 pesos—to go see everything. First came the turtles. We get to this beach, we walk along the plank and hopefully look down, expecting to see nests of turtles, or beds of turtles, or whatever bunches of turtles are called. All we see are two huge old turtles paddling around. Very disappointing; I took some pictures, for the record. Next—onward to the 'Mayan ruin.' We get to the other end of the island (maybe a ten-minute drive over bumps and around curves) and then walk over the rocks to a cliff-lookout point. There we see a small pile of stones—this is the 'Mayan ruin.'

Irving, Yucatan, 1980.

The sun is by now shining brightly and we are very sad not to be sunning ourselves in it. The place was a pretty spot and all, but what the hell.... So, onward to see the *pescados*. We get to Garrofan beach—a small stretch of sand, the usual thatched open-air huts, the usual tourists huddled over their *cervesas*. We descend the steps. We want to see the fish. We see some people in the water with masks, we see masks and snorkels for rent, and we understand the idea is to be in a bathing suit (we regrettably were not), rent a mask, stick your head in the water, and look at the fish. Marvellous. So we turn away, climb the steps, and drive back with our driver, who stops to pick up some friends on the way and blasts Spanish music out of his speakers in the back. Altogether a memorable adventure. Came back, put on bathing suits, and had a nice long swim in the pool here. We've decided to leave at the end of this week. I really didn't want Isla Mujeres to be all of Mexico I saw, for one thing. For another, the weather is spotty. For another, we're really isolated here, I mean you can't even get a newspaper or magazine, or get anything on the radio.

And the hotel seems to be falling apart. Sometimes the toilet doesn't flush, sometimes the door doesn't shut right, we've given up on trying to get a plug for the sink (I stuff the drain with a sock when I want to wash some things), or a bulb for the light by my bed. And forget hot water.

"So, what the hell. We're going to go to Cozumel. It's supposed to be a little more built up than this and we're told you can buy a bloody paper. I hope it's okay. If so, we'll stay there a week or ten days. Then to Merida as a base, while we see Chichen-Itza and Uxmal. We can see Tulum while staying at Cozumel. At least we'll see a few more places before leaving here, because I don't know about ever coming back. I mean it's been very nice and I'm certainly not sorry we came. But my stomach can't seem to adjust, for one thing. It's better than it was, but I still have to take the lomotil. Irving is fine, but that's still only one out of two. And if you have to be always so terribly careful, it takes something away from the overall pleasure of the trip. I spoke to my parents yesterday. They phoned, and it's established that we can go to the apartment after Doc Fogel leaves on Feb. 17. Which we've decided to do. So we have three more weeks in Mexico.

"I feel good about the decision to move on to Cozumel and so does Irving. I hope the mail he's expecting comes this week. Howard's supposed to be sending Adrienne's intro [to *For My Neighbours In Hell*]. We go to the post office and check every morning. This morning on the way we passed a beautiful young man sitting on the sidewalk, beer in hand (it was around 9:30) and a huge black bird sitting beside him. Turns out to be a pheasant—black with a white belly and a comb on his head that he made stand up and open like a fan when the man tried to touch him. Some other people passed and spoke to the man and he said he was sick and one of the others said he'd been sick a day before. Two days ago, while in the so-called lobby of the hotel here, a young man was at the desk asking for a doctor. Said he had a fever and diarrhea and vomiting; he was really in a bad way. So the desk man calls the one clinic here, gets off the phone, and says there is one doctor—but the doctor's sick too! Seems it gets everybody here, certainly all the tourists."

Later: "After dinner, which we didn't enjoy very much (Irving dreaming of steaks and saying if he doesn't see a fish again for a long time...) we took a walk over to Poc-na and got some Hershey bars. They were so utterly delicious and we were both enjoying them so much, Irving said if anyone had ever told him he'd be so thankful and happy for Coca-cola and Hershey bars, he'd have spat at them; however, they are the best tastes we've had.... Irving's just finished another poem, 'Ruina Maya,' that's come out of our explorations today and that I wrote about before. As we were walking back here, he observed that the problem here (aside from lousy food and no papers) [Note: it was Irving who had the great need for newspapers, by the way] is that there's no beauty, there's nothing beautiful except the sea, 'And you can't just look at the sea all the time.' He even said it's made him appreciate civilization! He also said he'd pack up and go tomorrow, if only we weren't waiting for the mail from Howard. God, how we hope the mail from Howard comes, already. It's beginning to be a bit of a drag. However, as long as it's good weather and we can take the sun and don't get sick again, it's okay."

Journal, Wednesday, January 30, 1980: "Yesterday was a lost day. It stayed cloudy and grey all day. We stayed in bed most of the time. Had one of the all-time worst suppers in a so-called restaurant we will not go back to. Today was perfect though, glorious, we took the sun all afternoon. Irving's working on yet another poem. I did one more, making the score thirteen for him, three for me. Today I wrote an article about our experiences [the good ones!] and am sending it off to the *Globe and Mail*; maybe they'll use it in the Saturday Travel Section. Irving says it's very good. He encouraged me to do it, after I read him a couple letters I'd written. He says I have a natural flair for it, a good style. *Nu,* who knows? We are enjoying each other. Considering we are together pretty much constantly, I think we get on amazingly well. Irving has taken to using the tape recorder, but not for his memoirs as planned. After he writes a poem, he reads it into the recorder, then we hear it—them—over and over. He's like a kid with a new toy, he's having such fun with it. Truly nothing gives him such pleasure as writing poems. Reading his books runs second, it seems. He seems to really have some kind of block about getting down to the memoirs. His new poem today is called 'Retribution,' and is a black prophetic poem. On the beach today, sun shining, feeling good, he was going on about how he smells burning flesh and foresees another world war. It seems the more beautiful the surroundings, the grimmer his visions and thoughts."

In reading those words, many years later, I was struck by a few things. How young my voice was; how consistent Irving always was; how a greater sense of humour would have helped me while living with him (although that kind of humour comes only with years); and how much in love we were. I have been on my own now for over thirty years and I have thought a lot about our years together and about what happened to end them, about whether I could ever be with another man in a lover or marital-type of relationship and about what it would take for me to embrace such a relationship, and about who I am now. I have thought about how Irving on the one hand didn't need anybody, but on the other hand, he always needed women. Understanding that, as his lover, his wife, his muse, or whatever, not only me, but any woman, was always going to come second to his writing. I did know that then and did fully accept that. That was never the problem, for us. I not only understood and accepted it, I embraced it as a part of him that I loved beyond explanation. There was the passion that kept growing over our years together, like a fire that feeds on itself. There was my love of Irving the poet, the creator, and my fascination with living with him, with being up close to that creative process, watching poems take shape. I was even fascinated with his fascination of chaos, the chaos he would either create, or just allow to happen, waiting to see what would emerge and if it would become another poem. I was crazy enough to enter his craziness, and be in that heaven and hell with him. Nevertheless, I was still young, no matter how mature I was for my age, and he knew this and it was part of our torture, part of his torture in particular, to want me so much, to want to be with me, and to be so afraid that we'd be doomed, if only because of the age difference. But the romantic in him wanted to override that, and did.

There is no way to rationally account for what draws a man and a woman together. Whether married or not, whatever the differences in age, or race, or ethnicity, if there is that connection, that fire in the belly, that melting into each other when they embrace, that shakes them to their molecules and takes them outside of this realm we recognize as the "real" world, then I believe they must be together. This sort of thing may cause problems, no question about it, especially if one of the people happens to be married. But I believe absolutely that when this passion, this connection happens—and it happens rarely, maybe two or three times in a lifetime, at most—it is a sin to ignore it. There are universal rules that override the moral conventions we impose, or allow society to impose, and which we conventionally accept. Those universalities operate from another realm, and a couple enters that other realm when they forge this kind of connection. They can try to analyze it, rationalize it, or reject what's going on seven ways for Sunday, but it's a waste of time and energy. And an even greater waste to lose something so precious as that connection. Some might say it is immoral, or amoral, but to hell with them I say. "There is a field beyond good and evil. Will you meet me there?" Rumi asked. If someone can't meet me there, well that's their decision, and I fully understand; but as for me, I will not turn away from that kind of connection, that kind of passion, that kind of recognition of the other once the line has been crossed and we enter that realm beyond rules and conventions. The sin is not in embracing such a connection, the sin is in turning away from it. Anyways, that's the way it reads in my book. And yet, our marriage ended even if the love did not.

18.

JOURNAL, TUESDAY, FEBRUARY 5, 1980: "Worlds away from the last entry. We left Isla Mujeres on Friday morning. Thursday night Irving was settling the bill and the so-called manager was there and Irving wanted to know what the bill came to in U.S.$ and the man said he didn't want to be bothered with that, and Irving persisted and the man began shouting at us, and I said he had no right to talk to us like that, and he said to me 'Fuck you.' He also called us 'scum.' So we went for a little stroll to calm me down and with the help of a lovely lady shopkeeper where we'd been buying our drinks, got the names and addresses of a number of very important people, including the owners of Posada del Mar, the heads of the tourist boards for the province of Quintana Roo and for the whole of the Yucatan, the governor and the head of the newspaper for the Yucatan. Then we proceeded to write a masterly letter to the owner, copies to all the others, recounting what happened and hopefully cooking the stupid son of a bitch's ass. We mailed it all off yesterday, so perhaps by *manana* the old shit will hit the fan. I hope so.

"Our journey began on Friday a.m. with another one of those memorable boat rides where far too many people crowd onto a little little boat! Really it's awful that they don't have proper-sized boats for the loads of people being transported. And there's no supervision or anything, no life preservers, nothing. I suppose it will take a disaster or two, the loss of a few hundred lives, before it changes. After all, people are expendable; their lives don't count for much. The boat was way down in the water with the weight. As we went, waves would occasionally wash into the boat, wetting all of us. I thought we might wind up shark food all through it. Miracle of miracles, after a mere one hour of fear, we arrived safely. Just made the bus for the next part of the journey. Another hour over very boring terrain, through Cancun onto Playa del Carmen, for the next ferry ride. With dread in our hearts we walked to the dock and who could believe it—a regular, appropriate-sized boat awaited us, with a boarding plank and two decks! Happily, marvelling, we got on board. The boat took off. It quickly became apparent why we were on a substantially-sized boat—a smaller one would have been smashed to smithereens. The waters were incredibly rough and if we didn't have good sea-legs, it would have been throw-up time. We rolled and pitched and at one point Irving grimly remarked, 'Wouldn't it be funny if *this* boat cracked in half,' after we'd been so relieved to see that it was so big and all. Along the way, a school of dolphins joined us and it really was fantastic watching them leap alongside of us. Finally we reached our destination—Cozumel—after a three-hour journey. Since Cozumel is another island, south of Isla Mujeres, it would seem reasonable to have a boat service from Isla Mujeres to here. But, as we have learned very well by now, just because something makes sense and seems obvious to us is no reason at all to expect to find it here. Thus the convoluted journey of ferry-bus-ferry.

"Upon clambering over tires to get up to the dock, we were besieged by people thrusting their cards at us, hustling everyone to take them to their respective hotels. We finally went with one of them. We got to the hotel, checked out the rooms, and walked out, fast. Trusty guidebook in hand, I left Irving with the bags and took off in search of a hotel. We settled in El Marques: it was clean, well-lit, and well-located. Dumped our bags and went for food, came back suffering slightly from culture shock. After Isla Mujeres, Cozumel was like coming back to civilization— more or less. Nice-looking restaurants and stores with all kinds of pretty things in them, paved streets, my God it was almost overwhelming. We eagerly grabbed a *Time Magazine* to see what was going on in the world. It must have been 5:00 or 6:00 when we dozed off, supposedly for a nap. We woke up briefly at 11:30

and went right back to sleep again and didn't get up till about 7:00 the next morning, never minding about dinner. I guess we were exhausted. When we got up, we decided to change hotels because El Marques was nice but didn't have a balcony and Irving likes to write on a balcony.

"We footed it again, round the block to Hotel Suites Elizabeth. The place was somehow sweet, the *senoras* were smiling and nice, and there was a clean room with a balcony and so in we moved. And what a balcony—in the 'garden' over which we looked, was an Irish setter and a monkey who amused us with his swinging on the clotheslines. We explored, then, some of Cozumel and discovered there is no beach access in town. In fact, the only places that have beaches, it seemed, are the luxury hotels, which at $75-$115 a night were definitely out of our price range. Yes, we learned, there are some lovely beaches. But they are located just far enough away so you can't walk, and of course there are no buses. You can rent a car or motorbike or bicycle, or take a taxi, or try your luck at hitching a ride.

"Meanwhile, we had some decent food in a cheerful, lively restaurant—no flies at all, good service and even a hot—I mean hot—cup of coffee or tea. Amazing to eat and not feel sick afterwards. We explored and went to sleep. Unfortunately, we were awakened at dawn, if that: first the rooster on our left started cock-a-doodle-dooing, then the dog started barking, and best of all—the turkey on our right started gobble-gobbling. That turkey kept up a racket non-stop. After two nights (even with using the ear plugs we bought), the turkey got the best of us, and we had to move again. Besides, there were only very narrow twin beds and they made fucking very difficult.

"Today we packed up again and moved into a good place with the incredible name: Hotel Barracuda! At last, peace and comfort. We have a nice-sized room with two double beds, and it's clean and there's hot water and a good shower and a balcony overlooking the sea and palm trees and even a tiny bit of beach, sand, even chairs to lie on! Also a mini fridge. We went to the stores and got sardines and rolls and peanut butter and jam and wine and beer and cokes and water and Kahlua, stocked up the fridge and enjoyed our lunch on the balcony. Heaven, at last.

Sunday we rented a jeep—a tin box with worn-out gear-shift—it was cute—and drove all over the island, saw two of the luxury hotels. We drove to a nice beach, took the sun all afternoon, had a good day. The island is mostly jungle wilderness, but the water is clear and unbelievably beautiful tourquoise in colour. There's even a good pizza restaurant and we delighted in every mouthful. Today, after we settled at the Barracuda, we went down to the tiny beach; the weather is very so-so, there was just a bit of sun. Irving went for a swim and came back exclaiming it was the best ever, anywhere, including Greece. [Note: This is typical Irving.] Then we came up and enjoyed the balcony, the food, the bed and the shower, in that order. I'm particularly delighted with how the sheets, towels, etc., are all monogrammed H.B. Obviously, this is the place for us. It's hard to believe, we finally seem to have found what we've been looking for."

Journal, Friday February 8, 1980: "While I've been quite lazy, just lying about and reading a lot, Irving has been writing and talking a lot. We're on the beach here at the Barracuda, Irving is sitting and shaking his head and muttering beside me, and he's just picked up his head long enough to tell me that the poem he's writing now is absolutely so great, so magnificent, it's the ultimate final statement on the theme he's been exploring. He keeps writing about the Holocaust. The other morning—and first thing in the morning is not my very best time—he began again with his images of 'tresses of murdered Jewesses,' and on about all the horrors and atrocities in man and that men do to men, and I'm afraid I didn't respond too terrifically. But in the evening he let forth a tirade on how he's not writing about the Holocaust only, per se, but using it to show the other things. Today he was saying how Dante could write about hell, and how difficult today is the hell we've created, where goodness doesn't save anyone, necessarily, from evil or torture or death. On the contrary, how many of the people in the camps were 'good' people, yet 90% were destroyed. He also said, the other night, how love is the ability to accommodate another's mania.

"Last night we went to the movies, to see *Same Time Next Year*, in English with Spanish subtitles. It was cheap—40 pesos for the two of us—and it was a nice big theatre, in good condition.

"Yesterday I went out to do some chores and when I came back Irving was on the phone. It was a woman from the *Toronto Star*, no less, interviewing him for an article on—us! To coincide with the *Love Poems* coming out on the 14th—Valentines Day. The *Star* wanted our story—older poet marries woman 36 years younger, etc., our meeting, our courtship, and so on. It sure is a good story, after all. Irving said he was really going great guns and saying the most beautiful things about me, and what a pity I wasn't there to hear him. I am sorry I missed it, but it'll be fun to see the article.

"Well, a few hours later now and Irving has just read me the poem 'Hells.' It came out of what he was talking to me about earlier, beginning with Dante and his vision of hell. The Holocaust as metaphor for our time. It's a biggie. And from there to how many poems, now, have come out of our talks—or his talking to me. And from there to how, because he felt [not that way with former partners], he'd seek out others to talk to, Dorothy or Eleanor or Marion or Musia, mainly Musia. How he regrets that through those years, so much was lost, what could have been turned into poems remained as just talk, and talk that vanished into the air; how Musia, in a way, got the best of him then, cause she'd give him a brandy and coffee and off he'd go, talking, and ideas would come and of course he couldn't just suddenly stop and go write a poem, so thoughts evaporated in conversation."

Journal, Sunday, February 10, 1980: "Today began grey and cloudy, the sand wet from rain. Irving began with prophesies to match. He says that Europe doesn't really want freedom, democracy and it's only a matter of time before they become communist—or rather, state capitalists. That, as in Russia, there is the privileged upper class, which has wealth and all the attendant comforts. What they don't have are labour problems, strikes, etc. No shit disturbers, because if there are any they get shipped off to Gulag. And he says that the equivalent wealthy, the power people, in Europe, will decide—what for do they need the aggravations that come with 'freedom?' And they'll opt for the same sort of state capitalism. He says he sees the French refusal to take a stand firmly against the Russian invasion of Afghanistan, and the French declining to meet with the U.S. in a joint united protest, as a sign pointing to his prophesy.

"The day stayed not nice. As the weather was lousy, we decided to do some gift shopping. We got something for David and Ken [my cousin who was arranging readings in Florida after we left Mexico], and Bill, then had lunch. When we got back to our room, we found it emptied of all znnour things. The woman at the desk didn't speak English, but we understood that there had been a previous reservation and the person was a diver and had to have a room on a lower floor, and so we were moved upstairs to another room. We've been in hotels before where we had to change rooms, but never was it done in such a manner! I was absolutely furious and so was Irving. We don't like someone going into our drawers, going through all our personal belongings like that. And we'd only been gone a short while. Why had nobody told us beforehand? It is the final straw for me. And that's not all, either: we can only have the room upstairs for three nights. After that, the hotel is booked and we have to get out. When we first arrived, the guy had said it [a change of rooms] was a possibility, but he'd also said there were usually some cancellations and that even if we did have to leave, he could transfer us to another hotel with which they were in some way associated, at the same price. Now, of course, there's no such talk. In response to my question where will we go, I got the answer, 'Wherever you want.' Well, I want out. We have this room for three more nights. Tomorrow, first thing, it's off to the Mexicana office to see if we can get out of here on Wed. a.m.

"We spoke to Ken the other night, who had the good news that he's gotten two readings lined up for Irving—at the catholic school, whatever it's called, and at Florida State U. Now that's good to hear. He's done more than anyone else, so far."

19.

JOURNAL, APRIL 9, 1980: "Well, I don't know what happened, I just stopped writing for no reason I'm aware of. We did get out a day or two after the last entry and it was bitter to the very end. Last-minute hassles with the bill and Irving had real murder in his eyes. Upon arrival in Miami, I called Ken [my cousin, dear friend, lawyer, and fan of the arts], who luckily was in and we went right to his apartment. Our foray to the supermarket was delirious delight and we had to severely restrain ourselves from grabbing everything in sight off the shelves. It took a few days before we could adjust to the culture shock. We were in Florida about three weeks or so and didn't look at fish—in spite of how good it is there—just ate a lot of meat and got healthy again.

"Irving did his two readings. The one at Barry College was really wonderful: great turnout, great response, good questions and request period afterwards. It was a great success. In the evening he read at Florida International University; it's a commuter college and the reading was at night. It's a monstrous army barracks-looking sprawled-out place. There were all of about twenty people there. But I bet those twenty people will long remember the reading they got that evening. Irving read as though the place was packed and he was marvellous. The audience had some requests ("Would you read more of your animal poems?")—not to be believed and we laughed it all off and went for Haagen Das ice cream afterwards, which is among the greatest ice creams in the world, and definitely one of my very favourite foods. While in Miami, we became very good friends with Ken, who really is a large cut above the average.

Irving, Harriet, and Ken at Florida State University, 1980.

We shared some really memorable moments and had a lot of fun with him.

"Since returning it's been a lot of running around up and back between Toronto and here [Niagara-on-the-Lake]. So much so, in fact, we've pretty much decided that we have to move to Toronto. It's just ridiculous. We spend as much—if not more—time there as here. The packing and unpacking, moving of things and all entailed is very wearying. Irving just leads too active a life to be anywhere but in the city. It's kind of a shame, as we really like this house—especially I love my kitchen and bedroom, and Irving loves the kitchen and his den—but maybe we'll get lucky and find a good place in Toronto. Anyways, it doesn't have to be for a while yet.

"The most incredible thing happened: Irving got a letter from the office of the President of the University of Toronto asking him to be Writer-in-Residence there for the 1981-82 academic season. We were bowled over—the U. of T., bastion of establishment WASPdom, who've tried their best to ignore Irving all these years ... well, we recovered from the shock and next day sent a letter of acceptance. Wonders will, I guess, never cease....

Irving and Harriet, after a reading at Florida State University, 1980.

For My Neighbours in Hell and *An Unlikely Affair,* the Rath book [Dorothy Rath wrote a book about her friendship with Irving] are both out. The former hasn't been reviewed yet; the latter was. A good review from Ken Adachi in the *Star,* and a super-bad, ignorant, distorted and slanted one from Duffy in the *Globe.* Irving wrote a letter to the Editor in response, and it was published today with a nice big headline. Duffy, whoever the jerk is, will be sorry he took on Irving, if he isn't already. Just wait till we're at the U. of T....

"Were in Montreal last weekend. The people who are active in keeping before the public eye the business of the Soviet dissidents held a symbolic Seder at the Sheraton Mount Royal and Irving was asked to read his poem for Scharansky and a couple others besides. The turnout was disappointing—only a couple hundred instead of the thousand expected. Irving said a few words and read his poems very strongly and beautifully, the people responded most enthusiastically. Irwin Cotler was there. He seems a serious, decent sort of guy. Irving is very proud Cotler is a former student of his. [Note: At Irving's funeral, Irwin came over to me, took my hand in his, and gently said he remembered the night Irving and I ran into him in downtown Montreal, and Irving introduced Irwin to me as 'his spiritual son.' It was very moving to me that Irwin remembered that moment and shared the memory with me. He is an exceptionally decent man, who made time, in the midst of a cross-country tour during an election, to come to Irving's funeral.] After the ceremony, we marched to the Soviet Embassy, with a police escort, along Sherbrook St. to Musee, with a tape recorder playing appropriate music and a CBC TV camera filming. However, it never was aired. Irving and I were in the frontlines— he holding high a torch they'd given him, me beside him holding high *Neighbours*. Figured a little publicity can't hurt. Too bad it wasn't used. Still, it was a truly moving evening and we were really glad to be a part of it.

"Yesterday two more nice things happened. I got a letter from Monitor Publishing Co. in Beverly Hills, California—they're assembling an anthology of American verse, garnered from all the various publications and wanted permission to use my poem 'Gladioli For My Mother,' which was in *Poetry Canada*. I'm delighted, of course, and so is Irving who says it's an important and wonderful thing. Then Irving got a call from Scharansky's cousin. He had turned on the radio recently and lo and behold there was Irving reading his poem for Scharansky. He called to say how much it had meant to him. Irving was very moved. Also Terry—our friend in Mexico—called to say hello and we had a nice chat with him. He did leave that wacko lady and is finishing his novel. One more life that Irving has profoundly changed. He really scared the shit out of Terry—or so Terry said.... He seems a really nice guy, so different from who you meet here. Very refreshing. I bet he comes to visit us this summer.

"Tomorrow Irving is off to Calgary for a reading and I'll spend the couple days in Toronto, playing with my mama. We're looking forward to the beautiful summer here [Niagara-on-the-Lake]—all those gorgeous fruits and veggies and sunbathing in the garden.

"We bought a new car—it should be ready in about a month. We plan on breaking it in by driving to New Jersey and Philadelphia. My Baba has expressed a strong desire to meet my husband and as Irving has never been to Philadelphia, we've decided to go. It's an interesting city, and there's that wonderful bookstore, so we should have a good time."

In a letter to Andrea, dated April 16, 1980, I wrote: "At last! It seems so long since I've written you a real letter. Today's a good day for it. Yesterday we returned home again after a few days in Toronto. As always, we were very busy and active, there always seem to be so many things to do, both chores and things we want to do. Now we're here for a whole two weeks and I have a chance to get things in order again. The running back and forth is really beginning to wear on us terribly. Especially me, since I do the packing and unpacking, most of the driving, and am after all trying to run a house here. Carting groceries up and back, trying to keep house and laundry clean etc., etc. But it's coming to a close. We've decided we have to move to Toronto. Irving (and therefore me) lead too active a life to be here. I'm afraid until he's ready to be a whole lot quieter than he is now, we have to be in the city. Also, he's accepted an offer to be Writer-in-Residence at the University of Toronto for the 1981 academic year. That really is a great victory for him, as the U. of T. is the bastion of establishment WASPdom and they've tried their best to ignore the outrageous Layton. He's really thrilled and so am I. This September he'll be giving one course at Sheridan, a community college in Oakville, just for the first term. It will mean once a week to Oakville (one hour from here) and then we'll probably go to Toronto for the night (half an hour from Oakville).

"We are looking forward tremendously to the summer here; it's such a beautiful place to be in those months. I wish you could come stay here for some time in the summer and see how lovely it is before we move. Beautiful farm and vineyard country, pick your own fruits if you want—the sweetest strawberries and raspberries, blueberries, all veggies. And the garden is so nice. And there's the Shaw Festival, lots of good plays to see. We'll be a little sorry to move, because we like the house so much." [Note to reader: Reading this now, it seems such madness.... We had worked hard and put money into making our home in Niagara-on-the-Lake so lovely—why did we not stick it out longer? Was Irving actually suffering from what he had previously identified as Aviva's "domomania"? I wonder, but will never know.]

Letter to Andrea continued: "But I hope we'll get lucky and find a house we like as much in Toronto. We know the area we'd like—the Annex—sort of mid-downtown, generally the ethnic and university area, west of Avenue Rd., around Bloor. Do you remember Toronto well enough to have an idea what I'm talking about? The good thing is we have lots of time for the move. We were talking about it last night and figured if we moved in the late fall—end Oct. or Nov., it would be good. But, if we don't find a house, it can wait a little longer. I don't imagine we'll have trouble selling this house for a good price. I'm a little sorry to give up the house, but sort of excited about moving back to Toronto too. Excited isn't exactly the right word—let's say it's the sensible thing to do and I'm not sad about it. Also, if I want to have a child—and I really do—it's better for me to be in Toronto, where my doctor is—and Uncle, who will see to it that I'm well taken care of. I stopped any forms of birth control after my Feb. period and thought I'd get pregnant first crack. Wrong. Got a period in March. Now we're on a diet. I was advised to take off some weight before getting pregnant. The big diet push is now, so I'm thinking maybe I should wait a month or so. But it's so nice, fucking without any diaphragms or pills or anything. I love the natural-ness of it. So maybe I'll just let it happen and if I get pregnant, that's that. I really do want to have a little girl.

"Got a letter from a publishing house [Monitor Book Company] in California, asking permission to use my poem 'Gladioli For My Mother' in a a lovely big hardcover book, *Anthology of Magazine Verse and Yearbook of American Poetry*, 1981 edition [edited by Alan F. Pater]. They go through all the hundreds of small mags and lit. publications in U.S. and Canada and make a selection for their anthology. They saw my poem in *Poetry Canada* and want to use it. Great delight for me. Also sent two poems (written in Mexico) to *Athanor*, a lit. mag. Published in Montreal, and they'll be in the next issue. Well, what do you know....

"Am writing some poems and they're good—but it's never as much as I like and it's not an easy process. Irving is a great help, very supportive and encouraging. Want very much to do a screenplay this summer. We plan to be pretty much here all the summer and I'll do less cooking and more writing.

"Have read and am reading some interesting books. Fania Fenelon's *Playing for Time,* a remarkable account of her experiences as a member of the orchestra in Auschwitz concentration camp. Quite a story and an insight into the horrors man can commit against man. Then I read Artur Rubenstein's autobiog, the second volume just published. What a beautiful man and what a great liver! I mean an appetite and zest for life that's beautiful to read about. Then I read some very good junk, a novel called *The Shining* by Stephen King. Terrific junk, I loved it. I wanted to read it because Stanley Kubrick (director of such masterpieces as *2001, A Clockwork Orange, Dr. Strangelove, Barry Lyndon*—biggies) is making a movie of *The Shining* and it's sort of a horror story that I love anyways and I was curious to read it and now I'm even more curious to see the movie. Presently into a book called *Prophets without Honor* by Grunfeld—a look into the intellectual life in Europe, especially Germany, up until the war, stories of many poets and writers—not just Freud, Kafka, and Einstein, but many lesser-known writers—most of whom were exterminated in the Holocaust. One woman in particular has so far caught my interest, a poet named Else Lasker-Schuller, who was a beautiful soul, wrote some lovely stuff, and was a real nut. I may yet do the screenplay on a sort of fictionalized but based-on-fact treatment of her story; if I do, the title to be *The Blue Miracle,* taken from a line of hers. There were so many great souls wiped out. And the thing is to read it and not just get depressed, but try to be aware of what happened and how it happened and what kind of people the Jews were and are. And what things people can do. Not to be aware of it all is a terrible lack, especially for a Jew. Have another couple dozen books lined up and oh my will there ever be time enough to read all the things I want to?

"...We've bought a car—or rather, have ordered it and are awaiting delivery, which should be in three to four weeks. It's a cute Chevrolet Citation, red outside and black inside with bucket seats, FM stereo, and a couple of other luxury options. Spent some fair time and energy looking around, asking questions, driving a lot of cars (it was suggested by one dealer that I get a job test-driving!), and checking the consumer guides. Citations got lots of points in important things and we liked the looks of it, and it seems to drive okay, a fair bit of spunk for a V6. Am eager for delivery. We've planned to drive to New Jersey when we get it—I have to see my Baba, it's been nearly a year and she's never seen Irving and wants to, and he's never been to Philadelphia, so we decided to make the trip and break in the car. [Note: My mother's family—her two sisters and her mother—my grandfather had died in the sixties—lived in south Jersey, just across the Philly border.] We're kicking around the notion of taking in Cambridge etc. while we're at it. This would maybe be mid-end May, or so, depending on if we get car when we're supposed to. Does this notion make any sense to you? Or is it a lousy paper-writing end-of-year bad time? We're easy. Do give thought to coming by this summer. I would love for you to see what was my first house and it really is pretty here. Your last scribble threw in something about a lover. *Nu???* Happy Spring! Miss you, and love you— Irving sends love, and wants to know how you are—and so do I— and "if Jake [Andrea's big black standard poodle] is farting with his accustomed vigour!"

Journal, May 11, 1980: "What happens to time? Yesterday the For Sale sign went up on our house. I've spoken to a couple of agents in Toronto and next time we go in, we will begin the job of looking for a house in the city. Irving just leads too busy a life for us to be here. *I'm* ready to retire, but *he's* not. He's into too many things, and it's impractical for us to stay here. It's a pity in a way, 'cause I like our home so much. But then again, I suppose it will be more exciting to be in the city, with access to all the action. We have to be lucky to find a house in the area we like for the price we can afford. If this house doesn't sell, we'll have to stay till it does. So the future is once again full of uncertainty and the sooner it's all settled, the better. I hate the uncertainty most of all.

"We are still awaiting our car, which the man said should be ready by the end of this week (for my birthday), but we'll see. I don't know yet if car men tell the truth but I won't be surprised if we have to keep on waiting. Spring as always is a beautiful miracle to watch happening, especially here in the country. Irving has been writing poems, two in the past couple weeks, 'Herzl' and 'Eternal Recurrence.' Both are for the next book, *Europe and Other Bad News.*

"This is the third month I'm not using any kind of contraceptive, hoping to get pregnant. Funny how I always thought right away, first month, I'd get pregnant and it hasn't happened. I would be happy to miss a period this month; that would be the nicest birthday present. I'll be thirty-two this coming Friday.

"I began, this past week, finally to write my horror story. It's going okay, some days a lot flows, some days a paragraph is pulling teeth with no gas. I must do it though, I must and so I am. We also have two cats now: Princess is eight or nine months old, white with black stockings like a whore on her rear legs and black markings on her face and green eyes. Tiger is a ten-week-old ball of grey fluff, all grey even his eyes and maybe part angora cause he's so fluffy. He has a nice little body and is growing fast. She's very maternal with him. He sucks her and jumps on her head and plays with her tail and she mumbles and carries on a non-stop verbal stream about everything in her cat universe. They're inseparable and a delight to watch together. The house was just too barren with no animals or anything. We went on a diet and have taken off about ten or eleven lbs. so far. It's a total drag, but what the hell, we have to do it and at least we're seeing results, which makes going on bearable."

Journal, May 18, 1980: "Just a brief entry so not too much time will go by and become empty space. Friday was my birthday, thirty-two now. It was a peculiar day, a little difficult. Irving and I had a little talk about thoughtfulness and the (however silly) importance of my birthday to me. We were not on the same wavelength and my needs were not being fulfilled, but I think it will be better now. The nicest part was the ice cream cone. Sheer heaven, after all the dieting deprivation. Spoke to the car man—they lie too—we have to wait another two weeks, he says now.... Parents called on the 16th [my birthday] as usual and sent a huge beautiful arrangement of flowers. They told me my present, amber beads, is waiting at the house. We have to go to Toronto tomorrow, so I'll see them. Irving is doing an interview for CBC radio, in spite of my very strong objections. After all the controversy in the *Globe* lately and nasty words between him and the CBC, ending with his saying they stink and he'll hold his nose every time he passes them on Jarvis St. It seems very wrong to me to do an interview there. However, he has not the sense of right and wrong that I do and, as usual, will rationalize and then do exactly as he pleases. So there."

Journal, May 29, 1980: "Well, he did the interview at CBC and we're going to listen to it tonight on the radio. It's a new show, the guy seemed nice and, as he's new at it, he hadn't become too CBC-pricky yet. [Forgive me dear CBC: in subsequent years, I loved the CBC and, in fact, still do. When I was raising Samantha alone and travelling all over Canada for my job, I used to say that the only two things that united Canada were the CBC, and hatred of Rogers [cable TV services]. As for the amber beads, they weren't at all what I wanted or had in mind, so I took them back to the store. Irving and I spent a day going a lot of places looking for the right amber beads. We didn't find them. Apparently what I want is very rare and so very expensive if they are found at all. But in my favourite jewellery store, Secrett, we did find a beautiful pair of amber earrings set in 18k gold and I loved them, and Irving is buying them for me, even though they cost quite a bit. They'll be the most special earrings....

"Our car is ready now and tomorrow morning we're off to Toronto again. We'll get the car and get haircuts and I'll stock up on meats and fish and cheese again and hopefully we'll see some movies and after brunch on Sunday will come back. It's two days to go to the end of the month and I haven't got my period yet, and I'm hoping so terribly much that I won't. It's very late now. I asked Uncle last night if it was time for a pregnancy test, but he said it was a little early yet, and if I had one it might come out negative, so rather than be disappointed I'll just wait another couple of weeks. Irving thinks I am. I've stopped smoking just in case he's right. My tits sure are tender.... He's working on poems, revising some that existed already. He's so delighted with the Else Lasker-Shuller one and the Herzl one."

Reading this journal entry, I am once again struck at how blithely I recount an event like looking for amber beads; at this current point in life, with my grey hair and being the same age

Irving was when we married, I have such a different perspective. Now, I can only shudder at the thought of his 'spending a day' looking for the 'right' amber beads, the ones I had in mind, and eventually buying me amber earrings. I wear those earrings to this day and I still love them, and all I would remember about them—were it not for the journal—is that he bought them for me out of love, and it was a happy time. Only now can I see and appreciate how devoted he was to me, to our love. I know now that he did things for me that he had never done for any other wife or lover. I also remind myself, however, of what I brought to him then: my youth, my beauty, my energetic devotion to his creative process, to the man he was, and even a child. And yet....

Journal, Wed June 4, 1980: "No period, hooray! Going to have the test on Friday and find out for sure if I'm pregnant. We bought some champagne today (Mumm's, yet), in anticipation of making the announcement to my parents at dinner. They don't know anything yet; we haven't breathed a word. I didn't want to talk about a 'maybe baby.' If the test comes out negative, I'll be disappointed. But I don't think it will. My tits are swollen and tender and I do feel a little weird.

"Irving has written two great poems already this week. Yesterday he wrote 'The Wheel.' It's about a few things: the Eastern notion of wheel of life, a wheel of torture, and the wheel going round the indifference of nature to man. The imagination in it is wonderful and original, and is so close in a way to the richness that was in some of Irving's poetry in the first wild flush at the beginning. He feels it to be so and says it makes him a little sad because he should have always been able to write like that, but because his life was as tension-filled as it was, his energies were diverted and fragmented. Only now, he says, he has sort of come into his own true self, with the kind of inner peace, sureness, and clear-headedness he needs to write these kinds of poems. They certainly are a departure from anything he's written in a lot of years. The imagination is just fantastic. The other poem he just wrote today. It's called 'The Annunciation,' and it made me cry when he gave it to me to read. It's about my (assumed but as yet not confirmed) pregnancy. We went for a walk to the post office; it was a beautiful day. When we came back, I went to work down here and he went to work upstairs and when he came down for lunch a couple of hours later he gave me the poem. It's very very very very beautiful. There are some enchanting images in it and the tone is so tender and loving, it should be a classic, a standard for all men to give to their wives when they become pregnant. He said to his knowledge there isn't another poem like it. There are poems to children, sure, but not to the pregnancy. So here we are. It was a beautiful day in all kinds of ways.

"A letter came yesterday from Rizzardi and today from Francesca. Both claim they don't know what happened—of course—to the plans for the tour. (Good old Freddie Prinze: 'Is no my job'). Anyways, we'll never know and it doesn't matter. Thanks to Francesca, we now have the names and locations of a number of the people from the various academies in Italy, so if need be we can communicate with them ourselves re: the proposed tour for next spring. And Rizzardi has written that it's important for Irving to be at Taormina in March '81. So we are talking—no, more than talking—we are actually getting it together for a trip to Italy next spring. I really was disappointed it fell through this year. It's been four years since Irving and I were in Europe together—*Four years!* And how did *that* ever happen?

"A few weeks back we were watching a show on TV, a CBC show called *Cities* and that Sunday night it was Melina Mercouri taking us on a tour of Athens. Well, Irving was loving it all so much. When it was over, I took one look at him and it was all over his face, the longing, so I said, "Look, if you miss it so terribly and you really want to go—go!" So we talked about it some over the next few days and we talked about my going too. But I really can't. Even if we could put together the money, our house is for sale and I can't be away for any length of time. And most importantly, if I am pregnant, in August I'd be three months or so gone and this being my first, I don't think I'd be keen on taking off for an extended trip to Greece (especially remembering the severe food poisoning I had there before). So, the conclusion of it all is Irving just got his letter from Canada Council saying they'll give him the money to go on the trip and he's gonna go in August for three weeks or maybe a month but I hope not cause that's really too long for me. And he says I'm very sweet to have said he should go. And don't I really mind. And I say look, I'd rather go with than stay behind while you go. But, there are some very good reasons why I shouldn't. And the Can Council money is there. If it could be converted to cash, nice, but it can't. If it could be deferred to another year, nice, but it can't. It's travel money and it's for this year and if it's not used up, it's just gone. Blown. So it really does make sense for him to use it and go. How rational and practical I am sometimes, it's horrifying.

"And we did get the car last Friday, and it's a delight. I love it. Irving hasn't driven it yet, he's afraid he'll bang it up first time out!"

On June 27th, 1980, I wrote to Andrea: "Have to spill it right away, no point trying to be cutesy about it—I am pregnant—and that's the happiest thing I've had to tell you in a long time. I really am knocked up, what do ya' know. Preggers. *Enceinte.* Happy, need I add. Somebody Amber (as she's being called thus far) is supposed to come in January, all going well. The 27th, doc said, give or take two weeks. I've been feeling mostly very well. For a while, I had some evening queasiness—backwards of course, being me—evening instead of morning. Felt great in the morning, but by dinnertime I had waves of nausea and couldn't eat meat or fish at all. That seems to have pretty much passed now and I'm doing really good. Irving is happy and proud and has written a poem called 'The Annunciation' that is one of the loveliest, most joyous lyrics possible. More good news: Gordon Weaver and Steve Rose phoned recently with an offer I have accepted, to be the Canadian (literary) representative for Barrich Productions. [Note: Steve Rose had been Senior Vice President of Worldwide Marketing for Paramount Pictures. Based in the Gulf and Western building, in Manhattan, he and I had met when I was handling Publicity and Promotions for Paramount Canada. We had developed a friendship that has lasted up to this very day. He and Gordon Weaver, who had been President of Worldwide Marketing at Paramount, teamed up after they both left Paramount, and created Barrich Productions, seeking scripts that would be produced under the Paramount banner.] Basically, I am to read mss., screenplays, stories, magazine articles, etc. and if I find something I think could make a good movie, to pass it to them for potential development. Theoretically, I could also become involved in setting up co-productions between U.S. and Canada. All of which is very nice, because it means I can have some involvement again with the film business, which I like, plus the writing scene and I don't have to be in an office at all, my time will be mine to organize as I will. I'm delighted, seems like a sweet deal to me. Maybe I'll even make some bucks, which sure would be nice too, since we don't exactly have an overabundance of $$....

"We have had no offers on our house yet. It will be much easier when it's sold. I really want to be settled in Toronto by Oct. I'm laying off looking for the moment—have seen a lot already and even if I found something, I couldn't do anything about it till this one's sold and I don't like playing with myself that much. Oh shit, what a nuisance it all is. I just want it over and done, is all. I despise domestic and financial matters like that....

"It's been—weather-wise anyways—an incredibly lousy summer so far. But I have this thing in me and when I think about it and I do a lot I feel very happy it's there and everything else is less important beside it. Beside *her.* So what's doing? Love, Harriet."

Letter to Andrea dated September 20, 1980: "Your letter ... came in the midst of my own blackness, which by the end of two weeks had me emotionally wrung out and which is only now beginning to be over, I think.... Briefly, here's the story. Every week—or very nearly every week—we've been going into Toronto. We stayed at my parents'. They, as you know, in spite of all their early resistance, have totally accepted Irving, and offered him all the kindness, generosity, thoughtfulness with which you are familiar. It became a pattern that each and every time we were in the city, off would go dear Irving for a whole afternoon or a whole evening (incl. dinner sometimes) with A. and, presumably, David. Oftimes when he'd return, it would come out that in fact the son had only been around briefly, or not at all. So, it was in fact, time with A. I was unhappy about it and said so and he'd gone on a harangue about how foolish that was on my part, etc., etc. and so I was just trying to keep a lid on it, but the tension was there and mounting. So here's the set up: we're at my parent's house and each time we're in, they see Irving leaving me and going off to A. For a long time, I tried to appease and placate them and convince them that it wasn't so important to me. But you know me and you know them and you know that if something is very much bothering me, it shows and they'll see it. So, two weeks ago we came in and it was Friday and my cousin Ken had come to visit. And Irving knew, 'cause I had told him, there'd been plans made for us all to go out for a good Italian meal on Saturday and a screening. But Irving meantime had made plans to take A. and David out to dinner and spend the evening with them. The scene is: we're all at the dining room table and my father mentions the following evening and Irving rather archly announces: sorry, he can't come, he's taking *his family* out. Well, at the moment, nothing was said but the next day plenty began to be said. My parents felt like they'd been slapped; they were very hurt by the statement. After all, they thought *they* were his family now, and *me*. It was the proverbial straw and all hell broke loose.

"My parents decided that they simply did not want to witness his unacceptable behaviour, or my resulting hurt, anymore. So they said we were not welcome to stay there; in fact, they didn't want to see Irving at all. My father spent about an hour and a half in the den, behind closed door, with Irving. Telling him his feelings about the whole situation. Irving, need I tell you, did not respond well or reasonably. He and his ego got on the highest horse available and rode into a flurry of hurtful statements. He got very mad indeed, and very very ugly. We left. Then I had him.

"He is, as you know, a very strong personality, very forceful, very articulate—a master wordsmith—very shrewd and incredibly stubborn and egotistical. Quote: 'Nobody will tell me, Irving Layton, what I can or cannot do.' That is, in his mind, what it was reduced to. Or so he tried to say. And a lot of bluster about *his* needs, *his* right to do as he wants and see whom *he* wants, *his* loathing of middle-class Jewish life, *his* rejection of middle-class Jewish life, etc., etc., etc. Truly I had to gather and re-gather all my forces and all my strengths to deal with him. It was impossible to get him outside of his own field of vision long enough to see what I was saying or understand how I was feeling. To me, it came down to: look, this and this hurts me. I don't understand it, I don't like it, and it hurts me. To say that's foolish of me does not make it so, nor make it go away. Either you care enough about me and my feelings to adjust your behaviour, or you don't. And if you don't care about my feelings, this marriage is over.

"Back he came with an attempt at reason: it's important to him that his son see that his mother and father, though not together, are friendly. Okay, I buy that. But you know, the son is not a child of nine or ten—he's a huge hulk of a sixteen-year-old. He's surely seen by now the friendliness. How about you take the son out and spend some time just with him. How about present wife, good old Harriet, goes with you and son and gets friendly too. Let son come visit father and Harriet. Harriet will delightedly have son whenever and as often as he wants. Son came once in the summer and Harriet made him very warm and welcome and he likes her very much. So? Well, I can't re-create for you all the scenes, or repeat all the words, but you have the essence of it.... I couldn't eat, I couldn't sleep, I cried a lot. I thought perhaps I'd made the most awful mistake of all in marrying him. I thought maybe the marriage was over. But I kept trying to make him understand and I kept trying to be able to stand listening to more of his onslaught. He was hurting too and I had to harden my heart at moments not to lose myself completely and fold under his will, not to subject myself utterly out of ... what strange combination of sentiments, who can say?

"Finally we began to crawl out of it. I think he values me and our life together enough to understand that some things just cannot be, if we are to survive together. He says I am precious to him, and he will not hurt me.... I want to believe that I'm important to him and that he values me and our life together enough to save it. Now all the words have been said and time will show the rest. So now here we are and we are quiet now, eating and sleeping again (me, that is—he never stopped) and I am hopeful that everything will be okay. We have pretty much made up with my parents. Actually, there was not a rift between me and them, only between them and Irving. And me in the middle—oh wonderful place to be. We just returned from Toronto. We went in and stayed in a hotel and it costs a lot of money to stay in hotels in Toronto. I went to see *my* family. We talked more. Irving came to pick me up there and said hello to them. And the next day was Yom

Harriet, six to seven months pregnant in her parents' Toronto home, 1980.

Kippur Eve, and my father gets a little emotional on the High Holidays and they were very grieved over how I looked and so they invited us to dinner. And Irving happily accepted and we went, all agreeing beforehand, with me, that we weren't going to talk about it any more. And then we came back to Niagara and here we are. It will maybe be a little tender for a while, but what can I say? I'm hoping.

"For myself, dear friend, deep inside in my most inner gut feelings, I have to tell you—and you alone—that I am altered from all this. A certain lushness of emotion, a totality of giving that was in me before is not in me now. It's like a little bit of me has been amputated. And that saddens me. Irreparably.... For me, as you know, having a child was always a terribly strong drive, one of the few really major events life has to offer. So that is the very most important thing happening to me, now. I didn't know it was so important to you, too. I guess maybe you did a neat job of not showing it too much, or maybe I wasn't sensitive or perceptive enough to see it well. Or maybe you didn't used to feel it so strongly as you do now. Anyway, I for sure understand your having the feeling and the need. I would be afraid for you to have a pregnancy without companionship, though. I mean, if you wanted to have a child and had no husband and you got pregnant anyways and wanted to have the baby, I would not like to see you do it all alone. I would like you to be near me, at least. So know that whatever thoughts you are having, slip this one in too—that wherever I am, you have a home and it would be joy in my life to have you near or with me. So there.

"Going into the sixth month in another week and looking it. Feeling not kicks, but stirrings and shiftings and having to pee all the goddam time ... still favouring Samantha as name for a girl, and Samuel Moses seems definite for a boy. Lots of time to decide, still. Am very glad the heat is over and beautiful autumn here...."

In another letter to Andrea dated October 17, 1980, I told her that we had rented a house at 21 Castlewood in Toronto; that our house in Niagara-on-the-Lake was neither sold nor rented, that I felt somewhat strange, not knowing really where I lived anymore. "Baby has begun to kick and I really get a kick out of that, let me tell you. It's a wonderful awesome feeling and I love it. Sometimes I just lie there and watch my stomach move, it's a gas absolutely. The past month has been a little rough and I lost a pound but saw the doc yesterday and he said the kid's heartbeat sounds delish and everything is very fine and okay. I'm working like a son of a bitch, and am enclosing a business card [the Barrich Productions card] for fun. It looks so classy and reminds me of another side of myself."

Clipping from the *Toronto Star*, Tuesday, December 9, 1980; Sid Adilman's column, Eye on Entertainment: "Irving Layton speaks an international language. His *Love Poems* collection is being published in Madrid in the spring. An illustrated bilingual version (Italian and English) of his *Selected Poems* is due also in spring from a leading publisher in Rome, translated by Alfredo Rizzardi, who introduced Italian readers to Ezra Pound's *Cantos* and T.S. Elliot's *The Wasteland*. All this is somewhat secondary in Layton's life at the moment because his wife, Harriet, is expecting the birth of their first child in January and it could well coincide with publication of his latest book, *Europe and Other Bad News*."

Clipping from *The Globe and Mail*, Wednesday, December 31, 1980, Zena Cherry's column, heading of which reads: "*Personality shows in cards*. And the one signed Harriet and Irving Layton and Somebody. Meaning she is expecting her first baby in two to three weeks. They were married in 1978. Their home is at Niagara-on-the-Lake and they've taken a house in Toronto for the winter. Harriet Bernstein Layton is literary representative in Canada for Barrich Productions of New York—she's responsible for bringing to Barrich original English and French-Canadian articles, novels, and screenplays for potential motion picture and TV production. Mr. Layton's newest book of poetry will be published by McClelland and Stewart next month. It's titled *Europe and Other Bad News* and dedicated "To somebody who made me want to change the title of the book." [And, no, he didn't change the title.]

20.

JOURNAL, JANUARY 1, 1981: "Finally January has come around. Our baby is supposed to be born this month. The pregnancy test I had just after the last entry was positive and we did drink our champagne with my parents and Marc and they got a bit wet-eyed and it was very happy. The summer was long and hot and Irving and I have very different memories of it now. He thought it was a wonderful summer—spent mostly with him in the garden writing in the sun, or writing in his den with the radio playing great music. He finished the book, *Europe and Other Bad News*. Some of what will no doubt be the all-time 'biggies' were produced this summer. I was merely uncomfortable with the early months of pregnancy nausea and major hormonal changes taking place in my body. Or, what used to be my body—I don't recognize it anymore. It was awfully hot and hard to sleep and we finally bought a fan that we carried from room to room—the kitchen in the day when I was working there—the bedroom at night, to sleep a little better. And I was deluged with hundreds and hundreds of manuscripts, screenplays, and stories from all over Canada, in my capacity—as of July—as literary rep. for Barrich Productions—hired by my old friends Steve Rose and Gordon Weaver. They came up here and did some interviews I'd set up to publicize the event [that announced my hiring and the production company's search for material]. We got national coverage, and the response was overwhelming. It took the next six months for me to crawl out from under! In fact, the last box load was just finished last weekend. Out of all the dreck—which unfortunately most of it was—there were a few things I thought interesting enough to send on to them in N.Y. There are four properties there now—maybe they'll like one of them. They haven't liked anything else so far enough to pursue it in any way."

Journal, January 3, 1981: To continue where I left off the other day—it was, anyways, a great writing summer for Irving. He wrote two more poems after 'Annunciation,' inspired by my pregnancy: 'Ashtoreth' and 'The Nativity.' This led us to thinking that perhaps *Europe and Other Bad News* was no longer an appropriate title for the book! So we thought and thought—for a while, it was *Beginnings*, then it was *To Make God Happen*. But he really didn't like anything as well as *Europe and Other Bad News,* so that's what the book will be called—with this dedication: 'For Somebody, who made me want to change the title of this book.' 'Somebody' is what we've been calling our child, until we know if we have a boy or a girl. If it's a girl, it will be Samantha Klara, and if a boy, Samuel Moses. First name after Mama's father, my zaidy Samuel, dear poetic prophetic soul that he was and second name after Irving's mother or father. Irving is frankly hoping for a girl—partly as it would balance things out and largely because he likes the idea of a sweet little girl child to dandle on his knee. I kind of like the idea of a daughter, myself—but if it's a son, well we'll be happy too. Like everyone says, as long as it's well and healthy. I'm very large and we thought maybe there were two babies in there, so I had a scan done, which shows a picture of the fetus. Well, there is just one big baby there, the picture showed. And, at that time—a few weeks ago—it was upside down, a breech presentation. Irving says, '*Nu,* it's showing its ass to the world already!' I'm to have another scan done this coming Wed., to see if it's still a breech, or has turned around. If it's a breech, I'll be due for a Caesarian, most likely. So, we'll see what sort of birth our child will have. Whatever it's to be, Irving is decided to be with me throughout. That'll be a first for him, too. I'm glad he wants to be there with me. His strength will help me. Meanwhile, the child is a very active one. It should be born anytime in the next two or three weeks."

At my next exam, there was some concern about the child, as Somebody had not shown any growth, nor had Somebody turned. At the hospital, I was hooked up and monitored and although it appeared that the child was doing well, it was decided not to take any chances since my due date was in the next week or two anyway. A Caesarian was scheduled, and Samantha was born on January 10th. Irving was indeed with me throughout the procedure. When I heard the words "It's a girl!" I wept for joy, as I had secretly been hoping for a girl most of all. I cannot begin to describe the expression on Irving's face when his newborn, perfect daughter was placed in his arms a few moments after her birth. It was a moment unlike any, and too personal—yes, even in the context of this memoir—to try to share.

Journal, Janurary 3, 1981, continued: "We have read the galleys for *Europe* etc., and had a meeting about the cover. Irving, as usual, had the idea for the cover and, as usual, had some difficulty making them understand clearly just what it was he wanted. He's rejected one so far; I hope the next one will be correct. It's astounding that at M.&S., supposedly Canada's largest and most important publishing house, there's no proper art department, even. And we know how limited Marta is as a publicist. We have to feed her ideas and then follow up on them, or next to nothing gets done. This time, we've also drawn up a list of places the book should be sent—including *Canadian Jewish News* and other Jewish organizations here: *Commentary* and *Encounter*; people like Lucy Davidowich and Dick Cavett, the N.Y. *Times Book Review*, and other U.S. publications. Seems to me important that those 'intellectuals' in the States are made more aware of Irving and what he's saying. Nobody there or anywhere is writing the sort of poems he is. Poems like 'The Search' or 'Sempre,' or the ones written in Mexico: 'Hells,' 'Reingemacht,' 'For Hans, Klaus, or Tadeusz,' 'Deliverance.' Super powerful things, like nothing else. Those from our Mexican sojourn/disaster have turned out to be some of the strongest. Irving says he'll always be grateful for the lousiness of that experience, because of the special edge of sourness and blackness it gave rise to in him, which is there in the force and tone of those poems. The poems written last summer in the garden are quite different—no less strong, but—like some of his earlier things—coming out of and having to do with nature. There is an exultation, and exuberance and affirmation and richness to them that I think hasn't been in his poems for a long time and never, in fact, to such a degree. It's a very great book. And I'm so happy he's dedicated it to this coming child. It made me cry, of course, when he told me.

"What else? Irving went to Banff for two weeks in November and once again felt it was worthwhile and enjoyed the experience. I was originally supposed to have gone too, but we decided against it. He's supposed to go back this summer and I expect I'll go then—with baby, hopefully. We did have such a nice time together there, I'd like to go back. And he taught the semester at Sheridan College in Oakville, the course he created, combining poetry, short fiction, and film. It was once a week, at night. He did some Lawrence, Babel, Kafka; some Frost, Auden, and Yeats; and *Five Easy Pieces, The Night Porter,* and *Apocalypse Now* for the films. A helluva course, seems to me. There were more people by the end than there had been at the beginning, which is a nice statement. I went with for about the first four or five, as we were still in Niagara-on-the-Lake. We'd drive in on Thurs., have a bite and go to the school, then stay over at the Holiday Inn and drive to Toronto the next day. Then when we re-located in Toronto, towards the end of Oct., it was already getting a little tiresome for me to schlep around, so I stayed here, and Irving would take the GO-train in. Mike Walsh [a professor at Sheridan College, and partner with Howard Aster in Mosaic Press] would pick him up and they'd have dinner, sometimes joined by Howard Aster and then after the class Irving would GO-train back. The first couple of classes, it was very interesting to see the faces. I mean, these are a mixture of adult part-time students, full-timers, and people from the community. Obviously none of them had ever seen anything like Irving. They came to him with sort of expressionless, blank faces—and I watched them begin to come alive, begin to twitch and stir and finally respond to him. He says that by the end they were a transformed bunch. He enjoyed the experience very, very much and I think will probably do it again. Still they were mostly non-Jews, and he yearns for the Jewish student *à la Herzliah;* that 'nervous, questioning mind' he enjoys so much and which seems to have pretty much vanished. But the other day he was visiting someone who teaches at Bialik, the Jewish school up Bathurst here and he saw some essays of some students there and was quite impressed. He's going to stop in at a class there this week. Maybe there he'll find the sort of student he really loves.

"So the autumn was quite busy, with Irving weekly in Oakville and also Banff, and after that he did a reading in Victoria as well, for Doug Beardsley [Canadian poet and educator, who studied with Irving at Concordia]. And there were other readings in Montreal and at Sheridan here and at Harbourfront, as part of the first International Poetry Festival. It was quite well attended; the poetry was largely most unimpressive. We did enjoy Stephen Spender, who Irving said had much changed from the many years ago when he'd seen him last—and changed for the better. Still, Irving towers above them all by miles and miles.

"We had a lot of people come see our house; but nobody bought it. So we found a house here (in Toronto)—an old couple going south for the winter who wanted to rent their place, furnished. And as the location was excellent (Eglinton and Spadina), and the rent was about half what we were afraid we'd have to pay, we took it and moved in the end of October. It's okay, but I am sad not to be in our own house, with our own things around us. Moving, even the little we did, is such an horrendous experience. And the place had forty years of filth to be cleaned—it took me the better part of a week, with Mama's two cleaning ladies helping, to make it liveable. And I'll have to move it all back again, when we return to Niagara in March. Dread chore. However, no help for it, it has to be done. Hopefully, this coming spring and summer the place will sell and we can re-locate to a house here. Pity we can't have two places, one here and our one there cause we do like it so much. But it really is too difficult, the back and forth all the time. The place had better sell this summer, or we'll be in a bit of a mess come next Sept., when Irving starts as writer-in-residence at the U. of T. Meantime, we're doing okay and I am not thinking too much about future worries. The main thing is to see this here child already. My parents are now getting very excited about their first grandchild. They've been south the past couple of weeks and in N.J. taking care of Baba, who had to have a D and C and was hemorrhaging and everyone was afraid it was serious but she came through again with flying colours, feisty soul that she is. They've been negotiating to bring her into a home here and it's now looking very good. She may be here in another month or so. We are all hoping so. Mama for sure would be terrifically happy. How great not to have to go to N.J. anymore. I think that pretty much catches up on our activities of the past few months. I don't know how or why so much time went by without my writing. I can make excuses of course, but what the hell? In my guts I have no excuse for myself, I'll just have to do better."

This is where my journal leaves off.

My marriage with Irving ended later that same year, although the divorce was not formalized for years. There was much publicity around our separation and divorce, all of it generated by a furious and deeply hurt Layton, who took our private matters into the public arena. It was beyond horrifying for me: bad enough to have my marriage disintegrate, and worse still to see all manner of distorted versions of the disintegration laid out in full page spreads in the newspapers, or hearing Irving talk about us on radio, on TV, in the papers.... Throughout it all, I never said a word publicly. I steadfastly refused all requests for interviews, I even declined meeting with Elspeth Cameron when she contacted me during her writing of Layton's biography. At times it was very difficult to maintain my silence. Naturally, I wanted to strike back, to defend myself against the stories that were told, stories that portrayed me as an uber-bitch who refused a father the right to see his child. Irving was never refused the right to see Samantha. I could not have achieved that even if I had tried, as the courts were clear on a father's rights to access.

On the front page of my journal notebook, Irving had written:

"'It does not seem possible to be an artist and not to be sick.'
—F. Nietzsche"

21.
Epilogue

M Y JOURNAL CONCLUDES DURING THE LAST DAYS of my pregnancy with Samantha. She was born on January 10, 1981, by Caesarian. Irving chose to be with me during the delivery, something he had not done with the births of his other three children. He held my hand throughout and when the doctor announced it was a girl child and placed her in his arms, he was tender, joyous, and clearly touched beyond words: a rare state for him. I took his wanting to be with me for her birth as confirmation that indeed he intended to be different with this child.

For the first few weeks after Samantha's birth, we stayed in Toronto, initially at my parents' house, where there was help and all I had to do was recover from the surgery and attend to my daughter, who I was breastfeeding. Then we returned briefly to the house we had rented on Castlefield before we went back to our lovely home at 9 Castlereagh in Niagara-on-the-Lake. The troubles began shortly thereafter. In retrospect, I accept blame for a lot of what happened. I had taken Irving at his word on certain things, and I had fully believed his intent and earnestness regarding this child we had made, and his intended involvement with her. It was not that he didn't want our child—he most definitely did. It gave him tremendous joy and delight to have her; it also, of course, fed his ego, to produce both a new book and a child at the age of sixty-nine. He had wanted our child, and he had wanted a girl, and we were blessed. Tragically, however, this was one of those times where I should have been able to differentiate between what he said and the reality of the situation. Unfortunately for both of us, I was neither mature nor wise enough to grasp those

Samantha in the Toronto apartment, 1981.

finer points. For example, when Samantha cried in the night, I would go to her, and bring her into our big brass bed to nurse her. My fantasy family included this kind of intimacy, this closeness, this shared warmth. Irving however would get up, grumbling that he needed his sleep, and go off to another room where he could continue his sleep uninterrupted. He delighted in her during the day, but had not the least idea what to do with her. This was, of course, perfectly understandable given his history and his lack of involvement with his other three children, particularly when they were young.

However, and this is significant, he had repeatedly told me that he regretted his behaviour with his other offspring. He had said to me that this time he wanted it to be different, and that he would make it be different; that this was another stage of his life and he would have more time, more patience, more understanding of how important the early years were for the child, and how desperately he wanted to be a fully engaged parent. This was an opportunity for him to do better than he had before, he said, a way to purge himself of some of the guilt he felt over how he had been with his other children. And I, of course, believed him. Who wouldn't? When Irving said all those words to me, I believe he really did mean them, every one. I did not and to this very day do not doubt him for one moment. It was part of his curse that he could not possibly fulfill those intentions; the three of us were denied so much, because of that curse. That is why I say, as I did on Don Winkler's documentary about Irving [in 2002], that he is a tragic figure, in the classical sense, a tragic figure inevitably doomed to tarnish that which shone most brightly for him.

The marriage went downhill. Irving went on a reading tour to Italy, which was good. I hoped the temporary time off between us would cool things down, bring some perspective to the situation, even though it was hard to be left on my own in a small town with a newborn. A wonderful woman named Becky came to help me out a few hours a week. She was from a large family of twelve or fourteen children. Her father had been a trapper and she came from the bush, from the North country. She was salt of the earth and heaven sent to me at that time. She allowed me the first rest I had known since Samantha's birth, and I was exhausted.

When Irving returned, things were still rough between us. I was resentful of his total self-absorption, although I should have known better by then, and now I wish I had tried harder to talk things out with him. Maybe hormonal changes explain some of my reactions at the time. I was resentful of Aviva calling our home several times every day, and of the extended phone conversations she'd have with Irving. If she did this intentionally to aggravate me, she was successful. I never had the gumption to tell her to piss off. When I would ask Irving why it was necessary for her to be so invasive in our life, why she had to call every single day, he'd always say it was because of David, how it was important for David to know that his dad was there for him, a part of his life for always, that he loved him, that he wanted to be involved. And, of course, that Aviva and Irving had a bond because of David and that bond was important to him. Irving would reassure me that I was the one he loved, I was the one he had married; after all, he had never married Aviva. Didn't that tell me something? He would ask and then he would dismiss my distress as immature and ridiculous. As I have already mentioned, there were other ways Irving could have nurtured his relationship with David that also included me (and Samantha), and I continued to suggest them to Irving, to no avail.

More and more I felt like Irving was pulling away from me and I could not bear it. I was non-confrontational by nature, and yelling and fighting was not my style. Instead, I withdrew. We had our arguments, and in one of the last, I finally did have at it with him, a table-banging argument that was much more his style than mine. But I was pushed to such limits of frustration, and I was fighting for our marriage. I told him that his dismissiveness of my concerns showed that he had absolutely no respect for my feelings, and how could I continue to live with someone who behaved that way. He said I was being silly. Couldn't I see that he loved me and wanted only to be with me? But I felt that we were being pulled down a whirlpool of a drain, a force that felt beyond our control was swirling around us, and I was going to drown unless I could find a way to extricate myself. I loved him beyond expression and my pain was probably matched—if not exceeded—by his. I could not bear to see our love destroyed. I could not bear to see what we shared go the route of all of his prior loves, wives, and lovers. I could not bear to see our unique relationship turn into something that resembled what he had had with everybody else. There was an inevitability to the situation, I felt. I began to realize that there was no way to rescue our love, to preserve it, except to leave it. I tried for a few more months to make it work.

Andrea, and her huge black standard poodle Jake, drove up from Amherst, Mass. to visit Samantha and me in March, when Irving was away reading somewhere. By then, the situation between us had worsened and I recall how wonderful it felt to breathe in the relaxed atmosphere, the loving air, the calm space of Samantha and me just being with Andrea, instead of the tension that had begun to undermine my life with Irving.

One day, in the spring or early summer—May I think it was—Irving called me from Montreal. I had never heard him speak as he did on that call. To this day, I don't know if he was drunk—though he was not a drinker—or what had happened to cause him to speak that way. He was like a madman and I was truly frightened. He said to me that "Things were going to heat up, and I had better not be in that house when he returned." I was scared. I didn't know what to do. It sounded to me like he was telling me to go away.

And so I did. I left, in fear and confusion, in a profound sadness that I would carry for years. Walking silently through our home, I looked at the matching couches in our living room, their earth-toned and cheery yellow fabric. The couch, where I had so often sat nursing Samantha in the evenings before going upstairs for the night. She would be napping in her beautiful navy blue English carriage, and when she woke for nursing, I would lift her out and sit on that couch with her at my breast, sometimes watching TV, sometimes listening to music. I stared at the couches where Irving and I had watched TV: news stories that ignited him, or TV Ontario movies, hosted by Elwy Yost, that would spark a later debate fueled by Irving's excitement, his sometimes marvelously insightful and sometimes utterly absurd interpretations of the films. Moving slowly from room to room, I stared at my tidy kitchen. Everything was ready for the next meal I would never make.

The renovations for the kitchen had been part of the wedding gift from my parents: the beautiful oak cupboard doors, the stacked washer/drier, the colourful Italian tiled backsplash. The kitchen where I really had been, as the saying goes, barefoot and pregnant, in some of the happiest times of my life. Where I made my tea and Irving's coffee in the mornings, the mornings he always greeted full of joy, grateful for me and for the good strong coffee, and where he would sing fragments of no song except the one inside him and he'd dance a silly little jig to celebrate the day. The kitchen with windows on two walls, so that it was always bright, and the side door that had been the warm welcome to us and to our visitors, to the heart of our home. I went upstairs to our bedroom, our beautiful bedroom. I will never forget how it looked. The soft yellow carpet, the wallpaper an old-fashioned yellow and white print. And most painful of all, our bed. Our beautiful brass bed, the bed where we had whispered our love and our dreams at night as a married couple, planning to be with each other forever. The bed where our daughter had been

Harriet and Samantha in the West Palm Beach apartment, 1981.

created, where we had loved and made love and giggled and felt grateful for how lucky we were; and where I had lain, alone with Samantha, when Irving was away or had gone off to find sleep elsewhere in the house. I think it was only because I was a mother now and had this miraculous daughter to take care of, that I did not stop breathing in those moments. I was in shock, and in despair. I left our home with Samantha in my arms. I did what I thought I must do. I walked out and never returned to our home, to the house that had held the dreams Irving and I shared for our future. I walked away from that house with our infant daughter, and I never lived there again.

We separated, and then my parents became involved, in an effort to help me. Once again, I wish I had handled it all differently. I left Niagara-on-the-Lake with nothing but my infant daughter and the clothes I could carry. I wanted nothing—none of the material things—that had been part of my married life, other than a few things that either were mine since before Layton and I had met, or things my family had gifted me with, like the big brass bed, the headboard of which Samantha uses to this day. Although my parents were in Europe, I went to their house—where else had I to go? There is no doubt that their subsequent involvement made things worse as far as the breakup was concerned. They meant well, and I would not have been able to manage those raw, ravaged, decimated days without their help, especially financially, from my father. I found an apartment to rent, which he paid for, as I had no money and Irving was certainly not offering any. When the courts ordered Irving to pay child support, he regularly defaulted on those payments. I understand why: he was angry and he was hurt. However, he did not behave responsibly, and if not for my father, I would have been God knows where. There were huge legal bills, as Irving took our private problems to the public forum. I tried over and over again to stop the publicity, my lawyer argued that taking our private matters into the public forum was not in the best interests of our child. But Irving was a poet inflamed, enraged, and stubborn and there was neither anything nor anybody who was going to stifle him, even if it wound up hurting his own case. His fury and defiance were uncontrollable. He wrote open letters to the Prime Minister that were printed in the papers. He gave television and radio interviews, discussing our life and the dissolution of our marriage. I remained silent. I remained silent when he said that I denied him access to our daughter, which was untrue. I remained silent when he portrayed me as a she-devil, an über-bitch. Ironically, some of those articles appeared on the very same day he would come to visit Samantha. Of course, he had access. The courts were very clear on the matter of access to a child. Irving could visit Samantha two times a week, for two hours each time—or at least, that was what the court had dictated. Whether or not he did it is another matter.

Whatever anger I felt for those lies has long, long ago died. I understand why he lied. I have forgiven all. He was enraged, hurt, bewildered as I was, but his fury morphed into a brutality and dishonesty the force of which was overwhelming, and I could not fight fire with fire. Of course, the press was all standing at attention, all too ready to print or broadcast whatever stories he told, regardless of accuracy. I don't blame them either. Business is business, and our private business, which he chose to make public, sold papers, got viewers or listeners and Irving gave good media.

I had to chase after money all the time, because he regularly defaulted on his child support payments. This too I kept to myself. He portrayed me as a shrew who drained him of much of his savings through legal fees, but the legal fees were initiated by him: by his defaulting on child support, by his refusing to adhere to court rulings that he desist from giving interviews about our private matters, which the court did finally rule on. Once again, he brought chaos on himself, and this time the poems that resulted were not so great. *The Gucci Bag* is one of his worst books, (with my apologies to Ellen Seligman, who had the no doubt very difficult task of editing that book with him). It is certainly not in the same league as the preceding ones he had produced both before we met and when I was his muse, lover, wife. It was a horrendous time. Samantha was teething and crying because of it, and I was crying myself to sleep night after night for what seems like years.

The courts ruled that I should ignore all the publicity, ignore things like the anonymously sent Rosh Hashanah (Jewish New Year) card I received, wishing me and my family to be sealed in the book of death (traditionally the sentiment is that one be inscribed in the Book of Life for the upcoming year). The court said I should ignore the letters sent to my employer, and to my father's business place, letters disparaging us and that said ugly things.

Now, I feel only sadness about it all, and think what I might have done to make it less ugly, less painful. What a colossal waste of money and energy. But I was hurting too, alone with our child, and devastated, completely devastated, by the end of our marriage. Here is the ugliest confession of all: ultimately, Irving gave up access to Samantha in exchange for not having to pay child support. His decision. Recently, I was told by my lawyer that had Irving challenged it and pursued his right to access, that court ruling would never have held up. But he did not. I raised Samantha alone. I had full responsibility for her in every way, including financially, other than that period immediately following our separation when my father helped me so I could be with Samantha that first year and a half of her life in our new home together.

I went back to work in the film business when Samantha was approximately a year and a half and I have supported us ever since. It pains me deeply that our daughter did not know her biological father, that she did not have the privilege his other children had (whether they recognize it as such or not) of benefiting from his vast realm of knowledge and his enthusiasm of sharing it; that she did not get to experience the excitement of traveling with him; that she did not know his joy in the mornings when he awoke, that she did not get to share a glass of wine or ouzo with him and engage in the sort of impassioned, lively conversation he so relished and at which he was so brilliant and stimulating. And it also pains me that he did not share in the joy Samantha is, and how much of him there is in her, which he would have so immensely enjoyed. When she and I engaged in lively conversation or heated discussions, which thankfully we did pretty much daily until she moved out and married, I often enjoyed playing devil's advocate, enjoyed getting her going; it is both to fill myself with the pride and delight I take in seeing what good brain power she has, how alert and articulate she is, and also because I enjoy seeing some of him in her. I tell her whenever she says something or responds in a way that is akin to what he would have done or said, because I want her to know those parts of him, and I want her to know they are in her, even though she did not learn them first hand. Of course she is more, much more than the sum of her parts. She is a marvelous, lovely, kind, generous, thoughtful, brilliant creative woman making her way in a world that is more beautiful because she is in it. A few years ago, she was asked to participate in a panel on Irving, part of the Montreal literary festival. Although she agreed to participate, she said to me that she felt like an imposter, because what right does she have really to speak about a man she did not know? I told her that she has a perspective nobody else in the world has, and that is worth a lot, whether she sees it or not at this juncture.

When Samantha was about ten years old, Irving called our home out of the blue. I was not entirely surprised because I had always felt that this would happen one day. My heart tore again at the sound of his voice, even given the struggle I was having, working hard, raising and supporting our daughter on my own. Still his voice made my heart beat hard and fast as it always had. There were legalities in place that I understood were binding, but in spite of those, I allowed the conversation to take place, and I never told anyone about it, never advised the lawyers, even though Irving could have been penalized for making the call. I was cordial to him. It broke my heart all over again to hear him. How could it be otherwise, when I still and always held love in my heart for him? He wanted to speak with Samantha. I asked her if she wanted to speak with him; she agreed, and I passed the phone to her. They spoke for a short while. He asked to see her. I got back on the phone and said maybe she should have a couple of days to think about that, since it was a big decision to have to make on the spot, and such a surprise after all to hear from him. He agreed.

She thought about it, and we talked about it. I did not try to talk her out of seeing him, but neither did I try to persuade her to do it. Maybe I was wrong to let it be her decision. Maybe she was too young, and maybe I should have made the decision for her. But she was a smart kid, strong in herself, and I felt she had the right to see him if she chose to, or to decline if she didn't want to. She decided she did not want to see him. I asked her if she wanted me to call and tell him to make it easier for her, but she said no, she'd tell him herself, which she did. He tried to persuade her to change her mind, and I remember her miming that motion of putting her finger down her throat like she was vomiting, while listening to him. She got off the phone and told me she didn't like the way he was trying to persuade her to change her mind. Stubborn daughter meet stubborn father, I thought to myself.

When Samantha was in her early teens, she came home from school one evening and said to me that the brother of a friend of hers, studying at University of Toronto, stated that he was studying Samantha's father in school, and she wanted to know if that was possible. I explained to her that it most definitely was possible, and likely in fact. We talked about his books, his place in the Can Lit world. It was not as though I had kept him a secret up to that point; on the contrary, whenever she would ask me

Samantha and Irving at his house in Montreal, 1997.

anything about Irving, I had always answered her as honestly, fully and age-appropriately as possible. I never spoke disparagingly about him to her. This particular evening, or shortly thereafter, Samantha asked me how would I feel if she wanted to see Irving. I told her that she could see Irving anytime she wanted, that she had always had that right, and certainly there was no reason I would stop her, as long as he also wanted to see her, which I felt he probably would.

The day came. Samantha was sixteen and planning a trip to Montreal with her friend Bri. Samantha was going to visit Irving. I had his phone number and I asked her if she wanted me to call, or she wanted to call. She wanted to do it herself. Of course she did, gutsy girl! I stood near her, just in case his reaction was not favourable or she needed me to take over the phone. She had to identify herself as his daughter before the woman who answered would allow her to speak with him. He was warm, receptive, and enthusiastic about seeing her; as I recall, she told me he said, "Nothing would delight me more," and an appointment was made. That was quite an emotional experience for me, standing beside her, watching her have her first mature, adult conversation with her father. Shortly thereafter, off she went to Montreal. I

Samantha and Irving at a tribute for him, Jewish Library, Montreal, 1999.

was nervous about how it would go for her. I couldn't stand to be alone, so I was with my friend Marie Formosa, pacing her apartment. I had asked Samantha to call me after she was done the meeting with her father, just to check in with me and let me know how she was after their visit. When she called, she was somewhat subdued, but said she was fine. The words uttered afterwards cut to my heart and have remained burned there from that moment to this day. She said, quietly, "It was harder to say goodbye than it was to say hello." She never spoke in much detail to me about that visit, but my sense was that they connected in a profound way. He was beginning then to fade with early dementia, but they were still able to have some good conversation. We have a couple of pictures that were taken of them together that day. When she returned from Montreal, I asked her if there was still enough of him functioning well, alert, and mentally alive enough for her to understand, for the first time, how it was that I could have loved him so much. She said, "Yes," and I was so very happy for that. More than happy, I was grateful that my daughter could begin to unravel the mystery of who this man was, what was it that made me love him so, and what drew us together in spite of the age difference. When she was a child, and we would see him on television, Samantha would ask me how I could love that "ugly

Samantha at the launch of her book, Here We Are Among the Living, *2012..*

old man." He was no longer a stranger who wrote a lot of books.

She saw Irving several more times, the last one being in Maimonedes with her then boyfriend and now husband Michael Bobbie. When they returned from that trip, she said "Mom, I totally just lost my shit this time. He didn't know me, he doesn't know anything anymore, and I had to leave the room and I just cried and cried." She has written eloquently about it all, about our lives, her journey, in her own book *Here We Are Among The Living,* published by Tightrope in the summer of 2012.

In what turned out to be the last time I saw Irving alive, in November 2005 when Musia and I went together to see him, she and I spoke of the breakup. She told me that she and Leon had phoned me at the time, had lengthy conversations with me trying to persuade me to stay with Irving, to keep the marriage together, to give it another chance. They had signed our marriage certificate, they had been friends of Irving's for so many years, they felt a responsibility. Musia said that she felt in her heart that I was the only woman Irving was ever with who really understood him, who understood how to love him, and who really was capable of giving him the kind of love he needed. They said that Irving had shown up at their place like a demented man, telling them that I wanted to leave him, and that he was beside himself with torture. I have no recollection of their phone call or the conversations they tell me about. I have, I guess, blocked these things so completely they cannot be retrieved. I cannot reconcile what they tell me about Irving and what he said to them, with what he said to me. It's not that I think they are not telling the truth—I have absolutely no doubt that every word they say is truth. But it is not the same truth Irving said to me. Therein lies the mystery. Therein are the imponderables. Therein lies the sadness, the loss.

In her book *The Lives of The Muses,* Francine Prose writes:

> How brave and resourceful the muse must be to balance, year after year, on the vertiginous high wire that her calling requires—to navigate the tightrope between imminence and absence, to be at once accessible and unobtainable, perpetually present in the mind of the artist and at the same time distant enough to create a chasm into which the muse's devoted subject is moved to fling propitiatory, ritual objects: that is, works of art.... Except in extremely rare cases ... tenure is not an option in the careers of the muses.

Between the truth an artist speaks, the truth of what he writes or paints or creates in whatever his medium, and the truth of who he is, therein lie all the mystery, pain and tragedy, and of course, also the greatest of ecstasies and passions: *la balance,* it's an ongoing attempt to maintain *la balance. The Tightrope Dancer,* the book Irving published in 1978 and dedicated to me, Gypsy Jo, is supremely representative of that notion—not only the artist, but his muse, is a tightrope dancer, and the dance is multi-leveled. Perhaps I was best as a muse and lover, and ought to have maintained that role. To me, it was worth all the pain and heartache, because we also shared such joy, and because it was such a remarkably prolific, creative time for him. The poems live on and I read them and re-read them to this day, as people will, in many languages, for years and years to come.

Irving Layton was a great poet, and however difficult or impossible it may have been to live with him, I am blessed and lucky to have what we had. Few people ever know anything remotely like a love such as we shared.

And then, of course, there is our daughter, Samantha, the miraculous blessing of Samantha. She comes to know her father largely through what he wrote, and from the stories I tell her. She has inherited some of those genes of his, including the writing gene, so who is to say what yet may come from this Irving Layton and Harriet Bernstein story?

All this I have kept to myself, holding the silence inside, until now. It is time to tell the story. It is time to close the circle.

Acknowledgements

My motivation in writing this book was to set the record straight. I am deeply grateful to Inanna Publications, and Luciana Ricciutelli in particular, for publishing it, for her enthusiasm, and for her invaluable editorial input.

Thanks to the special early readers: Vanessa Shields, Gianna Patriarca, Susan Swan, and George Elliott Clarke for reading, liking, and providing wonderful comments; particular thanks to Susan Swan for her very early encouragement, and manuscript suggestions.

Thanks to my medical team, who help keep me physically as able as can be: Dr. Carol Kitai at Women's College; Dr. Daphna Gladman at Toronto Western; Dr. Jose da Costa Reis (Zeca), and "Dr. Perspective" who keeps reminding me, at the most stunning moments, to breathe. Thanks to Drs Harold Berenstein and Yair Lenga for keeping my mouth working. Thanks to Crystal Hawk, EFT/TT teacher, friend, and healer through some really hard times.

Thanks and deep gratitude to all my spectacular women friends: Andrea Gilbert and Caryne Chapman Clark who have shared life with me for over fifty years. Franceszka Kolatacz (Auntie Broom), who has become family over the past twenty-five or so years. Some relatively new friends like the tenacious BabaYaga Place gals; and the QiGong circle, a widely disparate group of women who found, for seven years, common ground and caring in the sanctuary of Mrs. Ruth Frisch's home; special gratitude to Annette Romano, from that circle, for her love.

Thanks to my film biz friends: Patricia Gonzalez, "the rose among the thorns," who taught me much; Venka Galic and Jennifer Hofley; "Little Lady" Marie Formosa, who goes way way back with me; and the "other H," the amazing Heather Macgillivray, for whom I have the deepest admiration and love. Thanks to the French family, in particular Keira, who brought a new dimension of friend and family to my life.

Thanks to all my men: I am happy I did all that I did with you, loved and was loved, passionately. Thanks to Peter Roy, dung beetle and lawyer extraordinaire, for his restraint and advice.

Above all, thanks to my miraculous daughter Samantha, without whose support, fine input, encouragement, and endorsement this book would never have seen the light of day. You, Michael, Ida, and Nell bring inexpressible joy to my life, and I am grateful beyond words for the privilege of being Mama and Bubbie, my most favourite jobs.

I would like to also acknowledge the quote from Francine Prose's book, *The Lives of the Muses: Nine Women and The Artists They Inspired* (©Francine Prose, Harper CollinsPublishers, 2002).

Also, I acknowledge the permission obtained to quote from the following poems:

"Adam," "Adonis," "For My Incomparable Gypsy," and "In Praise of Older Men" from *For My Brother Jesus* by Irving Layton, Copyright © 1976 Irving Layton. Reprinted by permission of McClelland & Stewart, a division of Penguin Random House Canada Limited. All rights reserved.

Madman on Mithymna Beach," "Return to Eden," and "The Perfect Mouth" from *The Tightrope Dancer* by Irving Layton, Copyright © 1978 Irving Layton. Reprinted by permission of

Photo: Keira French

Harriet Bernstein is a romantic feminist who married Irving Layton for love and for art. A former film business executive (the first female General Manager of a major film distribution company), she was for many years a single, working parent whose most important job and joy was being a mother, and now, a Bubbie. She lives a full, powerful, and vibrant life in Toronto, despite having to manage many physical challenges. Her goals are to keep writing and to continue to make great soups.